H.D. between Image and Epic

The Mysteries of Her Poetics

Studies in Modern Literature, No. 111

H.D. between Image and Epic
The Mysteries of Her Poetics

by
Gary Burnett

UMI Research Press

Ann Arbor / London

Produced and distributed by
UMI Research Press
an imprint of
University Microfilms Inc.
Ann Arbor, Michigan 48106

Library of Congress Cataloging in Publication Data

Burnett, Gary Dean.
   H. D. between image and epic : the mysteries of her
poetics / by Gary Burnett.
      p. cm.—(Studies in modern literature ; no. 111)
      Includes bibliographical references and index.
      ISBN 0-8357-2042-X (alk. paper)
      1. H. D. (Hilda Doolittle), 1868-1961—Criticism and
interpretation. I. Title. II. Series.
PS3569.T9S6737   1990
811'.52—dc20   89-27653
                                                                     CIP

British Library CIP data is available.

The paper used in this publication meets the minimum requirements of
American National Standard for Information Sciences—Permanence of Paper for
Printed Library Materials, ANSI Z39.48-1984. ∞ ™

Contents

Acknowledgments

More than a few people have played a role in helping me write this book. I am only able to thank a small number of them.

For introducing me to the work of H.D. and teaching me from the beginning that there are settings outside the University in which poetry has its first life, a number of poets: Michael Davidson, Michael Palmer, Robert Duncan, and many others, both in print and in person.

For support, exchange of ideas, and friendship, the community of H.D. scholars, especially Diane Collecott, Eileen Gregory, Susan Stanford Friedman, Rachel Blau DuPlessis, Jennifer Clarvoe, Susan Schweik, and Cassandra Laity. And special thanks to H.D.'s daughter, Perdita Schaffner, for her interest and blessings.

For tangible and intangible sustenance, my friends and colleagues: Siobhan Kilfeather, John Archer, Madeleine Brainard, Brian Bremen, Danny Goldberg, Chris Go-Gwilt, Robert Spoo, Carol Barash, Marie MacAllister, and many others.

For their support, careful readings, suggestions, and interest far beyond what could have been expected, Sandra M. Gilbert and A. Walton Litz.

And for my family, Kathy, Joshua, and Jerusha.

Portions of this book have appeared in print previously. A shortened, revised version of chapter 1 was published in the special H.D. issue of *Agenda* (25, 3/4, Autumn/Winter 1987). A version of this material was read at the Emily Dickinson/H.D. Dual Centennial Colloquium in San Jose, California in October 1986. An early version of small portions of chapters 3 and 9 appeared under the title "H.D. and Lawrence: Two Allusions" in *The H.D. Newsletter* (1, 1, Spring 1987).

Grateful acknowledgment is made to New Directions Publishing Corporation for permission to quote from the following copyrighted works by H.D. (Hilda Doolittle): *Collected Poems, 1912–1944*, copyright © 1982 by the Estate of Hilda Doolittle; *By Avon River*, copyright 1949 by Hilda

Aldington; *Hedylus,* copyright © 1980, 1982 by the Estate of Hilda Doolittle; *HERmione,* copyright © 1981 by the Estate of Hilda Doolittle; *Notes on Thought and Vision,* copyright © 1982 by the Estate of Hilda Doolittle; *Nights,* copyright © 1986 by Perdita Schaffner; *Tribute to Freud,* copyright © 1956, 1974 by Norman Holmes Pearson; *Vale Ave,* copyright © 1957, 1958 by the Estate of Hilda Doolittle. Previously unpublished material by H.D. copyright © 1988 by Perdita Schaffner; used by permission of New Directions Publishing Corp., agents.

Acknowledgment is also given to New Directions for permission to quote from the following: By Ezra Pound: *The Cantos,* copyright 1934, 1937, 1940, 1948, copyright © 1956, 1959, 1963, 1966, 1968 by Ezra Pound; *Selected Letters,* copyright © 1950 by Ezra Pound; *Gaudier-Brzeska,* copyright © 1970 by Ezra Pound; *Literary Essays,* copyright 1918, 1920, 1935 by Ezra Pound; *Personae,* copyright 1926 by Ezra Pound; *Ezra Pound and Dorothy Shakespear, Their Letters: 1909–1914,* copyright © 1976, 1984 by the Trustees of the Ezra Pound Literary Property Trust. By William Carlos Williams: *The Autobiography of William Carlos Williams,* copyright 1951 by William Carlos Williams; *Imaginations,* copyright © 1970 by Florence H. Williams.

Grateful acknowledgment is also made to the Beinecke Library at Yale University for their permission to examine and quote from the H.D. manuscripts that are in their possession.

Introduction

Enter H.D. wrapped in a palimpsest.
                                        Harry Crosby

Considering the stature of some of her work, the critical history of H.D.'s poetry has been remarkably spotty. Her earliest work—published in Ezra Pound's anthology *Des Imagistes* in 1914 and her first volume, *Sea Garden*—met with immediate critical approbation.[1] This auspicious beginning, however, was to do just as much harm as good to H.D.'s reputation. It did present her to the public in a context almost tailor-made for her earliest, "laconic" poems,[2] but it also locked critical reaction into the narrow boundaries defined by the imagist manifesto; "H.D. Imagiste" became simply that and nothing more to the critics, so much so that her then-husband Richard Aldington was able to say years later that to many "the Imagist movement was H.D., and H.D. the Imagist movement" (*Life for Life's Sake,* 136). Though her poetry changed dramatically over the years—she was prolific until her death in 1961—this imagist label would haunt her so thoroughly that Randall Jarrell could dismiss her in 1945, simply saying that "H.D. is History," and suggesting that she had no business, as nothing more than an "Imagist," continuing an outmoded poetic career (130).

While Jarrell's assessment of H.D.'s worth has long been a central expression of the critical *status quo,* many other poets have consistently found a place for H.D. in their pantheon. Denise Levertov, Barbara Guest, and Alicia Ostriker—to name only three—have all written extensively on her work and on the place of that work in any accurate assessment of poetic modernism. And Robert Duncan, in what is certainly the most stunning display of one poet's reading of another in this century, spent nearly thirty years at work on his massive "H.D. Book," an undertaking which is one part extended autobiography and one part critical and spiritual appraisal of modernism in general and H.D. in particular.

In the 1980s, a growing number of academic critics—most importantly feminist critics like Rachel Blau DuPlessis (who is also a poet) and Susan Stanford Friedman, but also a significant number of others—have added their voices to this caring approach to H.D. and her work. In 1986 alone—the centenary of H.D.'s birth—four conferences were held in her honor, and at least four major collections of essays either saw print or were well on their way into print. Still, despite this flurry of activity, a significant gap remains in H.D. studies; surprisingly little attention has been paid to the poems of the years following the publication of *Sea Garden* in 1916 and preceding the *Trilogy* of the Second World War. The purpose of this study is to begin to fill that gap.

The impetus for such a project derives from two convictions concerning this period of H.D.'s work. The first is simply that the work itself is of great value; many individual poems stand out as exemplary achievements of H.D.'s particular genius, but, like the individual poems which make up *Trilogy* or *Helen in Egypt,* these poems gain immeasurably from being read in the context of the volumes of which they form a part. Like Yeats's later books—or like the collections of subsequent poets such as Jack Spicer, Robert Duncan, Adrienne Rich and a host of others—H.D.'s volumes are not simple, discontinuous grab bags of unconnected poems, but more or less articulate and coherent sequences. Each has its particular concerns and fashions a particular method or set of procedures through which it explores these concerns. And each, taking its place in the structure of one woman's life and work, grows out of the concerns and procedures of preceding volumes. H.D.'s work of this period, then, *can* be taken as a whole, as a single unit of sorts, though not simply as the monochromatic poetic treadmill of a woman stuck in her given role as the perfect imagist.

My second conviction grows out of the first; it is that H.D.'s work between the wars has never been adequately read. Not only has her way of building each volume into a single complex and interconnected whole gone unacknowledged, but these volumes have by and large gone without any critical attention at all. Two early book-length studies, Thomas Burnett Swann's *The Classical World of H.D.* and Vincent Quinn's *Hilda Doolittle (H.D.),* do contain useful chapters on this period, but neither is able to escape a manifestly false view of H.D. as a woman afraid of sexuality and with, in the words of Quinn, "a narrow play of intelligence" (147), a view which undermines all of their readings. More recent criticism—much of it of great value and perception—has tended to concentrate on the work of the latter portion of H.D.'s life, beginning with her work with Freud and the onset of the Second World War. Susan Friedman's *Psyche Reborn* provides an indispensable perspective on H.D.'s interest in and work with Freud, and on her nearly lifelong study of occult religious traditions without devoting much detailed attention to the poetry between the wars. Rachel Blau DuPlessis's *H.D.: The Career of That Struggle* undertakes a reading of this middle period, but is simply too short to cover everything adequately. Both books are important, groundbreaking studies, but both necessarily leave a great deal of work still to be done.[3] And, of the many, many shorter essays written and published in the renaissance of H.D. studies, only a handful—most importantly the excellent pieces by Eileen Gregory—even attempt to deal with H.D.'s poetry between the imagist years and her late epics.

Growing out of these two convictions, this study attempts to find a way of reading the poems of H.D.'s middle period without falling prey to the limitations of a narrowly conceived *a priori* understanding of Imagism. That is to say that, although the tenets of Imagism of course impinge on H.D.'s work after the First World War, they are not the only determining factor in that work. Other concerns—details of H.D.'s life, her response to the war, her research into the ancient mystery cults at Eleusis, the work of her contemporaries—all merge to form the context within which her writing takes place, and all push her writing well beyond the confines of Imagism. The purpose of this book is to trace the development of these concerns and to use this context as a way into the poems themselves.

The poet Kenneth Rexroth, in an introduction to a selection of D. H. Lawrence's poems, suggests that H.D.'s "images are purified of conflict; then the intensity which has been distilled from the sublimation of conflict is applied from the outside" (15). He goes on to suggest that her poems are mysterious constructs impervious to examination: "What results is a puzzling hallucination of fact, a contentless mood which seems to reflect something tremendously important but whose mystery always retreats before analysis" (15). It is my premise that, on the contrary, though H.D.'s poems are based on her reading of the ancient mysteries and are often apparently hallucinatory meditations built around a missing center, of indeterminate or inaccessible meaning, they *do* respond to analysis, to reading, and that it *is* possible to develop a way of understanding what they are about, or at least to draw on H.D.'s own terminology in an attempt to find out what *she* thought they were about, to participate in her orbit around the missing center and thus to speculate about what the poems say and the ways in which they say it.

Though H.D. has never been known as a critic or theorist of poetry, her work is full of meditations on her art, about what it is and what it can and cannot do. Her novels, short stories, essays, memoirs, and studies of ancient literature are all, in one way or another, studies in poetics, exploratory works in which she reflects on the significance and possibilities of the practice she has chosen as her own. When she writes about another poet—whether Euripides or Marianne Moore—she is always also writing about herself; in addition, her fictional characters are almost always poets, versions of herself, providing important insight into her thinking about art. Any reading of her poems, then, or any reading of her poetics, must turn to this other work as a source, as a way of approach, and as a primary context. This book grows out of such a necessity and, as a result, alternates chapters devoted to each volume of poems with contextualizing chapters that focus on H.D.'s other work. The scheme is chronological; the content of each of the framing chapters is determined and controlled by the composition and publication dates of the books of poems.

Such a method has its benefits. There is a surprising correspondence between the volumes of poems and other, quite different, work of the same time. It is as if H.D., instead of working in many different modes and undertaking many different projects, were consistently at work on a single poem, a massive long-poem in the modernist—or even post-modernist— tradition, weaving together verse and prose in a single diverse fabric, a tapestry of disparate and yet related materials, discontinuous but with each part impinging upon and transforming all of the others. In my alternation of chapters, I hope to suggest some of the richness of this skein of poetic material, or—to change my metaphor—to chart the landscape created by H.D. in the years between Imagism and epic.

1

A Poetics out of War:
H.D. after "Imagisme"

Plants and trees make countries, for us poets, at any rate and if everyone had just a little seasoning of the poet in his make-up, there would be, could be no more war.

H.D., letter to May Sarton, April 21, 1943

In 1921, writing as Helga Dart, H.D. began her first novel, *Paint It To-day*, with a directive for her own aesthetics:[1]

A portrait, a painting? You can not paint to-day as you painted yesterday. You cannot paint to-morrow as you paint to-day. A portrait, a painting? Do not paint it of yesterday's rapt and rigid formula nor of yesterday's day-after-tomorrow's criss-cross—jagged, geometric, prismatic. Do not paint yesterday's day-after-tomorrow destructiveness nor yesterday's fair convention. But how and as you will—*paint it today.* (chapter 1, 1)

As a credo, H.D.'s mandate to "Paint It To-day" has for an immediate context the work of her contemporaries, particularly of two men with whom she grew up in the early years of this century, Ezra Pound and William Carlos Williams. Pound's most characteristic statement of this definitive modernist doctrine comes only many years later, in a famous passage of Canto 53:

> Tching prayed on the mountain and
> > wrote MAKE IT NEW
> on his bath tub
> > Day by day make it new
> cut underbrush, pile the logs keep it growing

(264–65)

Williams's version appears in his 1918 prologue to "Kora in Hell: Improvisations":

> Once when I was taking lunch with Walter Arensberg at a small place on 63rd Street I asked him if he could state what the more modern painters were about, those roughly classed at that time as "cubists": Gleizes, Man Ray, Demuth, Duchamp—all of whom were then in the city. He replied by saying that the only way man differed from every other creature was in his ability to improvise novelty and, since the pictorial artist was under discussion, anything in paint that is truly new, truly a fresh creation, is good art. (8)

In the wake of the extreme aesthetic conventionality of the earliest years of the century, the power of novelty—conveniently schematized by Mina Loy in her "Aphorisms on Futurism" as "DIE in the past / Live in the Future" (272)—became for many the primary end of an artist's work. For Pound, as for Williams, it would lead to a radical poetics of the new in extended poetic forms flexible enough to accommodate new material, accidents of fortune, and wild shifts of poetic interest. Such urgency—which later in the century would lead to Charles Olson's Poundian theories of "Projective Verse"—manifested itself in the early Pound years as a continual ferment, a ferment seen clearly in the extraordinary range of the modernist *annus mirabilis* of 1922—a year which saw the publication of work as varied as Eliot's *Waste Land* and Gertrude Stein's *Geography and Plays*—as well as in a lively and sometimes confused outpouring of poetic theory. Pound's own work shifts swiftly in emphasis from his densely worked imitations of Provençal and Victorian poetry, to the miniaturist poetics of Imagism, to the energized images of Vorticism, and further to the increasingly dense *Cantos*. The force of the new, in the visual art scene of which Pound himself was part, manifested itself in a plethora of "isms," with Vorticism, Futurism and Cubism in the forefront.[2]

H.D.'s version of the modernist imperative makes substantial revisions in its emphasis. Her "Paint It To-day" neither insists on novelty for its own sake, nor emphasizes a push into the future at the expense of the present; her terms implicitly set her against the abstractions of the "isms" in a middle-ground aesthetic between conventionality and what she calls "yesterday's day-after-tomorrow destructiveness." The project she thus sets for herself relies on a shifting poetics—"You can not paint to-day as you painted yesterday" nor can you "paint to-morrow as you paint to-day"—but without the passion for sheer novelty of Williams's "Kora in Hell."

Williams himself realized the difference between the two aesthetic positions, and wrote the prologue to his "Improvisations" in part as a response to an exchange with H.D. He writes, quoting a letter she had written to him:

As assistant editor of the *Egoist* she refers to my long poem, "March," which thanks to her own and her husband's friendly attentions finally appeared there in a purified form:

14 Aug. 1916

Dear Bill:—

I trust you will not hate me for wanting to delete from your poem all the flippancies. The reason I want to do this is that the beautiful lines are so very beautiful—so in the tone and spirit of your *Postlude*—(which to me stands, a Nike, supreme among your poems). I think there is a *real* beauty—and real beauty is a rare and sacred thing in this generation—in all the pyramid, Ashur-ban-i-pal bits and in the Fiesole and in the wind at the very last.

I don't know what you think but I consider this business of writing a very sacred thing!—I think you have the "spark"—am sure of it, and when you speak *direct* are a poet. I feel in the hey-ding-ding touch running through your poem a derivative tendency which, to me, is not *you*—not your very self. It is as if you were *ashamed* of your Spirit, ashamed of your inspiration!—as if you mocked at your own song. It's very well to *mock* at yourself—it is a spiritual sin to mock at your inspiration—

Hilda

Williams answers:

Oh well, all this might be very disquieting were it not that "sacred" has lately been discovered to apply to a point of Arrest where stabilization has gone on past the time. There is nothing sacred about literature, it is damned from one end to the other. There is nothing in literature but change and change is mockery. I'll write whatever I damn please, whenever I damn please and it'll be good if the authentic spirit of change is on it. (12–13)

Williams responds angrily—and rightly—to H.D.'s misunderstanding of "the entire intent" of his work, but he also, as if in return, misunderstands *her* position, reading her emphasis on the spirit as nothing more than a retrograde stasis.

The critical tendency has always been to take Williams's side in this disagreement, to see H.D.'s Hellenism as "too staid, too chilly, too little fecundative to impregnate [Williams's] world" (12), to respond to her revisions of his poem with a sort of bemused outrage, as if the impregnation of *his* world were the only thing at stake. But the distance between the two poets emerges from something much more fundamental than H.D.'s meddlesome and naive revision of Williams's poem, justified or not; it is a sign of the profound differences between a poetry which is "damned from one end to the other" and a poetry conceived of as "a very sacred thing." In the terms of H.D.'s *Paint It To-day*, Williams's push for continual change or "mockery" is nothing more than "yesterday's day-after-tomorrow destructiveness"; "sacredness" is not, to H.D., a static anachronism, but a responsible inhabitation of the present, in the terms of today rather than of tomorrow.

Much of H.D.'s limited critical writing takes up this position against what emerges in Williams's riposte to her revisions. Though H.D. is not at all known for writing criticism, early in her career she did produce three short reviews—published in *The Egoist* in 1916 when she, with her husband Richard Aldington, was an editor—as well as one unpublished review of William Butler Yeats's *Responsibilities,* and two more general critical manuscripts, *Notes on Thought and Vision* and the largely unpublished "Notes on Euripides, Pausanius, and Greek Lyric Poets."[3] In indirect dialogue with the dominant modernist poetics of her contemporaries, these writings elaborate upon the aesthetics of *Paint It To-day* and the exchange with Williams.

The review of Yeats's *Responsibilities* most clearly addresses the issues raised in this dialogue. Undated and bound into a volume containing heavily revised drafts of *Notes on Thought and Vision* and a number of poems which would later appear in *Hymen* and *Heliodora,* this manuscript is only nominally a review of Yeats's book.[4] It is, rather, a strong polemic on the relation between poetics and politics in a world defined by war. The essay begins with a memory of Yeats's earlier books, and quotes lines from his "When Helen Lived" which repeat a key word from H.D.'s letter to Williams, "beauty":

> That men desert
> For some trivial affair
> Or noisy, insolent sport,
> Beauty we have won
> From bitterest hours.

H.D. then suggests that Yeats's responsibility has "only just begun," and turns to a long discussion of poetic responsibility:

"For we, 'the young' of this generation are sick of self-analysis, self-torture, self-appreciation. The ill-starred nineties which, historically speaking, claims Mr. Yeats, was a band of robust virtue compared with our own decade. For what are we, *les jeunes* in ourselves? First, a memory of the few, the really great, who have gone irreparably from us, next the hope that some may return, not broken by the bitterness of their experience but taut and aflame for the creation of beauty, and then, crouched as in a third line of battered trenches, are the few of us who are left, hanging on against all odds, in the wavering belief that we are the link, the torch-bearers. And upon us, almost with us, is the enemy.

"For us the enemy is not the great mass of inert life, the so-called middle-classes and general heaviness of the world against which the artist has always a legitimate quarrel, but for us, there has been a more treacherous force at work, a more subtle adversary. The chief enemy is not the middle-classes and the Philistine upon whom the young men of the nineties whetted their gift. It is the great overwhelming mechanical daemon, the devil of machinery, of which we can hardly repeat too often, the war is the hideous offspring.

"This daemon took for its own the most robust talent of our generation. It crept upon us and claimed its own. From our band, at best a few against many many millions; it has taken the most stalwart. The nineties was at one for all its internal, personal friction—the nineties at least held one common law as sacred, at least never condescended to the worship of material efficiency. The nineties, thank God, were not efficient, neither did they fall down before some Juggernaut of planes and angles. The nineties were ill-starred, but they had at least a star.

"And what has all this tirade to do with Mr. Yeats and his responsibility? A great deal. For Mr. Yeats and we few, the remnant who still persist in the worship of beauty other than the grace of the steel-girder are in somewhat the same position. For Mr. Yeats may be said to represent the last line of trenches for his own defeated generation as we for the present generation. Though our generation, inasmuch as its cubes and angles seem a sort of incantation, a symbol for the forces that brought on this world calamity, seems hardly worthy to compare with the nineties in its hopeless stand against the evil of ugliness. Our generation did not stand against the enemy—it *was* the enemy.

"But I will not say that it is the enemy. For it has merged into this struggle with its own much lauded guns and aeroplanes, it has become a part of the struggle and is no longer a self-willed agent. The guns they praised, the beauty of the machines they loved, are no more as a god set apart for worship but a devil over whom neither they nor we have any more control. The black magic of triangles and broken arcs has conquered and we who are helpless before this force of destruction can only hope for some more powerful magic, some subtle and more potent daemon to set it right.

"They called it to life but we are none the less responsible, we are all a part of this world calamity, we can not stand apart with Pharasaic gesture. But we can do this. We can wait, endure, confess the past was all a mistake, turn to the future and hope for the generation to follow.

"And this is why I feel that Mr. Yeats's responsibility has only just begun. For it seems in moments of despair that we have no past, no future. But Mr. Yeats has both. Can we not spiritually join our forces, and chastened with old calamities, redefine and reconstruct boundaries and barriers, and reinvoke some golden city, sterner than the dream-cities, and wrought more firm to endure than those riveted of steel and bleak with iron girders" (*Responsibilities*, 52–53). [The typed initials "H.D." follow.]

The essay is remarkable for its interweaving of the aesthetics of her generation with the politics and destruction of the war. H.D.'s "memory of the few . . . who have gone irreparably from us" anticipates Pound's "Hugh Selwyn Mauberley," but with a different tone. Pound's scenes of the lost nineties are superceded, in H.D.'s vision, by the figure of the one survivor—Yeats—of that "ill-starred" decade. And his very survival, beyond anything that his poems may or may not contain, marks Yeats for H.D. as one of the "torch-bearers" carrying on despite the "efficient" advice of Pound's Mr. Nixon and the "Juggernaut of planes and angles" of her own generation.

H.D.'s understanding of war's destructiveness also differs substantially from Pound's; where he angrily laments the death of artists like Gaudier-Brzeska in the trenches, H.D. attacks the very foundation of what she sees as an irreducible conjunction between aesthetics and militarism. Not only, she says, has the war claimed the lives of artists, it has taken as its own the aesthetic values of a generation, values which have been taken up by the spirit of war and have thus become intrinsically destructive. What she calls the "sacred" in her letter to Williams is precisely the ability of the "torch-bearer"—Yeats or, we are to understand, herself—to carry on with the responsibility of art in the face of this destructive spirit, to forge an art which is new without being violently severed from the past. The *other* new art, the art claiming to be the most of its time, denies its sacred ties with tradition.

Though H.D.'s essay projects a future, it is a future which maintains its relation to the past, a future made possible by endurance, by waiting things out rather than by an unrelenting thrust into the new. The planes and angles of a cubist or futurist canvas depend on what is, for H.D., a terrible and dangerous pun: their planes mimic the "aeroplanes" of the war;[5] together they comprise the "Juggernaut" before which her generation has fallen— what D. H. Lawrence once called the "mechanical, obsolete, hideous stupidity of war" (*Letters*, vol. 2, 218). The identification of the arts with the machine initially created a fecund unity between the arts and the enemy but this unity has lead only to a complete submergence of art into the destructiveness of the war itself: art "has become a part of the struggle and is no longer a self-willed agent." Thus, for H.D., the art that is the most directly of the times—that art which most reflects and is most determined by the militarism and industrialism of the early twentieth century—can only undermine the sacred responsibilities of the artist. In her Yeats review, the obligation for the maintenance of this sacred art falls not on the few—the "most stalwart"—who represent the new aesthetic, but on another few who, like Yeats, are able to wait and thus reinvoke "some golden city" of eternal beauty. The same ideal—a desperate vision of hope for a restored city—closes H.D.'s first volume of poems, *Sea Garden:*

> And in these dark cells,
> packed street after street,
> souls live, hideous yet—
> O disfigured, defaced,
> with no trace of the beauty
> men once held so light.

The sacred counterpart of the contemporary, disfigured city endures in the memory of the "torch-bearer":

> Though we wander about,
> find no honey of flowers in this waste,
> is our task the less sweet—
> who recall the old splendour,
> await the new beauty of cities?

$$(CP, 41)$$

In both her autobiographical novels and the Yeats essay, H.D. "Paint[s] It To-day," writes directly to a present world. H.D.'s Europe, a landscape literally containing both present and past, is her version of the great modernist perception of the contemporaneity of all ages; her variant on Henry James's American in Europe—visiting, in *Paint It To-day,* museums, cathedrals, and other sites of an abiding history—inhabits a multiplicity of times in which present and past are superimposed one upon the other in sacred fashion.

In the poetry, this temporal scene takes a quite different form; it is, after all, the poetry which has led critics to dub H.D. alternately "The Perfect Imagist" and—perhaps consequently—an anachronism or escapist.[6] And the landscape of her poems—not a historically present Europe, but an idealized, distant Greece—bolsters the epithet. But, given her sense of the responsibility of poetry, this distant Greece is also always a presence, both a memory of the Eastern American landscape in which she grew up and an elaborate metaphor for the world of the poet.[7] The "sacred" demands a political or timely dimension, an implicit if sometimes obscure response to the actual world in which the poet finds herself. In one sense, this kind of reaction against the narrow terms thus imposed on her poetry—the narrow terms of her "Imagism" as commonly understood—could be said to have defined H.D.'s career. As Robert Duncan contends in his "H.D. Book," for most readers of her poetry "there was, past the 'image' thing, the 'Greek perfection' thing. . . . For most readers, the Hellenic thing in H.D. was all 'clear,' 'frigid,' 'pure,' 'beautiful,' 'inaccessible.' It set her apart" ("From the Day Book," 126–27). Set her apart, as we have seen from her Yeats essay, erroneously. Such a classification not only limited expectations of the kind of work H.D. could produce, but was, as she herself noted, a misunder-standing of even her earliest work:

> I grew tired of hearing these ["imagist"] poems referred to, as crystalline. Was there no other way of criticizing, of assessing them? But perhaps I did not see, did not dare see any further than my critics. Perhaps my annoyance with them was annoyance with myself. For what is crystal or any gem but the concentrated essence of the rough matrix, or the energy, either of over-intense heat or over-intense cold that projects it? The poems as a whole . . . contain that es-sence or that symbol of concentration and of stubborn energy. The energy itself and the matrix itself have not yet been assessed. ("H.D. by Delia Alton," 184)

Even as late as 1949, when this note was written, H.D. clearly found it necessary to work both within and against the definitions of Imagism. Thus the tangling of the note's prose: she rejects the label of "crystalline" only to re-cast it in her own terms. An H.D. poem, she implies, is indeed "crystalline," but not because it is a stable anachronism or some kind of "well-wrought urn" perfect for a new-critical exegesis; if her poems are Greek, they are not of the nature of Keats's Grecian Urn, signs of a romanti-cized past perfection persisting in spite of the exigencies and upheavals of time. They are, rather, individual crystallizations of a very present over-intensity, versions of the "rough matrix" into which H.D.'s own idiosyn-cratic energies may be channelled. They may even be akin to what Ezra Pound called the Vortex, but a vortex uncolored by the planes and angles of the vorticists themselves.

H.D.'s 1949 note suggests that her poetry—even in its earliest forms— goes far beyond the simplicity of an imagist project. Crystalline poetry, as she points out, suggests a poetry of stasis, a poetry metaphorized as "crystal or any gem," as an objectified artifact. Such a false suggestion does recall the dominant version of Imagism; T. E. Hulme's earliest formulations of the new verse underscore its sculptural stasis: "This new verse resembles sculp-ture rather than music; it appeals to the eye rather than to the ear. It has to mould images, a kind of spiritual clay, into definite shapes" (*Further*

Speculations, 75). Hulme's further declaration that "Man is an extraordinarily fixed and limited animal whose nature is absolutely constant" (*Speculations*, 116) marks a quite different aesthetic extreme than the planes of the futurists, but one which is just as removed from H.D.'s "responsibility" or "sacredness" as that other more kinetic art. For Hulme, the art which works best within such a limitation is one of solid forms:

> In art this state of mind results in a desire to create a certain abstract geometrical shape, which, being durable and permanent shall be a refuge from the flux and impermanence of outside nature. The need which art satisfies here, is not the delight in the forms of nature, which is a characteristic of all vital arts, but the exact contrary. In the reproduction of natural objects there is an attempt to purify them of their characteristically living qualities in order to make them necessary and immovable. The changing is translated into something fixed and necessary. This leads to rigid lines and dead crystalline forms, for pure geometrical regularity gives a certain pleasure to men troubled by the obscurity of outside appearance. The geometrical line is something absolutely distinct from the messiness, the confusion, and the accidental details of existing things. (*Speculations*, 86–87)

The "dead crystalline forms" of sculptural art—so different from H.D.'s redefined crystals—are a kind of dead-end or spectre haunting Hulme's aesthetics; his classicism is *too* solid, as potentially dead as the traditional verse forms he would replace with his own free verse.

Ezra Pound, in his formulations of Imagism, also resorts to the sculptural metaphor. In "A Retrospect," he writes:

> As to Twentieth century poetry, and the poetry which I expect to see written during the next decade or so, . . . it will be harder and saner, it will be what Mr. Hewlett calls "nearer the bone." It will be as much like granite as it can be, its force will lie in its truth. . . . At least for myself, I want it to be so, austere, direct, free from emotional slither. (*Literary Essays*, 12)

In his 1914 essay "The Later Yeats"—an essay apparently unrelated to H.D.'s Yeats review—Pound adds a second kind of poetry to his canon, based on the music of words: "There have always been two sorts of poetry which are, for me at least, the most 'poetic'; they are firstly, the poetry which seems to be music just forcing itself into articulate speech, and, secondly, that sort of poetry which seems as if sculpture or painting were just forced or forcing itself into words" (*Literary Essays*, 380).

In another essay of 1914, "Vorticism," Pound explicitly defines the poetry of sculpture—what he was later to call "Phanopoeia" or the "casting of images upon the visual imagination" (*Literary Essays*, 25)—as

"Imagisme" (*Gaudier-Brzeska: A Memoir,* 82–83). And yet Pound is concerned in this essay to make Imagism over into something he can call Vorticism, an art of motion in which one "record[s] the precise instant when a thing outward and objective transforms itself, or darts into a thing inward and subjective" (*Gaudier-Brzeska,* 89). If Hulme's aesthetic transforms the visual into the solidifications of his sculptural metaphor, Pound mixes *his* visual sense with a very different notion of what constitutes vision.[8] In his famous description of the composition of "In a Station of the Metro," Pound utilizes the terminology of the visual arts, but with a twist, aligning his poetry with the non-representational paintings of Kandinsky, the vorticists, and the cubists: "That evening, in the Rue Raynouard, I realized quite vividly that if I were a painter, or if I had, often, *that kind* of emotion, or even if I had the energy to get paints and brushes and keep at it, I might found a new school of painting that would speak only by arrangements in colour" (*Gaudier-Brzeska,* 87). As his description suggests, Pound's vision does not necessarily equal sight.

Despite his emphasis on "Objectivity and again objectivity" (*Selected Letters,* 49), Pound is always capable of an opposite sense of the image as a nearly mystical force in poetry. In late 1914, in a short prose piece titled "Ikon," published in the only issue of the *Cerebralist,* he emphasizes precisely this sense:

> It is in art the highest business to create the beautiful image; to create order and profusion of images that we may furnish the life of our minds with a noble surrounding.
> And if—as some say, the soul survives the body; if our consciousness is not an intermittent melody of strings that relapse between whiles into silence, then more than ever should we put forth the images of beauty, that going out into tenantless spaces we have with us all that is needful—an abundance of sounds and patterns to entertain us in that long dreaming; to strew our path to Valhalla; to give rich gifts by the way. (*Ezra Pound and Dorothy Shakespear,* 277–78)

Such a conception of art takes Pound far along the way from Hulme's sculptural metaphors toward a visionary Imagism, one which may almost qualify as "sacred" in H.D.'s sense.

One of the first reviews of H.D.'s poetry, John Gould Fletcher's "H.D.'s Vision," appearing in *Poetry* in 1917, carefully distinguishes her poetry from Hellenism and Hulmian Imagism, seeing it as something closer to Pound's images for the soul: "The unpractised reader, picking up H.D.'s *Sea-garden* and reading it casually, might suppose it was all about flowers and rocks and waves and Greek myths, when it is really about the soul, or the primal intelligence, or the *Nous,* or whatever we choose to call that link that binds us to the unseen and uncreated" (267). H.D.'s poetry, that is, is a visionary poetry of the "sacred," fully engaged with the world of what she calls "beauty," an eternal and present world in which the soul moves and which does not depend upon "planes and angles" or "aeroplanes." The distant "Hellenic thing" of H.D.'s critics—"Greek myths" in Fletcher's review—is the sign of a very present spiritual reality. If Yeats's spiritualism gave him "metaphors for poetry," then H.D.'s "escapist" Hellenism fulfills the same function; both poets, both "wand-bearers," engage the world from a position other than the materialist.[9]

This aesthetic informs H.D.'s desire to "reinvoke some golden city." But if her position is not materialist, it is curiously not completely idealist either, for unlike Pound's "Ikon" it does not depend on a fully spiritualized space—an idealist's afterlife—for the significance of its images. H.D.'s city is neither an idealist "dream-city" nor a newly mechanized materialist city "riveted of steel and bleak with iron girders." As the city of an imagist—a city of images—it has its roots in that imagist's direct presentation of a material world while also maintaining extensions into a more ineffable realm.

One year before Fletcher's review of *Sea Garden*, H.D. anticipated his reading of her book while at the same time making of Imagism an art of the adept, touching both the visionary and the material. She begins her review of his *Goblins and Pagodas* with a short account of its first part in precise imagist terms: "Readers of *The Egoist* are already familiar with certain poems . . . particularly with the first part of the book where Mr. Fletcher presents with simplicity and directness a series of impressions" (183). Fletcher, in other words, follows Pound's first precept, "Direct treatment of the 'thing' whether subjective or objective" (*Literary Essays*, 3), using "things" which are both subjective and objective: "memories of a wistful, sensitive child's impressions of an old weather-beaten house and of the bleak spectres that dwelt within the shadows of the six white columns, that haunted bedroom, nursery, and attic, and crawled with the poison ivy about the roots of the old garden oaks" ("'Goblins and Pagodas,'" 183). But this classic Imagism is not, for H.D., the true achievement of the book:

> In the second section of his book, Mr. Fletcher deals with a more difficult and, when successfully handled, richer form of art: not that of direct presentation, but that of suggestion. Mr. Fletcher, in the very admirable Preface to this new volume, remarks, apropos of certain current opinions concerning the so-called "new poetry," "the key-pattern on a Greek vase may be beautiful, but it is less beautiful, less satisfying, and less conclusive a test of artistic ability than the composition of satyrs and maenads struggling about the centre."
>
> And as we come to a clearer understanding of the poet's method and his work,

we are almost tempted to continue his apt metaphor; to say to the artist: the images so wrought upon the body of the vase—the maenad, poised for ever, quietly for all the swirl of draperies and of loosened head-band, or the satyr for ever lifting his vine-wreathed cup—are satisfying and indeed perfect. But how much more for the lover of beauty is the wine within the great jar beautiful—how much more than the direct image to him are the images suggested by shadow and light, the flicker of the purple wine, the glint across the yellow, the depth of the crimson and red? Who would stand gazing at a satyr and a maenad, however adroit the composition of fluttering garment and poised wine-cup when the wine itself within the great jar stands waiting for him?

For it is no static vision that Mr. Fletcher seeks to give us. . . . (183)

Praising Fletcher for his art of suggestion, H.D. chooses the single reference in his "very admirable Preface" relating to *her* world—the world of Greece—for her discussion. While Fletcher's metaphor is primarily a defense of free verse—emphasizing the pictorial content of the vase over its more formalized aspects or the content of a poem over its meter—H.D.'s use of the metaphor literalizes it. She reads—or mis-reads—the metaphor as a defense of suggestion over presentation and then, in a step far beyond anything in Fletcher's preface, reads the illustration on the jar as presentation rather than suggestion. Misplacing the emphasis of Fletcher's "apt metaphor," H.D. is able to read the entire vase illustration, and not just the "key-pattern," as "static vision," and thus to invoke the more ephemeral wine (wine which is itself never really present other than as a suggestion in the "vine-wreathed cup" of the satyr) as the dominant metaphor for Fletcher's poetry and her own. And, cutting her poetics loose from Fletcher's pictorial metaphor—from what he elsewhere in his preface calls "definite material phenomena" (xviii)—she implicitly extricates her work from the even more static art of "direct presentation," the Hulmian Imagism of sculptural form.

Even as H.D. thus redefines her variety of Imagism, freeing it from the material stasis of these metaphors, she re-establishes its ties to a material world, finding in Fletcher's poetry materiality without stasis:

He uses the direct Image, it is true, but he seems to use it as a means of evoking other and vaguer images—a pebble, as it were, dropped into a quiet pool, in order to start across the silent water, wave on wave of light, of colour, of sound.

His poetry is not static, as I say—it is moving, whirling, drifting.

It is the whirling of flowers, of boats, of the sea-water, of rain slanting and beating, of birds swaying and drifting, of peonies springing like rockets, of rhododendrons, of orange-blossoms dashed with rain, seeming to me to be swaying above water, where again their broken reflections swirl among scattered images of straining clouds. It is the swirling of snow, of fire-flies, of forest trees. It is the drift and ripple of grass, and with it again, the flowers in the grass. ("'Goblins and Pagodas,'" 183)

Following these "vaguer images" of a materiality without stasis—and anticipating, in the process, D. H. Lawrence's 1920 demand for a poetry of the "immediate present" in which "there is no plasmic finality, nothing crystal, permanent" (*Selected Literary Criticism*, 85)—H.D. finds a connection between poetics and the war which resonates with her Yeats essay:

> In grimmer moods, it is the swirl of guns, cannon, terror, destruction. And through it all, it is the soul or mind or inspiration of the poet, knowing within itself its problems, unanswerable; its visions, cramped and stifled; the bitterness of its own insufficiency. Knowing indeed not whence it cometh and whither it goeth, but flaunting in the face of its own ignorance, its own undaunted quest. (183–84)

H.D. bases her images on Fletcher's book, but they are really her own. The choice of the Greek "great jar" links the review closely to her own Hellenic scenes, allowing H.D. to simultaneously materialize and etherealize the world of the poems. And more importantly, as in the Yeats essay she clearly defines the role of the poet in terms of a response to the war; the poet does not indulge in what Williams called "mockery," but endures—opposed to the war while aware of its destructive power—within what she knows to be the insufficiency of vision. As Yeats writes in "Per Amica Silentia Lunae," "we sing amid our uncertainty" (*Mythologies*, 331); H.D.'s poetry similarly maintains its "undaunted quest" by means of its very insufficiency.

Such a sense of creative ignorance or "cramped and stifled" vision persists throughout H.D.'s career, from the "stunted" flowers of *Sea Garden* through the flaw in the jewel leading Kaspar to vision in *The Flowering of the Rod*, and beyond, and it is regularly invoked in the context of war. Sometimes, as in the Fletcher review, the terrors of war threaten to dissolve both the quest itself and the ability of the poet to endure. At other times, "insufficiency" is nearly obliterated by the intensity of vision.

Late in *Paint It To-day*, after Midget Defreddy (the H.D. character) has recovered from a wartime breakdown, she defines what she calls the "visible world"—a world beyond the hindrances of war—for her friend Althea:

> Althea, this is a little tirade on the beauties of the visible world. The visible world exists; I have found since I have outgrown the period of war convalescence, that the visible world exists as poignantly, as ethereally as the invisible. When we can get the visible and the invisible together that makes another

world. I used to believe in the past and what I called the future; when you get the past and the future together, you get what I call, now for the sake of argument, the present, at least a poignant and ethereal present which I call the visible world.

There are hours which are drab nothingness. I used to call this the "present which is dead." There is a present which is dead, there is also the living present. (ch. 7, 21–22)

The "visible world" is doubly present: it both evokes a "present" enabling H.D. to "Paint It To-day" without either the anachronism of Hellenic poetry or the destructiveness of Futurism, *and* allows a "poignant and ethereal" material present. Thus Midget's retreat to the "invisible world" during the war is an escape not only from the war, but from the very reality of the present.

Still, inherent in the notion of a new, *visible* world set against the escapism of the invisible is a strong sense of engagement. Earlier in the novel, Midget's flight—from the world of her husband Basil (Richard Aldington) and of the war which comes, in her eyes, to define him—is described as a kind of sight: "So it was that Midget found a new trick of seeing. The trick was not altogether a good trick. I have my reasons for saying this. It shut her out from life" (ch. 5, 5). At the same time, Basil is able to see the "real" world of the war: "The tags that to her now seemed all of life worth keeping, left Basil with a faraway stare, perfectly listless, perfectly indifferent. He was seeing perhaps heroicly into the present, into the present that was dead. Into death itself" (ch. 5, 3). Both of them are able to see—one the dismal "visible world" of the war, the other the "invisible world" of her own hermetically sealed psyche—but neither has vision, which is possible only in the true "visible world" of combined inner and outer realities. This true vision dismantles the dualisms of ordinary sight (a positive value in Hulmian Imagism) and disembodied sight, melding the two poles into a single, more "responsible" or "sacred" whole beyond both the destructiveness of war and Midget's avoidance of its reality.

Two extremes make up Midget Defreddy's world: on the one hand the war, and on the other the escapism of an "invisible world." Somewhere in between these extremes—or, more accurately, somewhere far beyond them—is the ground whereupon H.D. would stake her claim for art. In somewhat different terms, she repeats this outline in her August 1916 review of Marianne Moore—a review written fully five years before H.D. and Bryher were to publish Moore's first volume under the imprint of the Egoist Press. She begins with the worry that Moore's poems may be meaningless, that they may, in other words, avoid responsibility: "[Readers of *The Egoist*] have read Miss Marianne Moore's poem again and again, and questioned, half in despair—is this a mere word-puzzle, or does it mean something? Does it mean something?" (118). Quoting the poem "Feed me, also, River God," she answers her own question: "I think that it does mean something." And, though she elsewhere criticizes the militaristic metaphors and techniques of the futurists, she here adapts her own battle metaphor—of fencing or sword-play—for a reading of Moore:

> I think that it does mean something. And if Miss Moore is laughing at us, it is laughter that catches us, that holds, fascinates and half-paralyses us, as light flashed from a very fine steel blade, wielded playfully, ironically, with all the fine shades of thrust and counter-thrust, with absolute surety and with absolute disdain. Yet with all the assurance of the perfect swordsman, the perfect technician, I like to imagine that there is as well something of the despair of the perfect artist—"see, you cannot know what I mean—exactly what I mean," she seems to say, half-pitying that the adversary is so dull—that we are so dull— "and I do not intend that you shall know—my sword is very much keener than your sword, my hand surer than your hand—but you shall not know that I know you are beaten."
>
> Yet we are not always baffled. Miss Moore turns her perfect craft as the perfect craftsman must inevitably do, to some direct presentation of beauty, clear, cut in flowing lines, but so delicately that the very screen she carves seems meant to stand only in that serene palace of her own world of inspiration—frail, yet as all beautiful things are, absolutely hard—and destined to endure longer, far longer than the toppling sky-scrapers, and the world of shrapnel and machine-guns in which we live. (118)

H.D. merges two distinct conceptions of poetry: on the one hand it is "absolutely hard"—a sculptural form or, in Hulme's words, "something fixed and necessary"—while on the other it is "as light flashed from a very fine steel blade," a dazzling, mobile work employed not only playfully in the stylizations of fencing, but "with absolute disdain" in deadly battle. Victory in this battle is a matter of subtlety rather than sheer force; the wielder of H.D.'s sword escapes both the absolute solidity of Hulme's theory and the overly dynamic, destructive thrusts of the avant-garde. H.D.'s term for her position here, as elsewhere, is "beauty," and she conceives of it as an absolute necessity in the face of war; her struggle for "beauty" does not escape the present world so much as it proposes an alternative justified by tradition and value:

> Miss Marianne Moore is an American. And I think in reading Miss Moore's poems we in England should be strengthened. We are torn in our ambitions, our desires are crushed, we hear from all sides that art is destined to a long period of abeyance, and that the reconstruction of Europe must take all the

genius of the race. I do not believe that. There are others here in England who do not for one moment believe that beauty will be one whit bruised by all this turmoil and distress.

Miss Moore helps us. She is fighting in her country a battle against squalor and commercialism. We are all fighting the same battle. And we must strengthen each other in this one absolute bond—our devotion to the beautiful English language. (119)

What gives this battle its significance for H.D. is its many-layered resonance. Clearly, it is in one sense aesthetic, a defense of poetry which is without question central to the poetic theory of her time, carefully elaborated with her own conceptions of tradition. On another level, it is a political poetics, engaged in a struggle against the devastation of the First World War. This conjunction of poetics and politics superimposes on H.D.'s awareness of the war a new and quite different understanding of tradition or history. In 1927, she was to give the title *Palimpsest* to her first published novel; the figure of the palimpsest—a parchment from which one layer of writing has been scraped to make room for another—is anticipated in these earlier writings of the war and early postwar years.

In a historical sense, H.D.'s palimpsest deploys a reading of her own time as a super-imposition over other times and of her own writing as a similar overlay; the writers she considers in the reviews are always substitutes for herself. For instance, H.D.'s use of Yeats's lines from "When Helen Lived" in her review of *Responsibilities,* an essay explicitly aligning his work with her own, works as a subtle palimpsest. Yeats's poem as a whole—not just the fragment quoted by H.D.—invokes a palimpsest-like relationship between the world of Homer's Troy and Yeats's own time:

> We have cried in our despair
> That men desert,
> For some trivial affair
> Or noisy, insolent sport,
> Beauty that we have won
> From bitterest hours;
> Yet we, had we walked within
> Those topless towers
> Where Helen walked with her boy,
> Had given but as the rest
> Of the men and women of Troy
> A word and a jest.

(Yeats, 108–9)

But while Yeats justifies the seriousness of war beyond the beauty of Helen, H.D.'s extraction, standing alone, not only emphasizes what are perhaps the most H.D.-like lines of all Yeats's early work, but rewrites the poem, turning it into a defense of H.D.'s own valuation of eternal beauty present not only in her early work, but throughout her life.[10]

In H.D.'s third 1916 *Egoist* review, of *The Farmer's Bride* by Charlotte Mew, she suggests another palimpsest, superimposing her own time and Alexandria:

> Originality is now rare, if not extinct. This is why we overestimate it. But in this, our present-day literary Alexandria, even the most "original" among us may take a sort of perverse delight in finding a new writer daring to discard his personality to follow, remotely or unconsciously perhaps, the tradition of an earlier generation. For the body is more than raiment, and the verse is more than its iambs, and the artist, if he be artistically mature, can follow a tradition—as Scopas, Polycritus, as Giotto, Masaccio—and remain as much Scopas, as much Giotto, as if he twisted his athlete into a gargoyle or reduced his angel into its original elements of an aureole and superimposed triangles. (135)

Twelve years later, H.D.'s "literary Alexandria" would become a part of the world of her second published novel, *Hedylus*, the city to which Hedylus and his friends, Sikeledes and Posidippus—all poets—travel to seek the patronage of a man named Demetrius. It is thus a city of the arts, but also a city which comes too late in time, a mere echo of the earlier Athens of Hedylus's mother Hedyle. It is, then, a place of outmoded tradition, a tradition always too late, distanced by war and time from its origins.

In H.D.'s review, however, the invocation of Alexandria cuts two ways. First, it implicitly places the work under review—and H.D.'s own—into the context of this tired, secondary tradition: "Originality is now rare, if not extinct." On the other hand, by invoking the poet's city, H.D. is able to claim a different kind of originality *within* tradition, a tradition including Giotto and Scopas as well as the Alexandrian poets incarnated in her novel twelve years later. And this traditional originality is, she suggests, superior to the mechanisms of the avant-garde; the vision of an angel "reduced . . . into its original elements of an aureole and superimposed triangles" evokes not only a false originary simplicity, but also the conscious primitivism of much cubist work. H.D.'s palimpsest obliquely recreates, in miniature, the argument of her Yeats review.

A third, more personal level of the palimpsest is at work in H.D.'s amalgamation of war-time poetics with her historical conjunctions and parallels. As some critics have suggested is the case for T. S. Eliot, H.D.'s concern here for the artist who dares "to discard his personality"—anticipating by three years his famous doctrine of the extinction of the artist's personality within tradition[11]—masks a deeply personal stake in her essays, as in her other work. It is well known that H.D. responded to the war as a deeply private event. Not only did she blame her 1914 miscarriage on the news that the *Lusitania* had been sunk, but many of her novels—including *Paint It To-day*—are fictionalized accounts of the breakup of her marriage to Richard Aldington in the direct context of the war.[12] Importantly, the first novel, for all of its autobiographical intent, begins with and is largely concerned with questions of aesthetics; the very aspiration to "Paint It To-day" is immersed, for H.D., in the problems of both artistic utterance and self-definition.

In the novels, the meshing of the aesthetic and the personal compels H.D. to tell her own story through fictional masks. In her essays, she does the same thing through the masks of the poets she reviews; H.D. herself appears in the motifs she chooses to emphasize: the lines from Yeats's "When Helen Lived," the Greek vase in Fletcher's preface, Marianne Moore's frail yet "absolutely hard" poems, and the literary Alexandria in the review of Charlotte Mew.

If in her review of Fletcher's *Goblins and Pagodas* H.D. praises his poetry for its evocative and vague images—for its ability to find a combination of materiality and the ethereal and thus to cultivate a middle ground between Hulme and Pound—if she praises it for its "moving, whirling, drifting" qualities, elsewhere she outlines an Imagism based much more closely on Poundian and Hulmian theory. Early in *Paint It To-day*, she uses the imagist metaphor of sculpture to set a simultaneously personal and poetic task for herself: "Which [of her worlds] was dead and which was living. Vaguely, she had of late years asked herself this. Now she set herself the task, like a problem in arithmetic, of answering the question not vaguely, groping into psychic layers of fog and probabilities, but sternly, with the emotions, it is true, but with the emotions of the sculptor rather than of the musician" (ch. 1, 13). Later in the novel, she describes, in a long underlined passage, the significance of sculpture:

> A work of art is the materialization of the electric force of the artist, electric force plus the directing impetus of the intellect.
>
> The material of the sculptor is the most definite of all. His electric impulse is materialized into definite form. The dynamic strength of his original impulse should therefore reach us less incumbered (as in the other arts) with our own impulses. In music, in painting, in poetry, our own emotions are apt to intrude, to cloud over the original impulse (or as commonly called, inspiration) of the artist.
>
> We should be able, more easily, to fall in love with a statue, than with any other work of art. (ch. 6, 6)

Struggling to find the difference between the dead and the living—to define for herself what she later in the novel calls "the present which is dead" and the "living present"—she literalizes the imagist figure of the statue, emphasizing in the process the connections she perceives between the personal and the poetic.

H.D.'s articulation of this task in the first chapter of her first novel follows Pound's imagist dicta precisely; in the place of his call for a verse which is "austere, direct, free from emotional slither," H.D. substitutes the stern "emotions of the sculptor." But her later formulation of the sculptural metaphor both extends and diverges somewhat from this austerity. While the statue is a materialization, a manifest and "definite form" which is "less incumbered . . . with our own impulses" and emotions, it also *incarnates* those very emotions; it is something we may "fall in love with." If the imagist poem aspires to the status of granite or a sculpture, then for H.D. this status defines the function of art as a materialization of emotional and psychic life. Though this inner life does not intrude or "cloud over the original impulse," it manifests both the impulse itself and the most appropriate response to that impulse. The emotions—even the "psychic layers of fog and probabilities"—thus *do* impinge on the formal stability of the work of art. This may not be Pound's "emotional slither," but neither is it his granite-like austerity or his spiritualized and neoplatonic "Ikon." Engaging the emotional life of both creator and audience, it is the ideal form of H.D.'s responsible or sacred art, melding the ethereal and the material, the intellectual and the emotional. Where Hulme's version of the sculptural metaphor solidifies and Pound's alternately solidifies and whirls off into the vortex, H.D.'s—to use her own word—crystallizes.

But the sculptural form is not, finally, a secure resting place for H.D.'s poetics. As metaphor, the solid figure of the statue continually threatens to resolve itself into the stasis repudiated by H.D. in her review of Fletcher. In her effort to "Paint It To-day," H.D. requires *both* the stability offered by the statue *and* the matrix of energy which it crystallizes, and it is in this combination of energy and possible stability that her poetics is possible. H.D.'s understanding of the energies of the futurist or vorticist endeavor rests on an understanding of those energies as a destructive force, aligned with the destructive transformations brought on by the war. Her own sense of artistic energies involves no less a transformational impetus, but melds with it a further sense of something eternal and unchanging in art. This melding is precisely what she calls the sacred.

At the end of *Paint It To-day*, she outlines the point at which the eternal cuts across the temporal and the artistic act becomes both a vehicle of transformation *and* something unchanging. Her terms are specifically personal—the passage is a dialogue between Midget Defreddy and Althea, who is a figure for H.D.'s companion Bryher—but resonate as well with her response to the war:

> "All things become beautiful if we, through the creative use of the intellect, transform them by a process of resetting them or reconsidering them in relation to what they have been or more important still, to what they may become. Nothing is static. All things change."
> "You and I change?"
> "You and I change," said Midget, "but the creative mind in us does not alter. You and I grow old but never to ourselves unsightly, if within us, the creative intellect, remains intact, unchanged, unchanging." (ch. 8, 6)

"All things change," and yet this energy takes place not, as for the futurists, in a mechanistic and militaristic ferment of novelty, but in a quite different matrix, conceived in terms of tradition and of a sacred and spiritualized material beauty. It is based on a projection of the self into its images, into the material with which it works. In her essays, H.D. projects herself into the poets she discusses, displacing their passing images into material for her own preoccupations. In her post-imagist "Imagisme," she situates herself within the sculptural metaphor and endows it with her own sense of a sacred poetry. H.D. conceives of her art as a working of prophecy, subject to neither the destructiveness of war and its related arts nor to the stultifying and static arts of the Hulmian mode. Her art "makes it new" or "Paints It To-day," while reviving a past; hers is a poetics directly of its time insisting on absolute presence and on its place within a palimpsest of all times. It is this which removes her poetry from the narrow definitions of a Hellenistic anachronism and which gives it its particular power.

2

H.D.'s Eleusis:
A Reading of the Mysteries

Mystery and a portent, yes, but at the same time, there is
Resurrection and the hope of Paradise.

                                      H.D., *"Vale Ave"*

H.D.'s insistence, in *Paint It To-day*, that "[w]e should be able, more easily, to fall in love with a statue, than with any other work of art" demarcates the "work of art" as an object of passionate engagement. At its most intense, its most mystical, H.D.'s relation to art becomes a vehicle for vision so powerful that it takes the form of possession, a literal inspiration. During her first trip to Greece in 1920 with Bryher, H.D. wrote a short prose sketch entitled "Helios and Athene," in which her engagement with the sculptural figure becomes just such a flight beyond the rational workings of the mind and the material stability of the statue itself. The second section of the sketch outlines the transformation, beginning with the physical fact of falling in love:

> The naked Greek, the youth in athletic contest, has set, accurately prescribed movement and posture. This convention made of him a medium or link between men in ordinary life and images of Pentallic frieze or temple front. We gaze upon this living naked embodiment of grace and decorum. We are enflamed by its beauty. We love it.
>
> When we have exhausted the experiences of personal emotion, we gain from the statue the same glow of physical warmth and power.
>
> The statue of Helios on the Olympic frieze, as the beautiful personality that once charmed us, acts as a go-between.
>
> The youth is a link between men (let us say) and statues.
>
> The statue is a link between the beauty of our human lovers and the gods.
>
> The statue enflames us. Its beauty is a charm or definite talisman. (327)[1]

A poetic manifesto, this second portion of "Helios and Athene" defines—insofar as it can be abstracted from H.D.'s impassioned declaration—
the scope and function of the arts, delineating three stages within the aesthetic process. The first of these is simply the direct reaction to the sculptural figure outlined so strongly in *Paint It To-day:* falling in love. But where
love's sexual force is submerged in the novel, here it is explicit, a direct and
immediate physical passion. This physical sexuality, however, arises
through the mediation of a representation; the statue substitutes for the
primary sexuality of the actual "naked Greek, the youth in athletic contest."
Such sexuality is once removed, held at a distance from "the experiences
of personal emotion"—a distance already praised by H.D. in her review of
Charlotte Mews's *The Farmer's Bride.* At this remove, physical response
becomes mental, a desire for rest, for the kind of stasis promised by the
materiality of the sculptural figure in the Hulmian metaphor:

> The statue was like a ledge of rock, from which a great bird steps as he spreads
> his wings.
> The mind, the intellect, like the bird rests for a moment, in the contempla-
> tion or worship of that Beauty.
> The mind grips the statue as the bird grips the rock-ledge. It would convince
> itself that this is its final resting place. (328)

But such security—such mental attachment—is unsatisfactory, and H.D.
proposes a third stage of response defined by a mystical or "inspired" passion:

> The mind, in its effort to disregard the truth, has built up through the
> centuries, a mass of polyglot literature explanatory of Grecian myth and culture.
> But the time has come for men and women of intelligence to build up a new
> standard, a new approach to Hellenic literature and art.
> Let daemons possess us! Let us terrify like Erynnes, the whole tribe of
> academic Grecians!
> Because (I state it inspired and calm and daemonaical) they know nothing!
> (328)

Her impassioned speech moves the artist beyond the intellectual stasis of
the "whole tribe of academic Grecians," beyond even the materiality of the
statue itself. As H.D. writes, the work of the artist begins "when his work
[is] finished" (327)—subsuming both physical passion and intellect into the
visionary state which is both the goal of H.D.'s art and the source of her
artistic passion.

In "Helios and Athene," these three stages are never quite stated as
such and can be deduced only through a reading of the text's gaps. One stage

of response to the statue does not explicitly give way to another, but simply disappears as the next takes over, leaving the reader to supply the steps between them. However, another text, *Notes on Thought and Vision*, which H.D. wrote on the Scilly Islands off the coast of Cornwall in 1919, outlines these stages explicitly, describing them as the stages of the Eleusinian mysteries:

> The first step in the Eleusinian mysteries had to do with sex. There were images set up in a great room, coloured marbles and brown pottery, painted with red and vermilion and coloured earthen work or clay images. The candidates for admission to the mysteries would be shown through the room by a priest or would walk through at random, as the crowd walks through the pornographic chamber at the museum at Naples.
>
> It would be easy enough to judge them by their attitude, whether it was one of crude animal enjoyment or hypocritical aloofness.
>
> The crowd that got through to the second room would be different, more sensitive, more fastidious. They would correspond to certain of our intellectual types of today. They would be interested because it was the thing to be interested—also to show their superiority.
>
> Any one who got safely through the mere animal stage and the intellectual stage would be left in a small room by himself to make his constatation. (29–30)

Following the first two steps of the process—the sexual and the intellectual—H.D. finds a third, inspiration:

> Socrates said, "There are many wand-bearers but few inspired." He meant, by wand-bearers, people who had passed the first two stages of the Eleusinian mysteries. We mean by wand-bearers today, intelligent people of normal development, who have looked into matters of life scientifically and with a certain amount of artistic appreciation.
>
> Today there are many wand-bearers but few inspired. (31)

The "constatation"—the declaration of faith or inspiration, as it were—of the initiate, demonstrating incontrovertibly the truth of the initiation, is at once the affirmation and the evidence of her inspiration, her vision of the mysteries. As in "Helios and Athene," the first two stages are necessary steps toward this vision but they are also only preliminaries to what comes next—the role of the prophet, H.D.'s ideal of the artist, stating truth through inspiration.

Though H.D.'s interest in Eleusis is not unique—certainly both Pound and Eliot shared such an interest, and James Frazer and Jane Ellen Harrison set the stage for their poetic work with groundbreaking research—the source for her three-fold division of the Eleusinian mysteries is obscure.

Harrison, in her *Prolegomena to the Study of Greek Religion,* divides them
into only two parts: the Lesser Mysteries devoted to Persephone, and the
Greater devoted to Demeter. She does, however, provide a possible gloss
for H.D.'s sexual reading of the mysteries; she cites the Christian commen-
tator Asterius's denunciation of the carnality of Eleusis: "'Are not the Mysteries at Eleusis the chief act of your worship and does not the Attic people
and the whole land of Hellas assemble that it may accomplish a rite of folly?
Is there not there performed the descent into darkness, the venerated
congress of the Hierophant with the priestess, of him alone with her alone?
Are not the torches extinguished and does not the vast and countless assem-
blage believe *that in what is done by the two in darkness is their salvation?'"* (563). Harrison's account places this sexual congress at the culmination of the second, greater, stage of the mysteries. H.D., shifting sexuality
to the beginning of the process, ultimately makes it the transformational
basis of her aesthetics, making it the ultimate grounds for the impassioned
constatation of the initiate.[2]

While H.D.'s poetics of the war years emphasizes a contemporary
"responsibility" within a broad tradition undefined and unsullied by the
violence of the war, her post-war writings attach the sacred to a single
definite tradition central to her Hellenism: the mysteries of Eleusis. Still,
like everything else in H.D.'s writing, Eleusis is a palimpsest and retains a
contemporary force. This contemporaneity takes several forms: the seeming
asides in *Notes on Thought and Vision* to modern "candidates for admission
to the mysteries," to today's "wand-bearers," and to the "whole tribe of
academic Grecians" who study Greece but do not live it. And H.D.'s own
constatation in "Helios and Athene" gives a directive which may stand with
her "Paint It To-day": "But the time has come for men and women of
intelligence to build up a new standard, a new approach to Hellenic literature and art." This "new approach" is nothing other than her own, creating
a Hellenism which is *both* historical *and* contemporary—in a word, a palimpsest. H.D.'s visionary mysteries are thus literally present to her, not the
distant artifacts of the "academic Grecians" she criticizes.[3]

H.D.'s Hellenism is thus a practice of revelation rather than of study,
a treatment of the past as present and alive rather than irrevocably dead. A
passage from her second unpublished novel, *Asphodel,* written between
1921 and 1922 and covering much the same biographical ground as *Paint It
To-day,* directly confronts this visionary imperative. Evoking both Hellenic
and Christian antecedents, her character Hermione—pregnant and wondering if she should allow the pregnancy to follow its course—decides that the
flight of a swallow into her room will be a sign that she should have the child.
In her ecstasy, she articulates a theory of vision and palimpsest:

Layers of life are going on all the time only sometimes we know it and most times we don't know it. Layers and layers of life like some transparent onion-like globe that has fine, transparent layer on layer (interpenetrating like water) layer on layer, circle on circle. Plato's spheres. Sometimes for a moment we realize a layer out of ourselves, in another sphere of consciousness, sometimes one layer falls and life itself, the very reality of tables and chairs becomes imbued with a quality of long-past, an epic quality so that the chair you sit in may be the very chair you drew forward when as Cambises you consulted over the execution of your faithless servitors. Cruelty and beauty and love of beauty is the common heritage of the whole race. Everything is to each but it is only in developing one's own genius, one's own mean personality (which is one's own innate daemon) that we can reach the realization of some sphere which is for all time, eternal, flowing as water, colourless, transparent which falling imbues the very common chair you sit in, the very ordinary book you lift and open with some quality that is one with the Revelation of Saint John or the orders of Sappho. Colour there is in this sphere world, colour of the red anemone, colour as seen under clear water, colour as sea-coral seen through crystal. World falls over your head and you are embedded in the world; you are its only imperfection yet your very presence giving quality, point, perspective to this otherwise so measureless luminous body. (pt. 2, 88–89)

The daemonic possession outlined in "Helios and Athene" is possession by a daemon of one's own; as H.D. puts it in *Asphodel*, the visionary is the "only imperfection" of this world, and yet it is the visionary who gives the world its "quality, point, perspective," who finally gives it its possibility of meaning.

The strengths of the first two layers of the aesthetic schema H.D. proposes in "Helios and Athene" and *Notes on Thought and Vision* come into their own in the third stage of vision or possession. The sexual arousal elicited by the statue becomes a metaphor for the passions of vision, a sublimated and yet sexually charged power. Similarly, the intellectual stage remains as the portion of the mind engaged in constatation, a visionary state akin to Saint John the Divine's Revelation and transformed by the passion of H.D.'s Sappho. In the constatation, all three stages merge; vision subsumes its antecedents without destroying them. Or, rather, it subsumes them by overwriting them in a palimpsest, revising and transforming them but retaining their traces and influences.

In H.D.'s system, the first stage, having "to do with sex," sets the pattern for the entire process, for it establishes the initial relation to the figure of the statue and thus to any initiation into the mysteries. H.D.'s images in these passages all depend on an underpinning of passionate attachment. "Helios and Athene" connects the god and the goddess as equals in H.D.'s vision, and posits Athene herself as a figure for the various powers of sexual connection. On the one hand, they stand as equal yet different incarnations of the divine, as in the third portion of the sketch:

> If Athene's citadel broke, Helios' temple crumbled. If Helios yielded to her, Athene herself was undone.
> Delphi and Athens were thus allied forever.
> Delphi, the serpent, the destructive heat, Delphi the devastatingly subtle seat of oracles, Delphi whose centre of religion was a centre of political intrigue, Delphi the lie, the inspiration, the music, found in Hellas, in the world, one equal: Athene. . . .
> To Helios alone could she open wide their splendour.
> He hated her because she stood unconquerable: he loved her as an equal. (328–29)

On the other hand, Athene contains Helios, and is thus a symbol on her own for the passion and engagement of the third stage of initiation:

> The greatest Athenians of the greatest period were initiates of the Eleusinian mysteries. Those great mysteries were protected by the Love of Athene.
> The love of Athene is symbolized by the arch of wings, for Demeter by the cavern or grot in the earth, and for Phoebus by the very essential male power. Love for Athene is the surrender to neither, the merging and welding of both, the conquering in herself of each element, so that the two merge in the softness and tenderness of the mother and the creative power and passion of the male. In her hand is the symbol of this double conquest and double power, the winged Nike. (330)

Helios and Athene remain linked intellectually and sexually, retaining traces of the two stages of initiation as elements of their relationship. Intellectually, their connection can be analyzed, as H.D. shows, in the political history of Delphi and Athens; sexually, Athene is a figure for the creative merger of mother and father. Each level of connection has its source in the sexual mysteries with which the initiation began; each is a version of the erotic, sublimated or intellectualized as it may be. And the mysteries themselves, "protected by the Love of Athene," in which all of these connections are joined, are sexual in their beginning and end, celebrating the restoration of links between the mythic mother and daughter—Demeter and Persephone—in the annual context of spring's fertility and regeneration.[4]

3

Hymen:
The Course of a Sexual Poetics

*Facing the path direct between intellectual greatness and
something . . . other.*

H.D., *Hedylus*

Notes on Thought and Vision was written in 1919; "Helios and Athene" in
1920. In 1921, H.D. published her second major volume of verse, *Hymen*,
through The Egoist Press in London and H. Holt and Company in New
York.[1] This volume, its title invoking both the classical god of marriage and
the physical "virginal membrane" (*O.E.D.*), shares with both of the earlier
prose works a preoccupation with the sexual stage of initiation into mysteries. Where H.D.'s first volume, *Sea Garden* of 1916, situated itself within
an imagist framework and explored figures of boundaries and intersections
suggested by the title image—the Sea Garden being the line where land and
sea merge[2]—*Hymen* re-explores these boundaries in terms of a new uni-
verse more fully inhabited by human figures. *Hymen* takes as its governing
metaphor the complex version of boundary or intersection suggested by the
figure of the hymen itself; it is a volume about human and divine merger, a
merger most clearly realized in the realm of the god Hymen: marriage in all
its aspects.[3]

In the March 1922 issue of *Poetry*, H.D.'s companion Bryher reviews
Hymen in terms which may as well be H.D.'s own, emphasizing her concerns with poetry in a time of war. Answering earlier critics' charges that
H.D.'s poems are "perfectly wrought but cold and passionless," Bryher
writes "Perfectly wrought the poems are. . . . But they are not cold, they are
not passionless; and apart from the color of some Attic names how are these
songs anything but the expression of the emotions and desires of an

extremely present age?" (333–34). And again, "Not cold, not passionless, but with emotion and thought perfectly balanced, *Hymen* can make even the 'disenchanted days' of which the poet writes, bright with beauty" (337). H.D.'s volume begins with just such a denial of the supposedly "passionless" state of the poet. On the first page of the first edition (though missing from the 1925 *Collected Poems*) a dedication appears: "For Bryher and Perdita."[4] The dual dedication—to companion and daughter—honors H.D.'s meeting with Bryher in Cornwall in 1918 and recalls the traumatic birth of Perdita and survival of both mother and daughter, nursed by Bryher, in March 1919.[5] More importantly, it places the names of the two other women at the head of *Hymen's* exploration of the marriage metaphor, binding the volume firmly to the personal passions of its author; it brings into *Hymen* both the history of the relationship between H.D. and Bryher—specifying it as a marriage of sorts—and the creative or procreative element of sexual passion in the figure of H.D.'s daughter, Perdita.

The mythic dimension of the passionate matrix suggested by the dedication to *Hymen* is the subject of *Notes on Thought and Vision,* which melds H.D.'s mysteries and aesthetics with her vision of the artistic and procreative passions. Developing a complex theory of what she alternately calls—sounding very much like D. H. Lawrence—"the overmind" and "jelly-fish consciousness," H.D. imagines the artist's immersion in "the world of pure over-mind" (18) as a kind of cap physically descending over the head:

> That over-mind seems a cap, like water, transparent, fluid yet with definite body, contained in a definite space. It is like a closed sea-plant, jelly-fish or anemone.
> Into that over-mind, thoughts pass and are visible like fish swimming under clear water. . . .
> I should say—to continue the jelly-fish metaphor—that long feelers reached down and through the body, that these stood in the same relation to the nervous system as the over-mind to the brain or intellect.
> There is, then, a set of super-feelings. These feelings extend out and about us; as the long-floating tentacles of the jelly-fish reach out and about him. They are not of different material, extraneous to the gray matter of the directing brain. The super-feelers are part of the super-mind, as the jelly-fish feelers are the jelly-fish itself, elongated in fine threads. (18–19)

A second "cap" ascends from the "love-region of the body," something which H.D. first experienced during the birth of Perdita:

> I first realised this state of consciousness in my head. I visualize it just as well, now, centered in the love-region of the body or placed like a foetus in the body.

The centre of consciousness is either the brain or the love-region of the body.

Is it easier for a woman to attain this state of consciousness than for a man?
For me, it was before the birth of my child that the jelly-fish consciousness seemed to come definitely into the field or realm of the intellect or brain. (19–20)

Artistic creation as a passional state, as a sexualized constatation, takes place within this context of relationship and birth. The reclamation of the daughter in the Eleusinian mysteries is equivalent to constatation itself; the rites of Hymen are thus the rites of poetry, a sign of the seriousness with which H.D. takes her own poetic initiation.

On the page facing the dedication—and still before either acknowledgements or table of contents—is a dedicatory poem. Separated from the body of the book, this poem moves *Hymen* directly into the mythic, setting a further context for what follows:

> *They said:*
> *she is high and far and blind*
> *in her high pride,*
> *but now that my head is bowed*
> *in sorrow, I find*
> *she is most kind.*
>
> *We have taken life, they said,*
> *blithely, not groped in a mist*
> *for things that are not—*
> *are if you will, but bloodless—*
> *why ask happiness of the dead?*
> *and my heart bled.*
>
> *Ah, could they know*
> *how violets throw strange fire,*
> *red and purple and gold,*
> *how they glow*
> *gold and purple and red*
> *where her feet tread.*

(CP, 101)

One typescript of this poem gives it the title "Pallas," specifying it as a poem to Athene, giving the volume—by extension—a divine dedication to go with the human dedications to companion and daughter. And "she," "high and far and blind," is indeed Athene; "doubly passionate" (*CP*, 330) as she finally turns out to be, the Athene of "Helios and Athene" is also initially such a distant, cold goddess, far beyond reach of the beings below her:[6] "We cannot approach her direct, so abstract, so cold, so beautiful. We approach her, if at all, through the medium of the mysteries and through the intercession of other Gods" (329). But this cold goddess is finally a passionate and *com*passionate figure, easily accessible to the one making her constatation, to the poet of a beauty set against those who "have taken life . . . / blithely" and who would claim that this bloodletting is more a part of the real world than the evanescent, "bloodless" ecstasies of the goddess and her poet. While thus melding the terminology of H.D.'s critical wartime writing to the passional visions of "Helios and Athene" and *Notes on Thought and Vision*, *Hymen*'s dedicatory poem also defends her in advance against the coldness of her critics' vision; her poems, like the violets near Athene's feet, are numinous with "strange fire," signifying the very real presence of both the goddess and the poet herself—physically and spiritually committed to the divine within the quotidian—in the company of the book's dedicatees.

One approach to the realm of Athene, H.D. writes in "Helios and Athene," is through the drama, "the outgrowth of the worship of Dionysius" (330). The body of *Hymen*, then, begins with a drama of sorts, a mini-masque which gives the book its title. The dramatic energy of this opening poem is minimal, but as a hieratic and ritualistic masque it clearly sets a stage for the volume's exploration of the marriage metaphor. In a succession of short, static scenes, small groups of women and girls come onto the stage and sing lyric poems, accompanied by a variety of musical instruments. Following the lyric singing, each group exits. The poems themselves are simple and stylized, both celebrating the impending marriage and lamenting the loss of the bride to the male world of the groom, "losing . . . her maidenhood" to his passion. One of the poems presents the bride as a cold, inaccessible goddess, as a version of Athene in her "white on white" guise:

> But of her,
> Who can say if she is fair?
> For her head is covered over
> With her mantle
> White on white,
> Snow on whiter amaranth,
> Snow on hoar-frost,
> Snow on snow,
> Snow on whitest buds of myrrh.

(106)

As could be expected, the antistrophe revises the vision, and the bride becomes a figure of passion beneath her veils:

> But of her,
> We can say that she is fair;
> For we know underneath
> All the wanness,
> All the heat
> (In her blanched face)
> Of desire
> Is caught in her eyes as fire
> In the dark center leaf
> Of the white Syrian iris.
>
> (106)

But if this passage marks a stage in the initiation rites of marriage, it also marks something quite different. The subtly sinister undertone of the antistrophe—the "wanness" of the bride, her "blanched face" at the threatening approach of the male—is echoed elsewhere in the early passages of the masque:[7] "Never more" shall the girls find the bride "bright / In the snow and wind"; the bride is "*Bound* with fillet, / *Bound* with myrtle," as if she were literally a captive of Love; the young women making up the bridal bed build it from scented wood so that

> . . . all the wood in blossoming,
> May calm her heart and cool her blood
> For losing of her maidenhood.
>
> (108)

The masque, like the marriage rite, reaches its climax with a consummation. The figure of Love as a tall male youth enters and sings an allegorized account:

> Crimson, with honey-seeking lips,
> The sun lies hot across his back,
> The gold is flecked across his wings,
> Quivering he sways and quivering clings
> (Ah, rare her shoulders drawing back!)
> One moment, then the plunderer slips
> Between the purple flower-lips.
>
> (109)

The moment fulfills not only the hopes of the earlier portions of the masque—the lyricism of this poem is, in the sequence, striking—but also its undercurrent of fear. The flower-bride, rapt by the solar beauty of Love, is also raped; the single word, "plunderer," turns the poem from celebration to lament as the voice of the poet breaks through and transforms the orgasmic song of Love. As the bride gives herself to the groom, she risks annihilation; he "seeks with honey-thighs to sway / And drink the very flower away," destroying the hymen—and the bride with it—even as he enacts the rites of Hymen.

The final portion of "Hymen" retains this ambivalence, wavering between ecstasy and annihilation. Following the climax of the plunderer, the stage becomes the domain of the male rather than of the female; for the first time, "A band of boys passes before the curtain," singing a final song of celebration and devastation:

> Where love is come
> (Ah, love is come indeed!)
> Our limbs are numb
> Before his fiery need;
> With all their glad
> Rapture of speech unsaid,
> Before his fiery lips
> Our lips are mute and dumb.
>
> Ah, sound of reed,
> Ah, flute and trumpet wail,
> Ah, joy decreed—
> The fringes of her veil
> Are seared and white;
> Across the flare of light,
> Blinded the torches fail.
> (Ah, love is come indeed!)

(110)

The orgasmic pun "love is come" punctuating the song shifts the masque's attentions from the preparations of the bride to the act of the groom, obscuring the drama of a woman who has endured the "losing of her maidenhood," whose veils "are seared and white." But the boys' song, celebrating Love's "coming," is also in a sense a song of the bride, lamenting her muteness and blindness "before his fiery need" simply by means of the unacknowledged but clear shift from her drama to the groom's. Following this transition, the masque ends on a distinctly dismal note, in darkness: "At the end of the song, the torches flicker out and the figures are no longer distinguishable in the darkness. They pass out like shadows. The purple curtain hangs black and heavy. The music dies away and is finally cut short with a few deep, muted chords" (110).

This scene—the marriage masque ending in the bride's desolation—

marks one end of the spectrum of *Hymen*'s images. The other end of the range is similarly laid out by the extreme celebratory tone in certain sections of the title poem. Such breadth of reactions to the marriage metaphor is inherent in the title figure itself—in the hymen, remaining intact in the rites and destroyed in the consummation. In this uneasy balance, *Hymen* echoes "Helios and Athene," where the two gods find a certain equilibrium moving back and forth between equality and an alliance built of hatred:

> So Delphi and Athens stood, existent, gaining power, gaining strength, through inter-dependence of hatred.
> But this hatred was clear, defined, removed from any hint of personal intrusion, intellectual, abstract.
> If Athene's citadel broke, Helios' temple crumbled. If Helios yielded to her, Athene herself was undone.
> Delphi and Athens were thus allied forever.

And again: "He hated her because she stood unconquerable: he loved her as an equal" (328–29). In different terms, such an uneasy balance is the stated goal of *Notes on Thought and Vision*: "Three states or manifestations of life: body, mind, over-mind. Aim of men and women of highest development is equilibrium, balance, growth of the three at once . . . " (17).

But while the two prose works foreground their concerns (though they are typically oblique in their presentation) and are explicable as arguments, *Hymen* takes the much more problematic poetic route through the same terrain. As a result, just as "Hymen" alternately presents passages of celebration and suggestions of despair, moments of the volume as a whole may occupy any point of the spectrum, may range to any position between the extremes. *Hymen* deals in incarnations rather than in arguments. The ending of the title sequence is a clear example. Are we to read the boys' song as a laudatory hymn of praise for the passions of Love, or are we to see only the seared fringes of the bride's veil falling from her in the masque's fading light? The two exist simultaneously; the ambivalence of the poem is insistent and inescapable.

The second poem of the volume, "Demeter," draws this pervasive ambivalence into an explicitly Eleusinian scene, bringing the primary characters of the mysteries into a pivotal place within *Hymen*'s framework. The poem's story, such as it is, contains two dominant elements—the loss of Persephone to the underworld and the adoption of "Bromios" (Dionysos) by Demeter[8]—framed by a consideration of Demeter as both an object of worship by men and an object mimicked by their representations of her. Section 1 is a retort to the marriage scene of "Hymen," emphasizing Demeter's disdain for the images men have made of her:

> Ah they have wrought me heavy
> and great of limb—
> she is slender of waist,
> slight of breast, made of many fashions;
> they have set *her* small feet
> on many a plinth;
> she they have known,
> she they have spoken with,
> she they have smiled upon,
> she they have caught
> and flattered with praise and gifts.
>
> (111)

But this disdain is not simply jealousy for the more traditionally beautiful images of another goddess (Aphrodite?);[9] it is, rather, the beginning of a complex set of relationships defined by both gain and loss within the framework of marriage and the divine family. This first section makes it clear that the danger of ruin is a given in the dominion of marriage—a danger metaphorized as a passer-by's ephemeral interest in Demeter's marketplace statue:

> But useless the flattery
> of the mighty power
> they have granted me:
> for I will not stay in her breast
> the great of limb,
> though perfect the shell
> they have fashioned me, these men!
>
> Do I sit in the market place—
> do I smile, does a noble brow
> bend like the brow of Zeus—
> am I a spouse, his or any,
> am I a woman, or goddess or queen,
> to be met by a god with a smile—and left?
>
> (111–12)

This marriage of the marketplace, in which the bride is in fact no more than a representation or image, requires the threat of abandonment to support it; just as the image of Demeter is less than Demeter herself, the image of the bride—the "spouse, his or any"—is less than real, more a simulacra than a real woman.

H.D.'s Demeter is, of course, an image, but of a different sort. Within the context of *Hymen* she is, like the H.D. who has recently given birth to a daughter, a figure of the mother, central to the kind of familial structure invoked by the volume's dedications.[10] Similarly, in *Notes on Thought and Vision* she is an embodiment of the mysteries, equivalent to the mother of Christ: "This is the mystery of Demeter, the Earth Mother. The body of the Eleusinian initiate had become one with the earth, as his soul had become one with the seeds enclosed in the earth" (52). Demeter is greater than the "shell" men have made for her, and the second section of the poem acknowledges her power:

> Do you ask for a scroll,
> parchment, oracle, prophecy, precedent;
> do you ask for tablets marked with thought
> or words cut deep on the marble surface,
> do you seek measured utterance or the mystic trance?
> Sleep on the stones of Delphi—
> dare the ledges of Pallas
> but keep me foremost,
> keep me before you, after you, with you,
> never forget when you start
> for the Delphic precipice,
> never forget when you seek Pallas
> and meet in thought
> yourself drawn out from yourself
> like the holy serpent,
> never forget
> in thought or mysterious trance—
> I am the greatest and least.
>
> (112)

Least in the marketplace and greatest in her own power, Demeter recreates *Hymen*'s marriage metaphor in its familial form—she governs a group parallel to the H.D./Bryher/Perdita trio, endowed with all the visionary marks of the true mysteries. At the time of Perdita's birth, H.D. was apart from both Cecil Gray—the father of her child—and her husband, Richard Aldington, but had acquired new alliances with Bryher as well as with Perdita. Demeter plays a divine version of the same role; the goddess faces the threat of abandonment in the poem's first section only to forge connections—to rectify abandonment—in the third:[11]

> Ah, small black head,
> ah, the purple ivy bush,
> ah, berries that shook and split
> on the form beneath,
> who begot you and left?
> Though I begot no man child

> all my days,
> the child of my heart and spirit,
> is the child the gods desert
> alike and the mother in death—
> the unclaimed Dionysos.
>
> (113–14)

Dionysos's role in the poem is clear: as Jane Ellen Harrison puts it in a discussion of a vase drawing of Dionysos with Demeter and Persephone, "Dionysos is accepted at Eleusis" (556–57); the reclamation of the abandoned child restores the gap left by the potential abandonment of the first section, a restoration signalled by the repetition of the phrase "and left" in both sections. As Demeter rescues Bromios, she reclaims much of her own power, restoring that part of her which had been threatened.

The story of the deserted child rescued by a protectress resonates with another story later dramatized by H.D. in *Ion* and, more importantly here, alluded to in "Helios and Athene": "The baby Ion, son of Helios, was deserted by his mother. She laid him among violets. Athene, the goddess, sent serpents to protect him. These serpents fed the child with honey" (326).

If *Hymen* as a whole situates itself in the domain of Athene rather than of Helios, then Demeter here substitutes for Athene, a figure through whom she becomes protecting goddess; both take it upon themselves to protect an abandoned male child, and both possess a power other than that ascribed to them by those who "have taken life . . . / blithely." The final section of the poem returns to the more familiar story of the rape of Persephone and the role of the mother in her recovery:

> *What of her—*
> *mistress of Death—*
> *what of his kiss?*
>
> Ah, strong were his arms to wrest
> slight limbs from the beautiful earth,
> young hands that plucked the first
> buds of the chill narcissus,
> soft fingers that broke
> and fastened the thorny stalk
> with the flower of wild acanthus.
> Ah, strong were the arms that took
> (ah evil, the heart and graceless,)
> but the kiss was less passionate!
>
> (114–15)

The addition of this story to the poem completes its cast of characters and solidifies its position within the marriage complex. In the completed sequence, Demeter emerges as the figure of a bride set on a "plinth" and abandoned, Bromios as the found and nurtured child, and Persephone as both lost daughter and "mistress of Death," the bride who has been raped and stolen from "the beautiful earth."

A significant image-cluster gives the poem much of its coherence and structure: recurring references to hands and arms move through the poem, adding to the resonance of the marriage complex. The first of these echoes the volume's title poem in its celebratory mood: "Soft are the hands of Love, / soft, soft are his feet" (112). But this delicacy quickly acquires an ironic edge as the line is repeated in reference to the terror of the abandoned Bromios:

> Soft are the hands of Love,
> but what soft hands
> clutched at the thorny ground.
>
> (113)

The soft hands of the child give the lie to the notion of the softness of a Love who could leave such a child on "the thorny ground." This antithesis carries over into the poem's fourth section, where the hands are no longer so soft. Here, Demeter's hands begin in the "Form of a golden wreath" encircling her daughter's head but quickly take on necessary strength as she searches for what she has lost:

> Now they are wrought of iron
> to wrest from earth
> secrets.
>
> (114)

The figure of Death—the god of the underworld who as a husband rapes his bride and steals her from her home—overwhelms the figure of Love, his strong arms "wrest[ing] / slight limbs from the beautiful earth." The apparent passion of Love, drinking "the very flower away" in "Hymen" is unmasked as an act of violence, a strong-arm assault motivated more by love of power than by a passionate Eros. Conversely, the figure of the mother emerges in the full power of her passion, with arms that can "wrest from earth / secrets," regaining her daughter and revivifying the earth. In the terms of H.D.'s wartime criticism, Death plays the role of the "daemon [who] took for its own the most robust talent of our generation," while Demeter becomes the carrier of a responsible and eternal beauty.

In *Hymen*'s particular reworking of the "Helios and Athene" paradigm, the ending of "Demeter" marks both a high and a low point. In its familial structure, its substantiation of the book's dedications, the poem contains great promise; the restitution of the mother-child connection brings with it nothing less than the re-animation of a war-torn earth. On the other hand, in the terms of the hymeneal metaphor, "Demeter" suggests anything *but* a Helios/Athene balance. The story of the abandoned Bromios, echoing the abandonment of Ion by Helios, indicts the god; he is not the equal of Athene, but the sinister figurehead of that "devastatingly subtle seat of oracles, Delphi whose centre of religion was a centre of political intrigue, Delphi the lie . . . " (*CP*, 329). The constatation of "Demeter" arises from something very different than the visionary powers of heterosexual passion suggested by H.D.'s reading of Eleusis; it is an attack upon the manipulations and violence masked by such passion.

But this dark scene—Helios and Athene entirely at odds and the "young hands" of Persephone imprisoned in the grip of Death—is simply one extreme of the hymeneal range. While "Demeter" would deny outright the possibilities of rapture and ecstasy within marriage, other poems— particularly H.D.'s version of Leda and the Swan—restore the joy of the other extreme. In "Leda," intercourse with the god is unmediated bliss, direct apprehension of his "kingly kiss" (121), the state called "vision" in *Notes on Thought and Vision*:

> We begin with sympathy of thought.
> The minds of the two lovers merge, interact in sympathy of thought.
> The brain, enflamed and excited by this interchange of ideas, takes on its character of over-mind, becomes (as I have visualised it in my own case) a jelly-fish, placed over and about the brain.
> The love-region is excited by the appearance or beauty of the loved one, its energy not dissipated in physical relation, takes on its character of mind, becomes this womb-brain or love-brain that I have visualised as a jelly-fish *in* the body.
> The love-brain and over-brain are both capable of thought. This thought is vision. (22)

The "physical relation" of Leda and the swan does not "dissipate" the poetic or visionary energy, but enhances it, allowing "no more regret / nor old deep memories / to mar the bliss" of vision (121). In the same way, "Evadne" recalls an encounter on the banks of the Erotos between the daughter of Poseidon and Apollo—H.D.'s Helios—as a lingering moment of visionary eroticism:[12]

> His hair was crisp to my mouth
> as the flower of the crocus,

across my cheek,
cool as the silver cress
on Erotos bank;
between my chin and throat
his mouth slipped over and over.

Still between my arm and shoulder,
I feel the brush of his hair,
and my hands keep the gold they took
as they wandered over and over
that great arm—full of yellow flowers.

(132)

"Hymen"'s plundering bee taking as his own the pollen of the flower-bride here becomes its opposite, as the bride savors the "gold" she finds in intercourse with the god.

Another poem, "White World,"[13] repeats the bee motif as a paradigm of union:

Yet not one wearies,
joined is each to each
in happiness complete
with bush and flower:
ours is the wind-breath
at the hot noon-hour,
ours is the bee's soft belly
and the blush of the rose-petal,
lifted, of the flower.

(135)

Standing by itself this image would threaten to sink into banality. Its place in the midst of *Hymen*'s bee imagery gives it weight; the figure of the bee stands variously for the male lover as "plunderer," the female lover, and the memory of the moment of conjunction.[14]

The very potential for triviality or sentimentality in the image gives impetus to another poem, "Fragment 113," which takes its lead from Sappho's "Neither honey nor bee for me":

Not honey,
not the plunder of the bee
from meadow or sand-flower
or mountain bush;
from winter-flower or shoot
born of the later heat:
not honey, not the sweet

stain on the lips and teeth:
not honey, not the deep
plunge of soft belly
and the clinging of the gold-edged
pollen-dusted feet;

not so—
though rapture blind my eyes,
and hunger crisp
dark and inert my mouth,
not honey, not the south,
not the tall stalk
of red twin-lilies,
nor light branch of fruit tree
caught in flexible light branch.

(131)

H.D.'s catalogue, based on Sappho's rejection of the excessive sweetness of the honey-bee image, moves systematically through the rest of *Hymen*, lifting out and discarding images. The poem's final stanzas, continuing the negations, intimate a different sort of visionary state:

not honey, not the south;
ah flower of purple iris,
flower of white,
or of the iris, withering the grass—
for fleck of the sun's fire,
gathers such heat and power,
that shadow-print is light,
cast through the petals
of the yellow iris flower;

not iris—old desire—old passion—
old forgetfulness—old pain—
not this, nor any flower,
but if you turn again,
seek strength of arm and throat,
touch as the god;
neglect the lyre-note;
knowing that you shall feel,
about the frame,
no trembling of the string
but heat, more passionate
of bone and the white shell
and fiery tempered steel.

(131–32)

As if in answer to "White World," these final lines translate the blandness of that poem's colorlessness into a "more passionate" whiteness in which the power of poetic vision supercedes both the easy bliss of a secure relationship and the "old desire—old passion" of Evadne's memory. *Hymen*'s marriage metaphor dissolves into the "fiery tempered steel" of a poem which can cut through the fantasies of "happiness complete" and replace them with something infinitely more powerful. The "shadow-print" of such negation is the "light" of "Fragment 113"'s vision.

Like the "doubly passionate" Athene of "Helios and Athene," the women of these poems—and others, like "Simaetha"—are passionate in both separation and connection, in both extremes of the hymeneal image. The most pervasive constellation of female figures appears in a sequence of poems beginning mid-way through the volume with "Hippolytus Temporizes" and continuing near the end with "Phaedra," "She Contrasts with Herself Hippolyta," and "She Rebukes Hippolyta." These poems comprise H.D.'s first working of the story of the triangle between Hippolytus, his mother Hippolyta, and Phaedra, a story she was later to use in her only original drama, 1927's *Hippolytus Temporizes*. In the play, Hippolytus is the central character, one of H.D.'s few major male masks; as it progresses, he, blindly in love with the virgin Artemis, is lured by Phaedra into a sexual encounter ending in his death and her madness. The poems in *Hymen,* on the other hand, focus on the two women, setting them in scenes determined by their relation to the hymeneal metaphor.

That this knot of characters is bound together through the mysteries of Eros in the first stage of the Eleusinian process is clear not only from the outlines of the story itself, but from the convolutions of the sequence's initial poem, "Hippolytus Temporizes." Each stanza begins with a statement of worship directed toward Artemis before slipping into an erotic aside spoken by Hippolytus to himself; the final stanza completes the pattern:

> I worship the greatest first—
> (suddenly into my brain—
> the flash of sun on the snow,
> the fringe of light and the drift,
> the crest and the hill-shadow—
> ah, surely now I forget,
> ah splendour, my goddess turns:
> or was it the sudden heat,
> beneath quivering of molten flesh,
> of veins, purple as violets?).

(122)

Hippolytus's worship of Artemis swerves into the "quivering" of his "molten flesh." In the murky context of the poem's asides, this graphically described orgasm may take place either in Phaedra's tent while she masquerades as Artemis, or more simply in Hippolytus's own mind.[15] His "temporizings" remain bounded by an obsession with the simply physical; what he imagines as a divine consummation—a true tryst with the goddess—is merely an onanistic version of the initial stage of H.D.'s Eleusis.

The sequence as a whole, though dominated by the erotic, does not remain in this first stage but, moving from the parent-child paradigm to an exploration of a relationship between two women, undertakes a journey through the mysteries. The three poems spoken by Phaedra late in the volume are constatations of the highest order, with Phaedra and Hippolyta as figures for the extremes of hymeneal passion moving through the stages of initiation. The first, "Phaedra," is a poem of vision or, more accurately, the poem of a woman possessed and tortured by the powers of vision:

> Think, O my soul—
> what power has struck you blind—
> is there no desert-root, no forest-berry
> pine pitch or knot of fir
> known that can help the soul
> caught in a force, a power,
> passionless, not its own?
>
> (135)

While Hippolytus is trapped by his own almost willful misreading of the erotic, Phaedra finds herself imprisoned by an Eros not of her own making, and prays for a restoration of control:

> *So I scatter, so implore*
> *Gods of Crete, summoned before*
> *with slighter craft;*
> *ah, hear my prayer:*
> *Grant to my soul*
> *the body that it wore,*
> *trained to your thought,*
> *that kept and held your power,*
> *as the petal of black poppy,*
> *the opiate of the flower.*
>
> *For art undreamt in Crete,*
> *strange art and dire,*
> *in counter-charm prevents my charm*

limits my power:
pine-cone I heap,
grant answer to my prayer.

(135–36)

Although constrained by the powers of Eros, Phaedra manifests a clear vision by the sheer insistence of her prayer; she may be a prisoner, but she knows it, and this makes almost all the difference. Still, despite her clear vision and strong voice, she does not escape. The image of the poppy—in the prayer a figure for her former strength—reverts in the poem's last stanza to an image of nearly absolute weakness:

The poppy that my heart was,
formed to bind all mortals,
made to strike and gather hearts
like flame upon an altar,
fades and shrinks, a red leaf
drenched and torn in the cold rain.

(136)

The two final, "imagist" lines—threatening like the images of "White World" to topple over into bathos—limit the reach of Phaedra's vision to the narrow bounds of her terrible possession.

This diminishment of the erotic to a scene of involuntary demonic possession provides the occasion for "She Contrasts with Herself Hippolyta," a poem which answers "Phaedra" and moves the sequence firmly into the second stage of H.D.'s Eleusinian initiation. While Eros entraps Phaedra, Hippolyta passes through the hymeneal rape intact; she is stronger, more passionate than her plunderer, and out of the clash with him comes a son bearing a masculine version of her own name:

Can flame beget white steel—
ah no, it could not take
within my reins its shelter;
steel must seek steel,
or hate make out of joy
a whet-stone for a sword;
sword against flint,
Theseus sought Hippolyta;
she yielded not nor broke,
sword upon stone,
from the clash leapt a spark,
Hippolytus, born of hate.

(136–37)

Hippolyta, like the Athene of "Helios and Athene," is equal to the encounter. Though Phaedra "breaks" under passion, the only thing to break from Hippolyta is her song, a prayer which, while it authenticates her as a kind of Phaedra-in-reverse, also establishes her as a version of the Demeteresque protecting mother (137). Though she is "twisted for [Hippolytus's] bearing," her prayer insists upon her stature. The prayer begins with a long, underlined song, clearly spoken by Hippolyta and repeated by Phaedra, to be followed by further prayer, more ambiguous in its derivation:

> You have the power,
> (then did she say) Artemis,
> benignity to grant
> forgiveness that I gave
> no quarter to an enemy who cast
> his armour on the forest-moss,
> and took, unmatched in an uneven contest,
> Hippolyta who relented not,
> returned and sought no kiss.
>
> Then did she pray: Artemis,
> grant that no flower
> be grafted alien on a broken stalk,
> no dark flame-laurel on the stricken crest
> of a wild mountain-poplar;
> grant in my thought,
> I never yield but wait,
> entreating cold white river,
> mountain-pool and salt:
> let all my veins be ice,
> until they break
> (strength of white beach,
> rock of mountain land,
> forever to you, Artemis, dedicate)
> from out my reins,
> those small, cold hands.

(138)

Phaedra's voice—as she recounts the story of Hippolyta and repeats her song—melds with Hippolyta's own; the underlined song is clearly the Amazon's, but as H.D.'s underlines disappear, Phaedra's voice vanishes, to be replaced first by the parenthetical "(then did she say)" and finally by the simple—though ambiguous—"Then did she pray." Through the substitution of one "she" for another, the "my reins" at the beginning of the poem—referring to Phaedra herself and creating the terms for her "contrast" with

Hippolyta—becomes a second "my reins," belonging to Hippolyta but, with this mingling of voices, *also* to Phaedra. Through such a subtle modulation of voice, poetic image, and thematic rhyme, "She Contrasts with Herself Hippolyta" suggests the culminating moment of *Notes on Thought and Vision,* in which "Christ and his father, or as the Eleusinian mystic would have said, his mother, were one" (52).[16] But if it echoes the moment of apotheosis in H.D.'s tract of visionary poetics, it also lingers at an earlier stage of initiation. Though neither Phaedra nor Hippolyta are "intellectual" in any strict sense, Hippolyta maintains a certain coldness—like Athene's ostensible aloofness in the dedicatory poem—which suggests that she is a figure for the second stage of H.D.'s Eleusis. She prays to Artemis, "grant in my thought, / I never yield but wait," and "let all my veins be ice"; she is a version of the cold goddess but is also, in the terms of *Notes on Thought and Vision,* "more sensitive, more fastidious" (29–30) than the tortured and eroticized Phaedra.

The third poem of the sequence, "She Rebukes Hippolyta," questions the assumption inherent in this suggestion; asking "Was she so chaste," it suggests that the chastity—or "ice"—of Hippolyta is nothing more or less than another form of erotic involvement. The poem becomes a direct constatation of passionate, intoxicated vision:

> She was mad—
> as no priest, no lover's cult
> could grant madness;
> the wine that entered her throat
> with the touch of the mountain rocks
> was white, intoxicant:
> she, the chaste,
> was betrayed by the glint
> of light on the hills,
> the granite splinter of rocks,
> the touch of the stone
> where heat melts
> toward the shadow-side of the rocks.

(140)

"She Contrasts with Herself Hippolyta" employs contrast as a subtle means through which to both distinguish between and conjoin Phaedra and Hippolyta; "She Rebukes Hippolyta" depends upon a similar twist. The "Rebuke" of the title—the judgmental vision of Hippolyta "betrayed by the glint / of light on the hills"—masks a deeper sense in which the poem re-unifies and re-eroticizes the entire complex of characters and images into a new sexually charged and visionary mystery. On several levels, the poem integrates the patterns and concerns of *Hymen* as a whole. It presents an Eros free from threat of rape, places a figure of the mother within an eroticized landscape unsullied by the rape of Persephone, reprises the parenthetical asides of "Hippolytus Temporizes" with Phaedra's vision in the place of his blindness, and situates Hippolyta within the context of the "white, intoxicant" power of "Fragment 113" and "Simaetha." And, as the culmination of a dramatic sequence—a trial run, as it were, for H.D.'s later play—it echoes the intent of "Hymen" without its static, masque-like traits.

Hymen thus begins with drama and moves to its end with a new, revivified drama moving its primary metaphors into a new setting emphasizing the visionary Eros of Hippolyta over the rapacious plunderer of the initial masque. This process of rebirth out of death—the process *Hymen* shares with *Notes on Thought and Vision* as well as the Eleusinian mysteries—forms the subject of the poem following "She Rebukes Hippolyta," "Egypt," where the connection of Egypt with Greece initially threatens "dream for life, / an opiate for a kiss, / and death for both" (140), but culminates in a restoration of the mysteries:

> We pray you, Egypt,
> by what perverse fate,
> has poison brought with knowledge,
> given us this—
> not days of trance,
> shadow, fore-doom of death,
> but passionate grave thought,
> belief enhanced,
> ritual returned and magic;
>
> Even in the uttermost black pit
> of the forbidden knowledge,
> wisdom's glance,
> the grey eyes following
> in the mid-most desert—
> great shaft of rose,
> fire shed across our path,
> upon the face grown grey, a light,
> Hellas re-born from death.

(141)

Evoking both the Judeo-Christian story of Exodus and Eleusinian tradition, this poem's promise of "belief enhanced, / ritual returned and magic" repeats the patterns of *Hymen*'s dance of mysteries, moving from rape— "Egypt had maimed us" (140)—to rapture and rebirth.

But this rebirth of the implicitly female "Hellas" does not mean that the climax of H.D.'s Eleusinian constatation simply patches over or forgets the plunderer of its beginning; nor does it move simply from the masculine figure of Eros in "Hymen" to the female landscape of the Hippolyta/Phaedra sequence. In the 1921 edition, *Hymen* ends with two poems, "Helios" and "Prayer": an homage to the male god of the sun followed by a final turn to the goddess. But in 1925's *Collected Poems*—and in *Collected Poems 1912–1944*—the order of these poems is reversed, ending the volume with "Helios." This new order gives the volume a suggestive symmetry, calling attention to itself as a counterpart to "Helios and Athene," beginning with the goddess and ending with the god. [17]

The effect of this transposition—aside from framing the volume and suggesting the field of its concerns—is to problematize the promise of visionary rebirth contained both in "Egypt" and in the new version of the marriage/family metaphor connecting Phaedra, Hippolytus, and Hippolyta. "Helios" begins as a direct and uncomplicated song of praise to the god, who "makes all things right" (142). The god, in this incarnation, is not only equal to Athene, but set above her as a faithful figure of the protector, a corrective to the complaint against *her* in the dedicatory poem; while she is "high and far and blind," dealing only with an elite of followers, Helios "makes all things right" both for followers and others. The god thus fulfills the promise of the volume's beginning, acting as a patron or sponsor for the visionary's constatation. But the final stanza brings him forward as "a treacherous god" and ties him back into *Hymen*'s dominant rubric of marriage:

> A treacherous god, they say,
> yet who would wait to test
> justice or worth or right,
> when through a fetid night
> is wafted faint and nearer—
> then straight as point of steel
> to one who courts swift death,
> scent of Hesperidean orange-spray.
>
> (143)

The irony of this "treacherous god" is that he is, in fact, treacherous. The seeming salvation he offers in the "scent of Hesperidean orange-spray"—a figure, like the traditional orange bough, for the joys of marriage in the islands of the blest—is metaphorized as a quick and painless death. The resonance of the lines compounds the irony. As the pun on "courts" suggests, a lover seeking marriage within this system also seeks death; thus all of the sinister aspects of the hymeneal scene re-enter the volume at the last moment, and Helios once again takes his place as an incarnation of the god of Death, the strong-armed figure bringing rape in the guise of rapture. And the designation of the orange-spray as "Hesperidean" masks a reference, not only to a joyful marriage celebrated with blossoms and praise, but also to something quite different. The Hesperides are the golden islands of the west, the site of the sunset and the home of the golden apples of Hera, one of which is the "apple of discord" associated with Paris's choice of Aphrodite's beauty over that of Hera and Athene and thus with the beginnings of the Trojan War.

This final Hesperidean scene, then, incorporates a new sense of merger into *Hymen*'s marriage metaphor, a merger which fully anticipates the conjunction between Eros and Eris—Love and Death—in H.D.'s late epic *Helen in Egypt*. And the ambivalence of this new merger sustains the antagonistic balance between Athene and Helios. Certainly the god here fulfills Athene's promise while also providing a "male" ending to the volume, thus establishing a kind of balance in its range of gender identities. But his presence here also threatens destruction, re-emphasizing the peril that "It was in Helios' heart to break"—to undo the protective power of the goddess. In the final line of the volume, the "scent of Hesperidean orange-spray" merges Eros and Thanatos, repeating the equivocal nature of the hymen in yet another insistently double image.[18]

The constatation which *Hymen* finally makes for itself is built up out of this doubleness. A variety of powers inhere in the materials H.D. works with—powers, primarily, of human and divine connection and possession—and these powers contain both great promise and great terror. In "Helios and Athene," H.D. insists "Let daemons possess us! Let us terrify like Erynnes, the whole tribe of academic Grecians," and yet when Phaedra is possessed by daemons she is terrified, reduced to "a red leaf / drenched and torn in the cold rain." Eros—or the erotic hymen—provides a figure for the double ground which finally defines this kind of vision; *Hymen* begins with the dual possibility of rapture and rape and ends with Helios as the carrier of both potentialities. The divine marriage is vision and, in another guise, simply death, the rape and disappearance of Persephone. In between these two poles, *Hymen* struggles to inhabit the truly visionary landscape of H.D.'s Demeter, "wrought of iron / to wrest from earth / secrets," and strong enough to sustain the weight of hymeneal possession.

4

Masks of the Eternal:
H.D.'s "Mediumship"

*Everything seems unrelated yet diametrically related, as you
slant one facet of a diamond into another set of values.*
                                                    H.D., "Ear-Ring"

Ezra Pound's work between 1908 and his declaration of the imagist principles in 1912 modulates from the elaboration of masks and personae in poems
like "Cino" to the pared-down constructions of "In a Station of the Metro."
That a connection exists between these two poetic modes—that Pound's
interest in the image is in part an interest in role-playing—is suggested by
his ultimate inclusion of all the work of the period under the single heading
of *Personae*. The title, first used in 1909 for a collection which is completely
in his early mode, lends a strong sense of continuity to his rapidly changing
work of the early years, insisting upon a link between his personae and his
Imagism. H.D.'s early work, on the other hand, clearly revolves around
certain connections submerged in Pound's poetry. Indeed, Cyrena N. Pondrom, in "H.D. and the Origins of Imagism," suggests that "H.D.'s early
poems were models which enabled the precepts of Imagism to be defined"
(74). If H.D. is thus the originator of imagist practice, it is her very existence
which makes it possible to see the otherwise obscure connection between
persona and image in Pound's poetry, because she, from the very beginning,
finds herself implicated in the images both in Pound's work and in her own,
finds traces of persona in even the smallest image.[1] Appropriately, then,
H.D. herself enters the fabric of the 1926 *Personae* as a figurehead for the
entire collection. Not only does Pound parody her in "Tempora" as the
"Dryad" who "with plaintive, querulous crying" cries from the court-yard

> "May my poems be printed this week?
> The god Pan is afraid to ask you,
> May my poems be printed this week?"
>
> *(Personae,* 110)

and possibly in the minimalist gestures of "Papyrus," but he places "The Tree," a poem dedicated to her, at the head of the collection, implicitly invoking her as a guiding spirit.

Susan Friedman has pointed out the ways in which this poem (given to H.D. by Pound as part of "Hilda's Book," probably in 1907) provides many of the images for H.D.'s novelistic critique, in *HERmione,* of the relationship between her own character, Her Gart, and the Pound figure George Lowdnes.[2] And, if "The Tree" is in part an origin for Pound's ultimate transformation of persona into image, it also provides a beginning point for H.D.'s own concern with that intersection. Cast as a tree or Dryad, H.D. must find her identity there, and must base whatever identity she does find in a reading of image; early in *HERmione,* Her Gart looks up into the body of a tree: "She lost the bird, tried to focus one leaf to hold her on to all leaves; she tried to concentrate on one frayed disc of green, pool or mirror that would refract image. She was nothing. She must have an image no matter how fluid, how inchoate" (5). What is at stake here is not simply the sense of limitation such a need for "image" implies; Her looks up into the tree, in part, to find her self-image as "Dryad," which is never anything more than an imposed self thrust upon her by George. But her gaze up into the tree—the investigation of her status as a literal "tree amid the wood" *(Personae,* 3)—also begins a process played out in *HERmione* as a movement from "inchoate" Dryad to a new birth of Her as writer of her own scripts and identities: "Her feet were pencils tracing a path through a forest. The world had been razed, had been made clear for this thing" (223). The Poundian assignment of the Dryad role thus *is* criticized, as Friedman suggests, but it is also written back into the end of the process in a whole new way. Late in the novel, the tree is once again a sign of identity: "The bushes held definite image, brought clear association" (226). Her remains "a tree amid the wood," but she is now her own tree rather than the one George Lowdnes had made:

> The great tree in itself was a world; Olympian. Her under it, looked up and up like a child in some tale of the Black Forest. Scent of snow (has snow a scent? It stings the nostrils, is an anesthetic), scent of needles, different sorts of wood smells. She recalled a red hibiscus with a sort of vicarious shudder. Red hibiscus seemed like a tissue-paper rose in some Nice carnival. Europe as she pronounced it in her consciousness seemed like that. Head bent back tried to

recall paintings, pictures upon ceilings. "Old paint, paint peeling off," she said aloud to the down-sweeping branches, "What's that to this thing?" Her hands uncurled and she caught at the great tree. George never could love anything quite properly. (227)

Within this framework of personal and literary borrowings, the Hilda of Pound's "Hilda's Book" becomes a source for the investigations of the later H.D., and the transformative assumption of persona enacted in "The Tree" determines a similar process in *HERmione*. The means through which such a persona is established is very much of a piece with the tenets of Imagism: the objective "thing," the tree, is central to whatever an identity can come to be. *HERmione,* thus, is in one sense very much a novel about the making of H.D.'s own personally marked and problematic Imagism out of a Poundian poetics of personae.[3]

H.D.'s other novels trace much the same process in somewhat different terms. *Paint It To-day* progresses through metaphors of painting. *Asphodel,* her second novel, employs writing itself as a dominant metaphor and explores the relationship between that art and the making of a life. The H.D. figure—again a "Dryad" named Hermione—begins with the proposition that writing is necessary for the constitution of identity: "If de Maupassant was true then life and letters met, were not sub-divided, hermetically shut apart. *Helen thy beauty is to me* was still hermetically sealed and a star . . ." (pt. 1, 3). One of the intents of *Asphodel* is to lessen the distance Hermione feels between the work of a poet and the life she lives, to break that hermetic seal and to make image equivalent to identity.

A third unpublished novel, *Pilate's Wife*—begun in 1924 and finally finished in 1934—has persona at its center. As H.D. writes in her "Author's Note" for the novel, its "theme is no new one" (n.p.), telling the story of a Christ who does not die on the cross but survives—the novel's titular figure, Veronica, saves Him by drugging Him with an opiate—and is transported out of his tomb to safety in another country.[4] The relationship between Veronica and Jesus comes about through her ongoing search for a religion allowing her a "way of searching a feminine counter-part of deity" (109), a religion which does not exclude women. Her search begins with an interest in the foreign cult of Isis—a goddess who is, H.D. writes, a perfect combination of Aphrodite and Athene (25)—and progresses through the occult arts and the ultimately anti-feminine Mithraic philosophy of light and dark. Veronica comes to Jesus through the graces of a woman named Mnevis— whose name chimes with "Isis" (29) and who is a worker in the occult art of palmistry. The Jesus of the novel allows women a place in his philosophy (126) and embodies the male figure desired by H.D. in the mysteries of *Hymen* and *Notes on Thought and Vision:* "This Jew seemed to combine

Greek intellectualization and occult wisdom in a curious precise manner";
he is "one with the Eleusinian Dionysius" (127). He is thus a figure for the
Eleusinian theatre which allows, as H.D. writes in "Helios and Athene,"
one "means of approach" to the mysteries (*CP*, 330). In other words, Jesus
picks up "Hymen"'s hints of drama, and turns that drama into a full-blown
mode of knowledge and vision. Acting—the taking on of personae—is the
quotidian equivalent of the mysteries; this is the art at the center of *Pilate's
Wife*.

Echoing the initial "I am Her" of *HERmione* (*HERmione*, 3), the novel
opens with a direct affirmation of the known identity of Pilate's wife: "I am
Veronica" (*Pilate's Wife*, 1). But where Her's name defines her role as
novelistic subject alienated into grammatical object,[5] "Veronica" both suggests that alienating distance *and* maintains an irreducible link between
subject and object. In her husband's speech, her name becomes "Vera-
ikon," or "true image," an image which is simultaneously at a distance from
Veronica and a legitimate mark of her identity:

> that Vera, Vera-ikon as [Pilate] sometimes ironically called her, seemed a self,
> apart in herself, something frozen in her to which she could speak, as to a statue
> in a shrine. She, this wife of Pilate, was a mass of contradictions, everything
> surrounding that inner statue, that self, was false. Only the Vera-ikon was true.
> Well, Memnonius had cleared that for her, she could act always. Deep in her,
> was another person that never acted. Who was that person? Veronica said, "I
> am Veronica." (146)

The name "Vera-ikon" initially comes to her, like Her's "Dryad," as an
imposition, given by her husband and reinforced by another man,
Memnonius. The very fact that this "other person" "frozen in her" is the
creation of another marks its separation from her. An insistent pun on "act"
sustains this sense: the outer Veronica both "acts"—takes on roles to mask
herself—and "acts"—undertakes positive action. She is continually implicated in the complications of this pun; if she is to be herself, she must either
indulge in the falsities of an actress or fall back upon the frozen self of her
internal "true image."

Veronica depends on the play-acting of public persona: "She was accus-
tomed to playing at being someone else, but knew all the time that the wife
of Pilate was adequately protected" (30). While her acting out of roles
mimes self-protection, it is superfluous. As Pilate's wife, Veronica is already
socially secure—she need not pretend to be anything other than what she
already is—and yet this socially valorized femininity demands her role-
playing: "Ladies of no recognized world, were encouraged to dramatize
imaginative ardour" (77). The ikon she makes of herself relies on the very

falsity of play-acting as a socially verified mode of constructing an identity: "That the character was a goddess, Ceres or her daughter, or a heroine of late mythology, didn't alter the fact that it gave opportunity for fantastic head-dress, painted fingers and jewels of fabulous exaggeration" (78).

On the other hand, Veronica automatically plays a role through her very name, a role which points to another effect of acting. H.D. takes the name for her character from Saint Veronica, who acquired an image of Christ when she wiped His face with a towel as He struggled up the road to Calvary; in Church tradition, the image adhering to her towel is indeed a "true image" or "Vera-ikon." H.D.'s Veronica, saving Jesus from his fate on the cross and finding her own identity through that act, re-invokes the notion of a truth inhabiting an image. The "Vera-ikon" which she gains through acting, thus, both is and is not herself. And she both is and is not the historical Vera-ikon of the Church; in the "Author's Note" to the first draft of the novel, H.D. writes and then crosses out: "I entirely disassociate in my mind, this Veronica, from the Veronica of church tradition" (n.p.). In later drafts, however, the disclaimer does not appear, allowing the connection to stand and resonate throughout the novel.

In a sense, Pilate's wife *does* gain Jesus's image to use as a sign for her own identity. His body resting in the tomb is called "The Image" (133), and His face comes to Veronica in revery as a sign of an Eleusinian revelation and as an answer to her speculations about love and recognition:

> Plato with his love and love, each a half, each about to find the other, seeking, searching, longing. . . . To Plato, it was possible to think of love, finding its own complement. To Veronica, it was different. No, to her each being was an entire entity, no half and half about it.
>
> There would come a moment, there might come a moment in the life of each one of us, when the normal pulse is stilled, burned or purified by passion if it needs be, or healed and strengthened by mere normal tenderness, a moment when man says "woman is not enough," when woman says "man is not sufficient." That moment is a phase past the mere Platonic intellectual enlightenment. There is or is not love contained within this germ of subtler recognition, just as there may or may not be honey in the flower's head. The bee alone can discriminate. (101–2)

Veronica's desire for something "past the mere Platonic intellectual enlightenment"—coupled with the image of the bee who has knowledge of the flower and the honey it contains—moves her revery into the mysteries explored by *Hymen* and *Notes on Thought and Vision*. Dreaming, Veronica hears someone calling her name and sees the face of Pilate as "the sun Image" or "sheer intellectual beauty"—as, that is, a sign of the second stage of the Eleusinian mysteries. In her dream, this face then becomes the face of Jesus crowned with thorns, both giving new meaning to the call she has heard—Jesus calls her to his religion—and acting as a gift of his image to her.

The novel ends with a reprise of this scene, as a new voice comes to Veronica: "It seemed, she could hear, as she heard, that weary day in her room, a voice speaking. It said 'Veronica.'

"'I am Veronica,' said Veronica, realising at last that she was that person" (165).[6] She is, in other words, not only the person called, but the person making the call, and her discovery of that fact is the novel's final gift of a true image. The end of the novel repeats its beginning, but with the Vera-ikon in place as a secure identity; just as Jesus does not exclude women from his philosophy, Veronica no longer excludes herself from her adopted masks. As her adoption of persona becomes a mode of self revelation, she becomes the very person she has been disguising all along.

Veronica's taking on of roles requires that role-playing transform itself into something greater, that it become "a moment . . . when the normal pulse is stilled, burned or purified by passion if it needs be," a culminating moment akin to the final stage of H.D.'s Eleusis. A short story written at the same time as *Pilate's Wife*, "The Moment" (1926), delineates this process. One of the characters in the story, Myra, is an actress, a representative of an eternal state manifesting itself in the figures of Greek drama: "The moment was hidden somewhere. One had to wait as it were, for this variety-show to end before the curtain was drawn back revealing an ancient temple. Jocasta and Antigone, Oedipus Rex and the discrowned Orestes were in the wings, waiting to be summoned by a gesture from this royal Myra. Of that, Myra was unconscious, perhaps even a little ashamed" (34).

The work of the writer—the H.D. figure in this story is named Vanna—fulfills exactly the same function; it is a kind of acting, a preparation of the self for "the moment" of revelation:

Maybe writing, maybe acting was a sort of outer precinct-service. Vanna said, under her breath, "acting, writing is outer precinct-service." Vanna knew that writing was a grovelling thankless sort of excuse for everything. Outside the temple, there are writers, actors. They wait, a slovenly, half-hearted crew, not for acclaim, not even for recognition. They wait actually for the moment, so that the moment, hovering with its resplendent wings, may not find them wanting. (39–40)

Just as the faces of Pilate and Jesus prepare Veronica for the revelation of her own identity, writing creates a context within which the eternal may break through time or the true face may be seen through the mask: "'What use is your writing, anyway?' It was this use. It made each moment a possible forerunner of the moment. It made mediumship, at rare intervals, legitimate" (41).

Of course, the use of personae is not unique to H.D. among her contemporaries—nor to Pound, though it is perhaps most evident in his work. T. S. Eliot's career begins with such an act; whatever else happens in "The Love Song of J. Alfred Prufrock," the voice of Prufrock takes on patterns of Eliot's own as it progresses. "The Waste Land" establishes and abandons a whole series of personae for its images and structures. And that concept so central to the "Four Quartets," "The point of intersection of the timeless / With time" (Eliot, 136), is remarkably similar to H.D.'s "Moment." D. H. Lawrence's novels of the period—from *Women in Love* through *Kangaroo*—invoke a series of semi-autobiographical masks as protagonists. Even William Carlos Williams works from the beginning toward a large conception of city-as-persona for his *Paterson*.

Still, H.D.'s interest in the mask in *Pilate's Wife* is closest to Pound's conception of the persona in that it is largely historical as well as autobiographical. But with this difference: where Pound's poems inhabit history so well that traces of autobiography are practically effaced, H.D.'s work invokes its personae primarily in order to establish connections between the historical past and H.D. herself. Her personae—like Veronica's—are never simply masks. Like Pound, she depends on a reading of history for her work; but, like Lawrence, she never forsakes a strongly personal stake in her characters. Veronica is at once a semi-historical character and an intensely personal figure for H.D. herself—as personally determined, for instance, as Lawrence's Rupert Birkin in *Women in Love*. And, in one of the first examples of the long series of transformations of her own name, H.D. even uses her initials as the core of the names of the dual protagonists of *Hedylus*, a 1927 novel which covers much of the same conceptual ground as *Pilate's Wife*.

Pilate's Wife utilizes a revised Biblical setting for its play of identity. Much the poetry of these years, on the other hand, is Greek in both setting and execution. *Hymen* depends on Greek mythology and mystery cults for its figures; *Heliodora*—published in 1924, the same year H.D. began work on *Pilate's Wife*—is built around a series of masks through which H.D. inhabits, transforms, and translates historical Greek poets, utilizing them as possible versions of herself.

As H.D.'s writing of the First World War makes clear, her Greece is never really the anachronism it seems;[7] the role of Eleusis in *Hymen* suggests something of the spiritual vibrancy (and dangers) H.D. finds in the Greek mysteries. But her most direct confrontation with Hellenism is a literary study, a largely unpublished manuscript begun in 1918, though "not finished until much later": "Notes on Euripides, Pausanius, and Greek

Lyric Poets." Perhaps the most important section of these notes is the first, on Euripides. Calling him a "problematic great-war Shakespeare," H.D. envisions him as a type of the modern poet with pacifist inclinations—as, that is, a version of herself: "Euripides lived through almost a modern great-war period. If Shakespeare had been born at the end of the nineteenth century and had come to maturity about 1914, his plays would hardly have been untinged with bitterness, with that especial non-partisanship, non-patriotism that creeps into the dramas of Euripides" (pt. 1, 3–4).

Modernizing her favorite classical dramatist, H.D. situates his work (and, by implication, her own) within the eternal realm of the sacred. Drawing on—though not acknowledging—Coleridge's *Biographia Literaria*, H.D. recreates Greek drama as an incarnation of the eternal: "Before Sophocles was, before Aeschylus and Euripides, I am. The *I am* of eternal beauty, of eternal striving toward intellectual and aesthetic achievement" (pt. 1, 6). Where for Coleridge the "*I am*" is an agent of "primary Imagination" transcending any hint of the personal, H.D.'s use of the phrase sets her own personal world securely within the eternal; and vice-versa—the very syntax of her sentence, "Before Sophocles was, before Aeschylus and Euripides, I am," sets H.D. herself, and her work, *prior to* the three classical writers. Her work becomes the act of a distinctly modern mind encompassing all time. For H.D., Hellenism is a means of reading, of finding herself in the distance—a kind of hermeneutics of the self. "Greece" no longer simply names a geographical and historical place, but a site of reading or play-acting, a spiritually conceived locale into which H.D. is able to set her own work:

> Look at the map of Greece. It is a hieroglyph. You will be unable to read it and go away and come back after years and just begin to spell out the meaning of its outline. Then you will realize that you know nothing at all about it and begin all over, learning a cryptic language. I am never tired of speculating on the power of just that outline, just the mysterious line of it, apart from the thing it stands for. (pt. 1, 4)

In another section of the notes, "A Poet in the Wilderness: Songs of Anacreon," H.D. explicitly detaches this act of reading the literary past from any hint of escapism or anachronism, claiming it as the grounds of her modernity:

> I am not fleeing for sanctuary across dead lintels of the past, into an unearthed temple, old lava-broken porches and courtyards, swept clean of scattered ashes, petrified corn grains, stone apple-cores and cinders.
>
> I am not fleeing from the present, pursued by present day art-theorists,

serpent-crowned Erynnes. I think myself rather beyond the fashion, ultra-modern. (3)

Emptying Greece of its expected significance, H.D. creates a landscape and a vocabulary—a "cryptic language"—accessible to her own concerns, an eternal realm stretching from the past of Greece to her own present situation.

The most interesting section of the notes on Euripides is a reading of his *Helen*, an essay significant not only because it is the first suggestion of H.D.'s interest in the figure of Helen in Egypt, or because of its close stylistic connections to her translation of and commentary on Euripides' *Ion* (published in 1937), but also for its elaborate imaginations of the play and of Helen. H.D.'s summary of the plot becomes a rapt encounter with her own visionary reconstruction of the ancient woman: "It is good to meet Helen face to face, for men and poets have visualized her so crudely" ("Helen in Egypt," 3). H.D.'s Helen is, in part, a version of the poet of *Hymen*, a figure with sexual and familial connections to the sacred: "Why must men and poets visualize her as a woman, this Helen? She is a spirit; she, who was hatched from an egg by Leda the mistress of God" (3).

Behind H.D.'s reading lies her discovery that Greece holds a life beyond the literary; it is a world experienced as an instrument of vision or mediumship:

> Perhaps in the opening of this study of Helen, I have been carried away too much by my own imagination, been unbalanced, intoxicated a little with my own idea, my own game, my toy, my discovery that the lines of this Greek poet (and all Greek poets if we have but the clue) are today as vivid and as fresh as they ever were, but vivid and fresh not as literature (though they are that too) but as portals, as windows, as port-holes I am tempted to say that look out from our ship, our world, our restricted lives, on to a sea that moves and changes and bears us up, and is friendly and vicious in turn. (7)

H.D.'s claim for the value of this endeavour as something "vivid and fresh not as literature" depends on a notion of reading as a dynamically reciprocal encounter; H.D. projects herself through the "portal" of the past, giving historical resonance to her own activity, while the Greek poetry which she reads simultaneously projects itself onto her, surmounting historical distance through intense personal significance. In her essay on Pausanius, H.D. invokes the metaphor of projection to describe this process of reading, calling it "this life within life." As she reads, "page after page of this fine print speed on with their miraculous treasure like some fine dull black and white screen-projection behind which, to the initiate eyes, gleam phantoms and treasures of colour and of magic. Again this life within life . . ." (4a–5).

A further passage echoes *Notes on Thought and Vision* as it affirms the dual nature of reading; like Eliot's intersection of time and the timeless, H.D.'s reading and writing—her play-acting—chart an occasion in which the eternal may come through to a poet who otherwise lives in a world of time:

> Ghosts to speak must have sacrifice. The odd thing is that the sacrifice is so exquisite a finding of oneself that one is willing to let everything go, friends, society, wealth or position in the pursuit of this Spirit. . . . So one feels, one is convinced . . . then things break across, we grow older, we come to realize (regretfully, looking back wistfully on the white flame of earlier enthusiasm) more and more that we must live too in life to preserve that "superlife" that seems to descend sometimes. ("Pausanius," 6)

Such a "superlife" is both the atemporal (or, perhaps more accurately, cross-temporal) "mythic method" of modernism in general *and* the mystically charged vision H.D. desires to find in the incarnation of the artistic object. It is the point sought by Her Gart in *Hermione* and by Veronica in *Pilate's Wife*, the point of intersection where image and identity meet, where a reading of image becomes acceptance of persona and persona becomes a gift of the eternal. "Greece" is H.D.'s name for this possibility.

Heliodora:
Translation and the Terrors of Song

> *However it came about, I found the thread and followed it*
> *through the labyrinth.*
>
> H.D., *The Sword Went out to Sea*

If *Hymen* explores Greece through its mythic figures as a form of desire, then *Heliodora* takes the somewhat different tack of charting the Greek landscape as it comes to be incarnated in masks and personae. The acts of masking—through translation and the use of historical figures—in this 1924 volume form a pervasive inquiry into the convergence between poetics and poetic identity; H.D.'s poetics, that is, emerges most insistently in this volume through the personae engaged by its poems.

In the story "The Moment," the legitimacy of what H.D. calls "mediumship" is more a matter of possibility than complete achievement. Similarly, in *Heliodora*, the ideal significance of Greece, though always present, is held at bay for critical inspection. While the book desires its "moment," it never denies the cost of desire; it is, largely, a study of submission to desire and of the dangers of that submission, all set in a Greek landscape of translation and personae.

Unlike *Hymen*, *Heliodora* begins, not with a dedication or dedicatory poem, but with an author's note setting a specific context in relation to Greek poetry:

> The poem Lais has in italics a translation of the Plato epigram in the Greek Anthology. Heliodora has in italics the two Meleager epigrams from the Anthology. In Nossis is the translation of the opening lines of the Garland of Meleager and the poem of Nossis herself in the Greek Anthology. The four Sappho fragments are re-worked freely. The Ion is a translation of the latter part of the first long choros of the Ion of Euripides. (*CP*, 147)

As this note suggests, *Heliodora* is from the outset concerned with translation, though not in any straightforward sense. Just as *Hymen* systematically complicates its governing metaphor of marriage and familial relations, *Heliodora* refuses to accept its mode of procedure—translation—as a given. The very *concept* of translation—and not simply the transposition of poetry from one language to another—as an act of assuming masks gives the volume much of its coherence.[1] Translations and adaptations are scattered throughout the volume and interspersed with other kinds of poems which flesh out the sequence and extend its resonances.

The first poem is, as in *Hymen,* something of a dedicatory poem to the goddess; but while *Hymen* claims to overcome the distance between the human and the divine, *Heliodora* accepts that distance, and intimates that the work of art may "grace" or mediate it:

> *intimate thoughts and kind*
> *reach out to share*
> *the treasure of my mind,*
> *intimate hands and dear*
> *drawn garden-ward and sea-ward*
> *all the sheer rapture*
> *that I would take*
> *to mould a clear*
> *and frigid statue;*
>
> *rare, of pure texture,*
> *beautiful space and line,*
> *marble to grace*
> *your inaccessible shrine.*

(147–48)

The passionate call of *Hymen* is chastened as the "strange fire" of its violets becomes something "colder than a rose," a tenuous yet beautiful life in a "glacial land" removed from other concerns. The project of *Hymen* is recast here into an antithetical passion: the sculptural figure is "frigid," and the goddess remote. It is as if *Sea Garden*'s mixing ground—that place invoked in H.D.'s first book where opposites mix and clash—forced passion to blend into its opposite, as if the fiery and inextricably problematic nature of *Hymen,* having played itself out, now required a retreat into the snow-bound landscape where a "*Wash of cold river*" takes over as the dominant figure. But this is not a space devoid of passion. The statue, frigid as it is, emerges from something more than dispassionate craftsmanship; it materializes out of "sheer rapture" drawing "intimate thoughts and kind" and "intimate hands and dear" into its curiously chilly setting.

The rapture of this poem is strangely distant from the sexuality of *Hymen;* it suggests an encounter of friends rather than of lovers, a sharing of "the treasure of my mind" rather than the intense physicality of "Helios and Athene" or *Notes on Thought and Vision.* Still, the rapture retains—as a trace of what has come before—more than a hint of the erotic despite the poem's attempts to efface or occlude it. Seemingly frigid, the poem enacts an encounter not only between friends but between two different incarnations of H.D.'s aesthetics. The sexuality of *Hymen* holds a residual power over the terms and terrain of the poem; in turn, the poem suggests the possibility of a desexualized creativity—the making of a "frigid statue," a craftsmanship side-stepping the problems of *Hymen*'s sexual aesthetics. The project of *Heliodora*—beginning with this encounter and pursuing its course through a series of masks—is to explore the connections and discontinuities between these two proposals, to see how intertwined or how distinct they actually are, and to examine the nature of the poetic identity uncovered in the process.

As if to prove that the sexual has not been completely erased from the world of *Heliodora,* the first poem after the pseudo-dedication echoes *Hymen*'s more blissful poems of sexuality with a sexual encounter between the human speaker and a representative of the numinous world of the gods almost grossly incarnated as a "Holy Satyr." The speaker makes "leaf-circlets / and a crown of honey-flowers" for the Satyr's throat, and gives up her song as an offering:

> hear this our song,
> accept our leaves,
> love-offering,
> return our hymn,
> like echo fling
> a sweet song,
> answering note for note.
>
> (149)

Though offering a vision of ideal reciprocity—an exemplary version of the encounter between a sexual aesthetics and an aesthetics of "sweet song"— this "love-offering" is rendered problematic by the sheer goat-like physicality of the Satyr. If the divine figure of Helios—who, in *Hymen,* offers a much more spiritualized sexuality—is difficult to reconcile with H.D.'s gender-based poetics, then the Satyr is even more troublesome. Still, in a curious way the promise of the poem's end rings true, an echo of the mirror imagery H.D. uses in *HERmione* to signal her hope for the personal wholeness a twin sister could bring.[2] And it is a vision of the ideal resolution of

Heliodora, in which the encounter between two systems engenders a poetic reciprocity where the poem may actually be "the moment."

H.D.'s mask in "Holy Satyr" is essentially one of anonymity, an identity as "inchoate" as Her's early in *HERmione.* She does give "love-offering" to the Satyr, but *he* dominates the poem, and the promise of the ending comes more from a potential she sees in *him* than in any aspect of her own role-playing. The next poem, "Lais," literalizes the hints of a mirroring art in "Holy Satyr" and for the first time explicitly employs translation, though here through the mediation of the grammatical third person. As Dale Davis has pointed out, "H.D., in 'Lais,' wanders through Plato's epigram, weaving in, out, and around it, though notedly not assuming the voice of Lais herself as epigrammatically spoken by Plato" (152). Both the woman Lais and the poet Plato appear only at this grammatical distance. In the translation by J. W. Mackail which is in H.D.'s library, Lais herself speaks directly through Plato.[3] The third person dominates H.D.'s translation, integrated into her own poem, as Lais and Plato are melded into the impersonal "one":

> *Lais has left her mirror*
> (so one wrote)
> *to her who reigns in Paphos;*
> *Lais who laughed a tyrant over Greece,*
> *Lais who turned the lovers from the porch,*
> *that swarm for whom now*
> *Lais has no use;*
> *Lais is now no lover of the glass,*
> *seeing no more the face as once it was,*
> *wishing to see that face and finding this.*

(150)

H.D. plays variations on the figures of the translation, emphasizing the failure of the mirror and Lais's abandonment of it to the unnamed "her who walks in Paphos."

"Holy Satyr" holds out the promise of an aural mirror in the echoing song of the Satyr, "answering note for note"; "Lais" subverts this vision of reciprocity into a failed narcissism. Where Lais once looked into her mirror to find a twin in the image of her own face—a "Vera-ikon" of sorts, but also an image of one who "laughed exultant / tyrannizing Greece"—she now sees herself, not as twin, but as dispirited other. These two opposite versions of the mirror—other as echo and self as other—form the boundaries within which *Heliodora* operates; the formative capacities of art, imagined as "song" in "Holy Satyr" and literalized as translation in "Lais," mark the terms in which the encounter is played out.

Appropriately, the most direct embodiment of this conceptual framework occurs in the title poem, where the mirror takes the form of an encounter between two poets, and H.D.'s more aesthetic concerns are played out in a poetic contest:

> We strove for a name,
> while the light of the lamps burnt thin
> and the outer dawn came in,
> a ghost, the last at the feast
> or the first,
> to sit within
> with the two that remained
> to quibble in flowers and verse
> over a girl's name.
>
>   (151)

There has been little critical agreement over "Heliodora." Vincent Quinn, for instance, reads it as an allegorized meeting between H.D. and Richard Aldington conveying "the joyfulness of two poets' comradeship" (40). Thomas Burnett Swann describes something similar, but with Meleager occupying the foreground of the poem, engaged in a poetic contest with a—presumably male—colleague (73–74). Bernard F. Engel, in "H.D.: Poems that Matter and Dilutations," takes the speaker to be a woman (516–17), while Rachel Blau DuPlessis—one of H.D.'s best readers—finds a debate "between two males" (*H.D.: The Career of that Struggle,* 21). And indeed, the poem supports all of these readings. It does not specify the speaker as either male or female, and depends, I would argue, on this very lack of specificity for its significance; a choice for either male or female speaker determines how one understands the poem. As I read it, it is a poem requiring two quite different readings, the first of which takes the speaker to be male, lost in wonder at the mastery of the other poet. The victorious poet ("He") is so taken by his powers that he abandons the traditional nine muses in favor of the girl Heliodora; the question "what was one girl to the nine?" (153) is ironically answered as she becomes the complete source of inspiration and they become nothing. The other poet watches the inspired carelessness of the master as he moves to the door, seeing the wine spilled on his robe as a visible sign of his immersion in "the moment"—a visible sign of what he has poured "in the vat / from which all poets dip and quaff" (152). The poem moves from grudging admiration—"the phrase was just and good, / but not as good as mine" (151)—through an exchange of visionary fire and its reflection—"Then he caught, / seeing the fire in my eyes" (152) and "So I saw the fire in his eyes, / it was almost my fire" (152)—to unquestioning awe.

Still, there are cracks in this seemingly straightforward poem through which an entirely different scenario emerges. To begin with, the very name of the "girl," Heliodora, like Hedyle or Hedylus, fleshes out the skeletal initials of H.D., specifying her as a mask for the poet rather than simply the source of inspiration for two other—male—poets. In this second scenario, a second "I," a ghostly incarnation of the historical Heliodora (she was a poet, though no fragments of her work are extant)[4] or the living H.D., hovers behind the speaker's praise for his friend. Thus the scene of the two who "strove for a name" (151) becomes the only means of incarnation for the figure who is otherwise effaced from a poem which purports to be in praise of her. As this figure emerges through the poem's interstices, it becomes clear that the lines written to immortalize her serve that function more for the poets who write than for their object. Heliodora becomes simply a name for which the two ambitious men may wrangle. As the poem is read a second time with the shadowy figure of a real Heliodora hovering behind it, the rhetorical question

> what was one girl faint and shy,
> with eyes like the myrtle,
>
> . . . .
>
> to vie with the nine?
>
> (153)

takes on a new irony: she simultaneously is effaced from the center of the poem *and* comes to exert a new control over the shape it takes. She is subtly transfigured, that is, from diminished muse to poet. And the poem's conclusion carries the irony to its fullest expression:

> I thought:
> there will never be a poet
> in all the centuries after this,
> who will dare write,
> after my friend's verse,
> "a girl's mouth
> is a lily kissed."
>
> (154)

Of course, H.D.—whose initials are buried in the name Heliodora even as Heliodora is buried in the poem—is the one who "dares" to write these lines, bringing the effaced "girl" once again to the poem's center, and constructing an intricate palimpsest where "the moment" of connection between the two women can flourish. If the poem is initially about two men who "strove for a name," it ultimately recaptures that name for Heliodora—

H. D.—herself and brings all of its figures together into an extended critique, constructing a strong poetic identity which cuts across time and gender.

My first reading of "Heliodora" ends on an affirmative note of praise; the second reading carries a new affirmation in its sense of collaboration and historical interconnection, but this new affirmation depends on a negation of the first. The figure of the woman who comes to dominate the poem in the second reading can only emerge as she obliterates—or writes over—the erasure she suffers in the first reading. Her appearance is a clear victory over the manipulations to which she was initially subject. Still, the friendly contest between the two male poets does exist, and does give form to the poem. Neither reading is able to eclipse the other fully; the two maintain an uneasy equilibrium similar to the balance of male and female in "Helios and Athene."

"Heliodora" depends heavily on intertextual resonances for its figures and patterns. As the author's note points out, its italicized portions are drawn from "two Meleager epigrams from the Anthology." In "Notes on Euripides, Pausanius, and Greek Lyric Poets," H.D. praises Meleager's poems to Heliodora as an act of love acknowledging her presence and resurrecting her after death: "He meets finally his Heliodora and it is from that meeting that arose the first, actually the first song-series of lyric love-poems" ("Garland," 3). Meleager's praise of Heliodora makes her an eternal figure able to sustain a presence through the agency of his text: "Heliodora is dead but Heliodora is not dead" ("Garland," 4). And, lest this seem too close to the objectification of Heliodora by the two poets striving in H.D.'s poem, H.D. praises Meleager for his inclusion of women as poets—not simply as figures of inspiration—in his anthology: "The list [of poets in the Anthology] is the more touching and exquisite when we take into consideration that this exquisite gesture was the first of its kind. Particularizing women not as equals but in some subtle way co-workers with men, struck a new note" (7). Like Euripides, Meleager is an important antecedent for H.D., one to whom she can turn for her masks, as justification for her poetics, and as an ur-figure for her play of poetic identities.

The other essential intertext for "Heliodora" is to be found in the translations of H.D.'s estranged husband, Richard Aldington, published as *Medallions in Clay* in 1921, the year of *Hymen*. In this volume, Aldington translates not only "Latin Poems of the Renaissance," "Greek Songs in the Manner of Anacreon," and "The Poems of Anyte of Tegea"—a Classical female poet who was the source for H.D.'s "Hermes of the Ways"—but also a nearly complete selection of Meleager's poems, including the two epigrams H.D. draws upon for "Heliodora."[5] H.D. must have seen her own public name emerging insistently from these epigrams, particularly since she and Aldington had together been the "ardent Hellenists" of the early imagist movement, and since her initials are displaced in Aldington's dedication by another set: "A.Y."—Annabelle Yorke, "l'autre" with whom Aldington was involved from 1917 until 1928.[6] Just as Heliodora is effaced from central position in a poem which bears her name, H.D. disappears from a volume which certainly has its roots in her relationship with Aldington. "Daring" to write a poem which subtly reincarnates Heliodora—and herself—she reclaims authority as both poet and translator and authenticates Heliodora and Meleager as clear figures for herself *after* their appearance as Richard Aldington's modest clay figurines.

Still, in "Heliodora" the woman herself never actually speaks except through subtle suggestion, and this problem is carried to its extreme in the following short poem, "Helen," where an eternal state of silence becomes the only hope for acceptance of the female Helen:

> Greece sees unmoved,
> God's daughter, born of love,
> the beauty of cool feet
> and slenderest knees,
> could love indeed the maid,
> only if she were laid
> white ash amid funereal cypresses.

(155)

The next major poem of translation, "Nossis," restores voice to the female poet and claims this restitution as a form of reincarnation, of legitimate mediumship. The poem, like "Heliodora," follows two characters—"he" and "I"—and includes translations; here, however, the translated voice belongs to Nossis herself, and her voice, coming through "his" as he reads, takes over the poem as its "moment":

> *"He sought for Moero, lilies,*
> *and those many,*
> *red-lilies for Anyte,*
> *for Sappho, roses,*
> *with those few, he caught*
> *that breath of the sweet-scented*
> *leaf of iris,*
> *to set beside the tablet*
> *and the wax*
> *which Love had burnt,*
> *when scarred across by Nossis:"*

when she wrote:

"*I Nossis stand by this:*
I state that love is sweet:
if you think otherwise
assert what beauty
or what charm
after the charm of love,
retains its grace?

"*Honey,*" *you say:*
honey? I say "I spit
honey out of my mouth:
nothing is second-best
after the sweet of Eros."

"*I Nossis stand and state*
that he whom Love neglects
has naught, no flower, no grace,
who lacks that rose, her kiss."

I thought to hear him speak
the girl might rise
and make the garden silver
as the white moon breaks,
"Nossis," he cried, "a flame."

(156–57)

"Nossis" presents a remarkably full version of that moment of conjunction in which poetic mask is poetic revelation and voices come together across time and space. Meleager's words do not, as in "Heliodora," forget their inspiration in their own fervor; they have been marked indelibly—like "the wax / which Love had burnt"—by Nossis as a living poet, "a flame" akin to the flame of Love burning her wax tablet. His passion is so strong that his interlocutor—despite the scoffing at the dead "girl" (155)—finally looks on in wonder at the visionary "flame."

From "*Wash of cold river*" through "Nossis," *Heliodora* progresses clearly, from ice to fire, from a cold claim for poetic incarnation to a passionate embodiment of mask and voice. The stages of this progression are easy enough to follow, and if the volume ended at this point, it could be argued that it had achieved its goal of integrating mask and voice, passion and art in one enunciation. But "Nossis" is followed immediately by a poem reprising the sheer physicality of "Holy Satyr," a love song to a centaur whose "horses's hooves / tread softer than a deer's" (158). And this curious poem is followed—in the first edition of *Heliodora* though not in the *Collected Poems* of 1925—by two definitively "Imagiste" short poems: "Oread," in

which sea, shore, and tree are so conjoined and mixed that they become
indistinguishable in the composite image of "pools of fir"; and "The Pool,"
which may be about Narcissus's gaze into the mirroring pool or about a
fisherman's marvelling scrutiny of the fish he is about to capture. In either
case, "The Pool" problematizes the promise held out by the mirror in "Holy
Satyr" and fulfilled in the mingling voices of "Nossis": if this is a poem about
Narcissus, it takes place just prior to his drowning, and if it is a fishing poem,
it takes place just before the fisherman removes the source of his wonder
from the only world in which it may live. The achieved fullness of poetic
identity of "Heliodora" and "Nossis" is almost immediately superceded,
placed at risk in these two short poems.

Even "Nossis," for all its affirmation of the power of poetic masks,
contains a suggestion that its quest may not be concluded after all. Meleager's words give the clue; the power of Nossis's art carries within it the
capacity for destruction. Meleager writes of

> the tablet
> and the wax
> which Love had burnt,
> when scarred across by Nossis.

(156)

Melded with Love's destructive flame and her own writing figured as a
scarring, the praise of Love in Nossis's song recalls Phaedra's dilemma in
Hymen; she may be "caught in a force, a power, / passionless, not [her]
own" (135), in the throes of a destructive poetic passion. Nossis holds the
power to enthrall Love, but Love holds the power to burn her in his turn.
This terrible power clouds the affirmations of "Nossis." The progression of
the volume reflects this complication; where its initial poems are practically
linear in their connections, the rest of the book—by far its greater part—is
more like a maze in its complex unravelling. It contains poems clearly
belonging to the sequence—poems of translation and of masking—interspersed with poems commenting more or less obliquely on more or less
obscure aspects of the process. Thus a series of adaptations from Sapphic
fragments are punctuated by poems like "Flute Song," in which H.D.
chases her daughter from the room where she is writing.

"We Two," a poem about a mysterious encounter, metaphorizes the
irregular and alogical progress of the sequence as a "maze of daedal paths":

> We two remain:
> yet by what miracle,
> searching within the tangles of my brain,
> I ask again,

> have we two met within
> this maze of daedal paths
> in-wound mid grievous stone,
> where once I stood alone?
>
> (165)

It is not possible here to account for each poem in this maze, nor to suggest the progression of the sequence in any but the broadest terms. It must suffice to focus attention on some of the poems in which translation—or role playing—takes a dominant role, and to trace the volume to a conclusion in the terms provided by these poems.

Both "Thetis" and "At Ithaca" allow secure points of reference—specific mythic and geographic placings—for the "daedal path" of *Heliodora*, as if the volume were a literal passage through a landscape informed by myth. Like Pausanius, whom she calls the "Baedeker of his time" ("Pausanius," 1), H.D. invokes these places as literal landscapes for her own eternal inhabitation: "Names live in eternity, are set there like stars" ("Pausanius," 4). *Heliodora* is filled with poems of this nature, appropriating resonant names for their terrain: "At Ithaca," "After Troy," "Toward the Piraeus," "At Eleusis." The practice situates the volume in a land sacred to H.D. and gives the figures from mythology and literary history a new authenticity; the poets who reside in this landscape are real figures, as true and embodied as the real places in which they are found.

Both "Thetis" and "At Ithaca" further embody the burning passion of "Nossis" within a mythically conceived masking of the poet. "Thetis" refers obliquely to her marriage to Pelius before moving to her desire for a son:

> *Who dreams of a son,*
> *save one,*
> *childless, having no bright*
> *face to flatter its own,*
> *who dreams of a son?*
>
> (160)

Thetis is the only one among the Nereids who wishes for a son rather than a daughter, and this gives her particular definition:

> *each would have for its own,*
> *a daughter for child.*
> *Who dreams, who sings of a son?*
> *I, Thetis, alone.*
>
> (161)

Similarly, "At Ithaca" is spoken through the figure of Penelope waiting for and desiring Odysseus:

> I see my lord who moves
> like Hector, lord of love,
> I see him matched with fair
> bright rivals and I see
> those lesser rivals flee.

(164)

While these two poems, like "Nossis," give voice to otherwise silent women, they implicitly take that voice away as they emphasize desire for absent men over the women's own encounter with the languages of art. Thetis sings, but only a song of desire for Achilles. She ends her singing and becomes an object—though fluid and with connections to the sea which is the source of her power—stretched out on the earth beneath his feet:

> Not I, the mother, Thetis self,
> I stretched and lay, a river's slim
> dark length,
> a rivulet where it leaves the wood,
> and meets the sea,
> I lay along the burning sand,
> a river's blue.

(163)

Similarly, "At Ithaca" emphasizes Penelope as seamstress of an elaborate tapestry, even as an artist in her own right in the absence of Odysseus. But her art is tied inextricably to the play of sexual desire, both for Odysseus and for the suitors who congregate in his absence:

> weaving his happiness
> within the stitching frame,
> weaving his fire and fame,
> I thought my work was done,
> I prayed that only one
> of those that I had spurned,
> might stoop and conquer this
> long waiting with a kiss.

(164)

Penelope's imagined submission—echoing "Holy Satyr" and "Centaur Song" in its mixture of desire and implicit revulsion—dissolves into a vision of Odysseus:

> But each time that I see
> my work so beautifully
> inwoven and would keep
> the picture and the whole,
> Athene steels my soul,
> slanting across my brain,
> I see as shafts of rain
> his chariot and his shafts,
> I see the arrows fall,
> I see my lord who moves
> like Hector, lord of love,
> I see him matched with fair
> bright rivals and I see
> those lesser rivals flee.
>
> (164)

The "lesser rivals" who flee are both the unwanted suitors who would ironically allow Penelope to keep her artistic work whole *and* her rivals for the love of Odysseus: Circe and Calypso, with whom he is "matched" during his wanderings. The ending of the poem denies Penelope's efforts as maker of art and redefines her as object of Odysseus's desire. Despite the power of her vision, it is clear that Penelope faces a choice between the role of maker of images and the role of desired object, and that neither option is fully satisfactory: the completion of her weaving leaves her vulnerable to conquest, and the acceptance of her husband requires her to deface her art, to accept an identity which is at least as much his as it is hers.

This is precisely the choice suggested by *"Wash of cold river,"* and which informs and molds the most important grouping of *Heliodora*'s poems, the four Sapphic adaptations, which move from the necessity of choice to a realization of its impossibility. The first of these, "Fragment Thirty-six," takes its lead from a fragment which might well serve as an epigram to the entire collection: "I know not what to do: / my mind is divided." The poem, spoken by a woman while her lover lies sleeping beside her, reveals the encounter between "song" and desire as clearly as anything in the volume:

> I know not what to do,
> my mind is reft:
> is song's gift best?
> Is love's gift loveliest?
>
> (165)

Echoing the images of *Sea Garden*, this expanded fragment metaphorizes its dilemma as a wave forever about to break and yet forever held back from breaking:

as a wave-line may wait to fall
yet (waiting for its falling)
still the wind may take
from off its crest,
white flake on flake of foam,
that rises,
seeming to dart and pulse
and rend the light,
so my mind hesitates
above the passion
quivering yet to break,
so my mind hesitates
above my mind,
listening to song's delight.

(167)

Though the poem is fundamentally about choice, it also strongly suggests that there is in fact *no* choice to be made, that the poet's vocation—"listening to song's delight"—is already an accepted fact. "Fragment Thirty-six" is a post-coital poem in which spent desire for passionate contact may re-emerge; and yet, its imagery complicates *Heliodora*'s initiatory identification of the artist's work with coldness. Here the poet's "snow"—the frigid statue she may take into her arms—is an unresponsive lover:

so shall I turn and take
snow in my arms?
(is love's gift best?)
yet flake on flake
of snow were comfortless
did you lie wondering,
wakened yet unawake.

(166)

Whatever sexual passion is hinted at in these lines, its realization remains securely at a distance. With no returning embrace, the speaker's desire continues only as an unfulfilled possibility troubling the music she hears in her wakefulness. The choice she must make is not finally between passion and song, but between the passion of song and the ghost of sexual desire; the speaker is clearly locked in the throes of her song, like Phaedra and Nossis, "caught in a force, a power, / passionless, not [her] own." Or, more accurately, she is caught up in a passionate art which is both an intense "moment" beyond her control and an instance of her own prophetic, visionary abilities; she is both subject and object of her utterance. Whichever possibility finally breaks the poem's deadlock, it will take the form of *this* passion rather than the passionless cold she finds in her lover's arms:

> I know not what to do:
> will the sound break,
> rending the night with
> rift on rift of rose
> and scattered light?
> will the sound break at last
> as the wave hesitant,
> or will the whole night pass
> and I lie listening awake?

(167–68)

If the sound which she hears "breaks," it will break into a visionary display of "rose / and scattered light," and if it does not break—if, that is, it continues unabated—it will simply sustain the song which already holds her in its power.

The potential terror of possession by song is clear in a poem which is separated from "Fragment Thirty-six" only by the short "After Troy": "Cassandra," subtitled "*O Hymen king.*" Taking on the mask of the never-believed Greek prophetess and invoking the title of her own previous book, H.D. presents a prayer for deliverance from the visionary grip of "Fragment Thirty-six." Possession by Hymen denies the possibility of a more human passion, and the poem calls for a sexual embrace to replace the terrors and isolation of vision:

> is there none left
> can equal me
> in ecstasy, desire?
> is there none left
> can bear with me
> the kiss of your white fire?
> is there not one,
> Phrygian or frenzied Greek,
> poet, song-swept, or bard,
> one meet to take from me
> this bitter power of song,
> one fit to speak, Hymen,
> your praises, lord?
>
> May I not wed
> as you have wed?
> may it not break, beauty,
> from out my hands, my head, my feet?

>   may Love not lie beside me
>   till his heat
>   burn me to ash?

>   (170–71)

Here sexualized passion is chosen rather than the passion of "the bitter power of song"; and yet, this is nothing more than a choice between two tyrannous masters, one which must result in consumption rather than consummation. The Love offered by "Hymen lord" (171) is not redemption from the tyranny of song, but is—as H.D. puts it in the next poem, "Epigrams"—"ruthless, perilous, imperious hate" which would "crush with bondage" (172) as implacably as the song which crushes Cassandra. Servitude controls all of the poem's options; as the prophet/poet reaches to escape the terrible bondage of her art, she is inescapably trapped within it by the very fact that she *sings* of her desire to escape. And the condition to which she would escape holds a power which is, if anything, even more terrifying: a visionary wedding which is also—as in *Hymen*—a wedding of destruction.

The aesthetic position of this poem is far from the de-sexualized, "frigid" art proposed at the volume's outset. Artistic and sexual passion are—as "Nossis" would have it—"flame." Each a version of the other, they are inextricably tied together and yet mutually exclusive. The one can only be conceived in the terms of the other and neither exists without the terror confronted in "Cassandra." The remainder of *Heliodora* roams this bleak domain.

"Fragment Forty" finds that Love is an uncontrollable, uncontainable power:

>   Could Eros be kept?
>   he were prisoned long since
>   and sick with imprisonment;
>   could Eros be kept?
>   others would have broken
>   and crushed out his life.

>   (173)

It is, rather, a force which itself imprisons those who come under its sway; "Fragment Forty" melds this realization with despair at the ending of love, finally intimating a dawning redemption:

>   I cried:
>   "I must perish,
>   I am deserted,
>   an outcast, desperate

in this darkness,"
(such fire rent me with Hesperus,)
then the day broke.

(175)

But the suggestion of the coming of day as a kind of salvation from the destruction wrought by Love is immediately engulfed by a new subordination to Love in a more visionary guise; the break of day signifies only a more sinister "breaking." The final section of "Fragment Forty" alludes to the story of Psyche in order to place the moment of vision under the command of the two tyrants, Love and song; the song emerging from this moment unveils as much destructive terror as it does legitimate and redemptive mediumship:

What need of a lamp
when day lightens us,
what need to bind love
when love stands
with such radiant wings
over us?
What need—
yet to sing love,
love must first shatter us.

(175)

The encounter between two aesthetic possibilities—between erotic vision and the vision of song—which gives *Heliodora* its structure and scope becomes, as it shatters the vessel through which it is incarnated, more a literal battle than the friendly contest between equals of the book's early poems. "Toward the Piraeus" openly conjures the destructive power of H.D.'s Greek masks:

Slay with your eyes, Greek,
men over the face of the earth,
slay with your eyes, the host,
puny, passionless, weak.

(175)

The "Piraeus" of the poem's title was built—and destroyed—as a stronghold for the fleets of Athens, and H.D. uses the site as a metaphor for her own situation.[7] The poem's final section defines the love relationship as a form of unintentional terrorism in which the speaker takes on the role of love-object faced with destruction at the hands of her soldier/lover. The vocabu-

lary establishing the nature of the self thus threatened refers directly back
to *Hymen's* "Fragment 113" in which the "fiery tempered steel" of a visionary lute is a sign of the tremendous power of the poet. Here, though, the
steel is more a sign of the poet's peril, an indication that the encounter with
either lover or song may end in disaster:

> It was not chastity that made me wild, but fear
> that my weapon, tempered in different heat,
> was over-matched by yours, and your hand
> skilled to yield death-blows, might break
>
> With the slightest turn—no ill will meant—
> my own lesser, yet somewhat fine-wrought,
> fiery-tempered, delicate, over-passionate steel.

(179)

The biographical resonance of this poem is insistent—the juxtaposition
of lover and military man makes it clear that on one level it addresses the
break-up of H.D.'s marriage to Richard Aldington during the First World
War. It is, in fact, tempting to pursue a biographical reading of all of *Heliodora*, investigating the disintegration of a relationship between two poets,
one of whom is caught up into the war while the other becomes more and
more involved with a poetics of prophecy. Indeed, suggestions of this relationship abound in the volume. Still, H.D.'s attempt to come to terms with
her failed marriage demands a simultaneous coming to terms with her own
involvement in poetry. In this sense, "Toward the Piraeus" is more importantly about art, about H.D.'s own poetic project, a project at this point
very much in danger of a failure more devastating than the ending of her
marriage.

The next poem in the Sapphic sequence, "Fragment Forty-one," gestures toward abandonment, leaving the unfaithful lover and his mistress
behind—an act greater than an offering of either art or the mirroring potential of "Holy Satyr" and "Lais":

> I dare more than the singer
> offering her lute,
> the girl her stained veils,
> the woman her swathes of birth,
> or pencil or chalk,
> mirror and unguent box.
>
> I offer more than the lad
> singing at your steps,
> praise of himself,

his mirror his friend's face,
more than any girl,
I offer you this:
(grant only strength
that I withdraw not my gift,)
I give you my praise and this:
the love of my lover
for his mistress.

(184)

Such renunciation, however, does not defuse the crisis of *Heliodora*, nor
does the Sapphic mask bring with it a full embodiment of the spirit of
Sappho through which H.D. may cut away the imprisoning complex of
passion and song; the poem which follows—intervening between "Fragment
Forty-one" and the next adaptation, "Fragment Sixty-eight"—incorporates
the entire range of the volume's interests in a single figure: a statue of the
poetess Telesila. A short note at the beginning of the poem confirms this
figure as one in which poetry and war come together: "In Argos—that statue
of her; at her feet the scroll of her love-poetry, in her hand a helmet" (184).
H.D.'s probable source for Telesila is Pausanius, who portrays her as the
head of an army of women:

> Telesilla was famous among women for her poetry, but still more famous for the
> following achievement. Her fellow-citizens had sustained an indescribable dis-
> aster at the hands of the Spartans under Cleomenes son of Anaxandrides. Some
> had fallen in the actual battle, and of the others, who took sanctuary in the
> grove of Argus, some had at first ventured out under a truce only to be slaugh-
> tered, and the rest realising the enemy's treachery had stayed behind only to
> be burnt to death when he fired the grove. By these means Cleomenes, pro-
> ceeding to Argos, led his Lacedaemonians against a city of women. But Telesilla
> took all the slaves and all such male citizens as through youth or age had been
> unable to bear arms, and made them man the walls, and gathering together all
> the weapons of war that had been left in the houses or were hanging in the
> temples, armed the younger women and marshalled them at a place she knew
> the enemy must pass. There, undismayed by the war-cry, the women stood
> their ground and fought with the greatest determination, till the Spartans,
> reflecting that the slaughter of an army of women would be but an equivocal
> victory and defeat at their hand dishonour as well as disaster, laid down their
> arms. Now this battle had been foretold by the Pythian priestess, and Hero-
> dotus, whether he understood it or not, quotes the oracle as follows:

> > When male by female's put to flight,
> > And Argos' name with honour's bright,

Many an Argive wife shall show
Both cheeks marred with scars of woe.

Such is the part of the oracle which refers to women. (237–39)[8]

A successful female militarist, Telesila is for obvious reasons interesting for
H.D. She stands, in part, as a corrective to the destructive male figure of
"Toward the Piraeus," an historical Amazon who was the salvation of Argos.
In H.D.'s poem, however, Telesila's dealings in war are sexual, and any-
thing but unequivocal. As military leader, she is subject to the desires of
War *and* of Love, and the kisses she receives duplicate the kisses of "Holy
Satyr" and "Centaur Song":

> War bent
> and kissed the forehead,
> yet Love swift,
> planted on chin
> and tenderest cyclamen lift
> of fragrant mouth,
> fevered and honeyed breath,
> breathing o'er and o'er
> those tendrils of her hair,
> soft kisses
> like bright flowers.
>
> Love took
> and laid the sweet,
> (being extravagant,)
> on lip and chin and cheek,
> but, ah, he failed
> even he,
> before the luminous eyes
> that dart
> no suave appeal,
> alas, impelling me
> to brave incontinent
> grave Pallas' high command.

(185)

Despite the sentimentalized tone of these lines, Telesila's decision to lead
her own forces is a matter of regret for her because the military life in which
she finds herself is as destructive and as sexually charged as a life subordi-
nate to Love; and War itself is subject to Love's terrible domination, an
indiscriminate, violent rape:

> War is a fevered god
> who takes alike
> maiden and king and clod,
> and yet another one,
> (ah withering peril!)
> deprives alike,
> with equal skill,
> alike indifferently,
> hoar spearsman of his shaft,
> wan maiden of her zone,
> even he,
> Love who is great War's
> very over-lord.
>
> (184–85)

The assumption of Telesila's mask is equivalent to an acceptance of the spirit of War—an act foreign to H.D.'s deeply ingrained pacifism—and the poem is cut through and through with hesitations and misgivings. The kiss of War falters before the eyes, ignoring the poet's visionary capacities. By the same token, the kiss of Love "ignore[s] the chin / and the sweet mouth" (186), denying the efficacy of the poet's words. As she accepts the kisses of these two, Telesila locks herself into the role of an ironically passive recipient of their power, replaying again and again her inability to give her own gentler kisses for fear of entrapping another woman:

> And yet,
> (remembrance mocks,)
> should I have bent the maiden
> to a kiss?
> Ares the lover
> or enchanting Love?
> but had I moved
> I feared
> for that astute regard;
> for that bright vision,
> how might I have erred?
> I might have marred and swept
> another not so sweet
> into my exile;
> I might have kept a look
> recalling many and many a woman's look,
> not this alone,
> astute, imperious, proud.
>
> (186–87)

H.D.'s awareness that any choice between Love and song leads to entrapment leaves little possibility for *Heliodora's* conclusion beyond a further involvement in that impasse. The legitimacy of the volume's "mediumship" hinges on the depth of such an entanglement rather than on any too-neat answer dissolving the dilemma. While the ending of *Pilate's Wife* seems to suggest a solution—Veronica's discovery that the voice she hears is her own after all—H.D. writes in "H.D. by Delia Alton" that this sense of solution is in fact illusory, that the novel's ending is unsatisfactory:

> Veronica speaks of love, this opiate. But we feel her emotions are in a sense as unreal or as real in a super-sensuous dimension, as the exotic fragrance contained in her imported crystal phials and boxes. She appears at the end, to break her alabaster-box, but her conclusions do not wholly satisfy us. It is as if in a wave or pre-vision of the next war, or the suppressed memories of the last, we endeavoured to build a shell, almost a tomb about her. (182)

The final acceptance of a secure identity derived from immersion in personae drops Veronica right back into the ambiguities with which she began. Similarly, *Heliodora* works its way toward an ending resolving nothing.

Following "Telesila," the Sapphic sequence asks for nothing more than the ability to die. "Telesila" itself ends with a "march to death" (187), and "Fragment Sixty-eight" presents death as an ultimate giving over of the self to a power beyond its control:

> I envy you your chance of death,
> how I envy you this.
> I am more covetous of him
> even than of your glance,
> I wish more from his presence
> though he torture me in a grasp,
> terrible, intense.
>
> Though he clasp me in an embrace
> that is set against my will
> and rack me with his measure,
> effortless yet full of strength,
> and slay me
> in that most horrible contest,
> still, how I envy you your chance.
>
> (187–88)

Such a vision is the apotheosis of both the "embrace" of sexual domination and the "measure" of a thralldom to song. Though it is desired as a final escape from the complexities of *Heliodora's* project, it is never anything other than an ultimate consummation of the terrors of that project. This is juxtaposed with a quite different vision of death in the following poem, "Lethe":

> Nor word nor touch nor sight
> Of lover, you
> Shall long through the night but for this:
> The roll of the full tide to cover you
> Without question,
> Without kiss.
>
> (190)

Even the finality of "Lethe," absolute oblivion undoing both word of song and kiss of sexuality, cannot be envisioned except as desire, set in a possible future rather than a present fulfillment.

Heliodora's ending resolves neither the encounter which gives it shape nor the complexities of an identity created by that encounter. The book's "maze of daedal paths" becomes even more convoluted as a variety of poems that don't "fit" take their places among those that do; a sculptor's homage to his brother's victory in a chariot race stands with a translation of the opening of *The Odyssey* and choruses from an unidentified Masque. In the *Heliodora* section of the 1925 *Collected Poems*, four poems from this portion of the volume (including "Odyssey") vanish. But the dominant quality of the ending is not changed after "Fragment Sixty-eight" and "Lethe." Most of the volume's final poems explore characters who are—as "Orion Dead," one of the poems removed in 1925, puts it—"poisoned with the rage of song" (56) even as they continue to sing.

"The Look-out" concerns Lynceus, a ship's look-out who, like Cassandra, is a visionary without the ability to compel either belief or understanding in others. His fate simply repeats Cassandra's rather than providing an alternative:

> O God, if I could speak,
> if I could taunt the lot
> of the wretched crew,
> with my fate, my work.
>
> But I may not,
> I may not tell
> of the forms that pass and pass,
> of that constant old, old face
> that leaps from each wave

> to wait underneath the boat
> in the hope that at last she's lost.
>
> (198)

What little ground this poem has gained beyond "Cassandra" involves acceptance rather than transcendence. Cassandra desires an impossible deliverance from her situation; Lynceus at least understands its necessity:

> Many and many a sight
> if I could speak,
> many and many tales I'd tell,
> many and many a struggle,
> many a death,
> many and many my hurts
> and my pain so great,
> I'd gladly die
> if I did not love the quest.
>
> (199)

Lynceus is a version of the poet continuing her search for "the moment,"
loving the act of creation even as she knows its terror:

> But Lynceus,
> though they cannot guess
> the hurt, though they do not thank
> the oars for the dead peace
> of heart and brain worn out,
> you must wait,
> alert, alert, alert.
>
> (201)

"The Look-out" negates "Lethe"'s desire for oblivion; the peace of Lethe
is the "dead peace" of the unseeing oarsmen who complain only that there
is "no work for Lynceus" (199).

But is this visionary—this poet—exalted or suffering in defeat? If *Heliodora* sets out to find a moment in which peace may come, in which the
complexities of a passionate art disappear as the time of the poet bisects the
eternal realm of her masks, then the project fails; as each poem takes on a
new persona in the effort to solve the impasse of H.D.'s poetics, it also takes
on—as an inherent part of this assumption of a mask—the entire predica-
ment it proposes to correct. In *Pilate's Wife*, Veronica's ability to act always
involves both positive action and the falsity of disguises. The same problem
inheres in *Heliodora*. Still, song does continue, and the sheer ability to

endure is a victory of sorts, one that is historically justified by H.D.'s indulgence in poetic masking. As H.D. accepts the figures of Sappho, Meleager, and others into her poetry, she also situates her own work in a tradition defined by them; she places herself at the center of the pantheon she invokes.

This poetic victory, while not meager, is by no means secure, as the ending of *Heliodora* makes clear. The penultimate poem, "Hyacinth"— which is *"From the Masque"*—repeats the confrontation between sexuality and ice initiated in *"Wash of cold river,"* and in so doing once more reiterates the very desire with which the volume begins. The poem addresses a female lover who is passionate both in anger and in her connections to a lush and creative life, and ends with a longing for the marginality and tenuous security of the snow:

> you have your tense, short space
> of blazing sun,
> your melons, vines,
> your terraces of fruit;
> now all you have,
> all, all I gladly give
> who long but for the ridge,
> the crest and hollow,
> the lift and fall,
> the reach and distant ledge
> of the sun-smitten,
> wind-indented snow.
>
> (205–6)

On one level, this is desire for existence apart from the entanglements of passion, where the anger of the lover neither disturbs nor interrupts the "ice, spark, or jewel" (204) of the poet's Mallarmean solitude. And yet, the journey through the *Heliodora*'s "maze of daedal paths" shows that poetry depends for its very existence on the workings of passion and cannot be separated from either its allure or its danger.

The book's final poem invokes the mask of the classical poet who is arguably the single most important figure for H.D.: it is a translation from Euripides' *Ion*, a play H.D. was to translate in its entirety and publish with elaborate commentary in 1937. The very choice of Euripides as the final persona for *Heliodora* suggests a grand culmination of the volume's role-playing, one last act of legitimate mediumship in which past and present poet collaborate, coming together in a single incarnation. But the passage of the *Ion* which H.D. chooses for this culmination, the "bird-chorus," puts more emphasis on the dangers she faces than on a successful integration of poet and mask. The young Ion stands on the temple steps, faced with the job of frightening the song-birds away. What these birds receive for their songs is not the bliss of a poetic moment, but the simple threat of death:

> swan, swan
> and do you really think
> your song
> that tunes the harp of Helios,
> will save you
> from the arrow-flight?
> turn back,
> back
> to the lake of Delos;
> lest all the song notes
> pause and break
> across a blood-stained throat
> gone songless,
> turn back, back
> ere it be too late,
> to wave-swept Delos.

(207)

Ion substitutes for the desired child of "Thetis" who can be

> *a stray self, furtive and wild,*
> *to dive and leap to the wind,*
> *to wheedle and coax*
> *the stray birds bright and bland*
> *of foreign strands.*

(161)

But here, the child is an agent of destruction rather than desire and song. Thetis, in her poem, became an enraptured "arrow's flight / straight upward / through the blue of night" (162); here the arrow is not romanticized. The "blood-stained throat / gone songless" is the final incarnation of *Heliodora's* danger. Neither simply the oblivion of "Lethe" nor the terror of conjoined militarism and passion of "Toward the Piraeus," it is an ending brought on by song itself, a silence which cuts the poetic utterance off in the middle.

H.D. criticized D. H. Lawrence's *Look! We Have Come Through* for not being "*eternal*, not sublimated: too much body and emotions" (*The Letters of D. H. Lawrence*, 3, 102). Neither *Hymen* nor *Heliodora*, for all their "eternal" masks, can escape the "body and emotions" through which they came to be written. This situation carries the poems of masking and translation inexorably to the threat of *Ion*'s Bird Chorus. *Heliodora*, facing the very danger which could be its destruction, can end with nothing more affirmative. Though she published her Euripedian drama *Hippolytus Temporizes* in 1927, H.D. would not publish another collection of her own poems for seven years.

6

After *Collected Poems:* Repetition and the Avant-Garde

Words, repetitions, framing of words means bars down.
                                        H.D., *"Mira Mare"*

In 1925, within a year of *Heliodora,* H.D. published a volume of *Collected Poems,* gathering the poems of her first three books together with a few poems and translations which had first appeared in pamphlets between 1916 and 1919. This collection, following her first book by only nine years, has the unfortunate appearance of a retrospective before its time, suggesting a career in eclipse rather than in mid-stride. Such a premature retrospective carries with it the implication that H.D.'s work prior to 1925 is all of a piece, that it coheres as a single poetic statement.[1] While this is in a sense true—H.D.'s poetry, through the first three volumes, is continually self-referential, each successive volume building on and answering aspects of the prior collections—the single rubric of a *Collected Poems* emphasizes continuity at the expense of variety and difference. Brought together, the three volumes flow almost indistinguishably into one another, and the relocation of a handful of poems from *Heliodora* into a new section titled "The God" makes this literally true. H.D.'s poetic trademarks, her habitual images and techniques, call attention to themselves as little more than repetitions, marks of obsessive attention to a very small range of experience closing in upon itself in a single hermetically sealed container. Stranded, enclosed within her own past work, H.D. becomes susceptible to such dismissive criticism as Randall Jarrell's vitriolic 1945 complaint against her continued existence: "H.D. is History, and misunderstands a later stage of herself so spectacularly that her poem [*The Walls Do Not Fall,* of 1944] exists primarily as an anachronism" (Jarrell, 130–31). Jarrell's dismissal of H.D. simply assumes the accuracy of the *Collected Poems'* suggestion of a career-ending closure and cuts her off from any possible future development; if his state-ment represents a dire misunderstanding of the pertinence of H.D.'s later work, it is also in one sense an appropriate response to the temporal and stylistic distance between *Collected Poems* and *The Walls Do Not Fall*, a distance that must have seemed to Jarrell and many others to be bridged only by the silence of an abandoned career.

A number of critics more sympathetic to H.D. have likewise found little more than silence between 1925 and 1944. For instance, Alicia Ostriker, in an otherwise indispensable essay titled "The Poet as Heroine: Learning to Read H.D.," moves from the early work to *Trilogy* with no mention of 1931's *Red Roses for Bronze*.[2] And Louis Martz, the editor of the massive and essential *Collected Poems 1914–1945*, finds that most of the poetry of the late twenties and the thirties is "pitiful, grasping for a response the words cannot command" (*CP*, xxiii). Even Robert Duncan, for whom H.D. is a master of poetry on a par with Pound or Williams, finds a "malaise" in her work of this period ("H.D.'s Challenge," 25).

Such an unease with the writing of the late twenties and thirties—and it is something even H.D. felt—is symptomatic of a larger problem marked by the appearance of *Collected Poems*. As the barely restrained despair at the end of *Heliodora* suggests, the possibilities inherent in H.D.'s begin-nings had largely run their course by 1924; the early closure of "H.D. Imagiste's" career leaves two options for future development: on the one hand, her work could simply continue, repeating in an ever diminishing cycle the modes and themes of her first three books or the career could start anew, undertaking a new mode, a new method of procedure, could "make it new" in the sense demanded by the avant-garde H.D. had rejected in the late teens.

Curiously, H.D. follows both options. Undeniably, portions of *Red Roses for Bronze* are weak repetitions of her earlier work. But in the late twenties H.D. also begins a flirtation with certain key forms of avant-garde experimentation, publishing her work in magazines like Charles Henri Ford's *Blues* and Eugene Jolas's *transition*. The pieces published in these little journals are not collected in *Red Roses for Bronze*, but do form a context for much of that volume, investing many of the poems with an aura of experimentation.

Why would H.D. move even tentatively into an alliance with the poetic avant-garde of the late twenties when she had so strongly rejected such an aesthetic as destructive in the years following the First World War? The easiest—and most accurate—answer is simply that the times had changed; for both H.D. and the practitioners of the avant-garde the purposes of art shift subtly in the decade after the war. As H.D. suggests in an answer to a questionnaire printed in the final issue of the *Little Review* under the title

of "Confessions—Questionnaire," art must hold out against formulaic response: "I fear always from the future and the present the fear of fear, I
suppose you would call it claustrophobia. I fear being caught in any one set
formula or set of circumstances . . ." (39). In this context, alongside people
like Gertrude Stein and George Antheil, H.D.'s avoidance of "one set formula or set of circumstances" sounds like an avant-garde manifesto, an echo
more of Pound's "Make It New" than her own "Paint It To-day." And yet,
her terms echo her earlier revisions of the imagist doctrine of the sculptural
poem. In 1916, she had praised John Gould Fletcher for writing a poetry
which is "not static," but "moving, whirling, drifting," refusing to be stuck
in the formulas of Imagism; in 1929, the formula against formula remains
substantially the same.

Another of her answers reflects the same belief, simultaneously singling
out modern art as something new and claiming that it is of a piece with
tradition: "Art to-day is what art always was and has been, what you or 'we'
choose to make of it. There has never, I am certain, been a more vibrant, a
more exciting era for the pure artist, to anyone who wants to make something out of nothing, something (to be more explicit) out of Chaos" (40). In
another answer, H.D. claims for herself a "reason" which in conventional
terms would better be called "unreason":

> Are you a reasonable being in a reasonable scheme? Oh, yes. Certainly. Some-
> times my own reason conflicts with the relative reason of the general scheme.
> That is not my fault nor their fault. If one perfected one's scheme one would
> be able to live a life "there" and a life "here" like two sets of wheels going round
> and round, each churning away to some purpose. Things get "unreasonable"
> when the wires or wheels get tangled. (40).

The distinctly modern art which makes something "out of Chaos" is an art
of the intersection between rationality and its opposite, very much an avant-
garde gesture, finding its place through a persistent exploration of alternative modes.

Another of H.D.'s answers repeats the point in terms of the self; all
individuals, she says, are identical, and yet all irreducibly different:

> I don't think I want to change places with anyone else because surely each one
> of us is a world to himself, a shell-fish of his own making. "We" are all the same
> at root, all just one of those protoplasmic germs or spheres or globes that Plato
> talks about. "We" differentiate one from the other only by the shell and as the
> shell is MY shell and as I have made this particular shell for my own particular
> line of defence, I can't see what I should or could want with anybody's shell
> but my own. (39)

This shell is a matter of both surface and essence, giving identity and significance to one's own reason against the imposed, too-formulaic reason of the social norm, a sign of a completely individualized identity consciously constructed out of the depths of unconscious "Chaos." In this sense, H.D. differentiates her art from more mainstream endeavors, allowing it special status because of its unique investigation of the relationship between those depths and her own reasonable or unreasonable constructions of self.

In clear contact with the avant-garde, H.D. further embraces "unreason" in an experimental "Prose Chorus" written in 1929, though not published until 1936 in the little journal *Caravel:*

> Which one of us will break before the unassailable beauty? You before Unreason and the spread of plumes and the purple sandal-strap and the ointment that drips still from the alabaster corner of a box that is not yet quite, quite, quite broken? Will you stay? will you go? Take heed . . . look close. Look close . . . take heed. Listen . . . let all the home-coming spirits buzz over the harp laid on the floor, let the homing spirits look and wait, bees in the aether, look and wait. They wait for the gold of the humm-mmmm of the note of the song that is Unreason; they stay for the note that is a ladder to heaven, the rule and square and parallel of lines of silver that mount with perfect equanimity toward Heaven.
>
> . . . tell me there is unreason in you and season and the return of season will be stricken by the unassailable notes of the song stricken in our two throats.
>
> *Antistrophe*
> . . . what have I laid on the altar called Unreason? Everything. Not this best gift. Listen to the will of the Soul leaving its earth garment. (n.p.)

Other portions of this "Prose Chorus" appeared as early as June and July of 1929 in Charles Henri Ford's *Blues*, a journal marketing itself from the beginning as a forum for experimental work.[3] But H.D.'s first appearance in a recognizably avant-garde context was in July of 1927 in the fourth issue of Eugene Jolas's *transition,* a journal most noted for its 1929 "Revolution of the Word" manifesto and for its early publication of Beckett and Kafka and its serialization of James Joyce's "Work in Progress." H.D.'s five poems in this issue include two in her most recognizable mode as well as three "Child-Songs" documenting conversations between H.D. and her daughter Perdita in which the child's irrational, freely associative statements answer her mother's more "reasonable" questions.[4] A single example demonstrates these atypical poems:

> "They cut it in squares,
> sometimes it comes

in little jars—"

"O—?"

"Under the trees—"
"Where?"

"By his *sheep*-pen."

"Whose?"

"The man
who brings eggs:
he put it
in a basket with moss."

"What?"

"Why,
the little jar."

"What for?"

"Why,
to carry it over—"

"Over where?"

"The field to Io's house."

"Then?"

"*Her* mother took it out
of the moss,
opened it—"

"What?"

"The little jar."

"And then?"

"We each *had* some."

"What?"

"Why the thing
in the little jar
they got
from the straw huts."

"What huts?"

"Why,
the little huts
under the apple-trees,
where they live—"

"Who live?"

"Why,
the *bees.*"

(*CP*, 347–48)

transition is a particularly appropriate place for H.D.'s first avant-garde
appearance, for many of Eugene Jolas's editorial pronouncements are strik-
ingly close in terminology to H.D.'s earlier statements. By 1932, Jolas
would announce the arrival of "The Vertical Age" in an anti-mechanistic
statement calling for "mediumistic experiments in life and language," a
"revolution of the soul" "in the face of machine-mammonism" (*transition*
21, 6). From the beginning, H.D. thought of her work as such a mediumistic
process, a living, incarnational work melding the eternal with the temporal.
More importantly, in *transition* 3—the issue immediately preceding H.D.'s
appearance—Jolas echoes her desire for a transmutation of the eternal into
time as well as her rejection of the destructive avant-garde of the Futurists.
In essence, he calls for an art which will "Paint It To-day" without a too-
mechanistic contemporaneity—a nearly exact repetition of H.D.'s program
in the late teens and early twenties in which "the immense lyricism and
madness of illogic" supplants "skyscraper spirituality": "We are not interested in literature that wilfully attempts to be of the age. Unless there be a
perception of eternal values, there can be no new magic" (*transition* 3, 178).
Jolas continues, in what could be taken as an exact description of H.D.'s
method in the "Child-Songs": "We need new words, new abstractions, new
hieroglyphics, new symbols, new myths. These values to be organically
evolved and hostile to a mere metaphorical conception must seek freer
association. Thus there may be produced that sublimation of the spirit which
grows imminently out of the modern consciousness" (179). As H.D. writes
in "Notes on Pausanius, Euripides, and Greek Lyric Poets," "I am not
fleeing from the present, pursued by present day art-theorists, serpent-
crowned Erynnes. I think myself rather beyond the fashion, ultra modern"

(3). Her work and the experiment of *transition* are of the same literary moment.

The fact that H.D. neither collected her experimental poems nor carried out further explorations of the more formal aspects of avant-garde writing suggests that her flirtation with the experimentalists was really little more than that. And much of Jolas's short essay is alien to H.D.'s sensibility in its demand for a "disintegration" of "the sterile world of beauty" (179). Still, the connection is suggestive. The avant-garde of the period *is* much closer to the psychic and spiritual realms that interest H.D. than the earlier avant-garde of the First World War; moreover, in 1931—the year of *Red Roses for Bronze*—the single most important revision of imagist aesthetics comes into being with Louis Zukofsky's *Objectivist Anthology.*

An apparently fortuitous juxtaposition with Zukofsky points to a thread linking H.D.'s experimental work of these years with the more cautious, more readily identifiable "H.D." collected in *Red Roses for Bronze:* in the July-September 1932 issue of *Pagany,* H.D.'s story "Pontikonisi: (Mouse Island)," written under the name Rhoda Peter, appears immediately preceding the first installment of Zukofsky's "A." This significant bit of synchronicity suggests an important alignment of poetic interests.[5] In William Carlos Williams's words, the objectivists saw themselves as correctors and revisers of a weakened imagist tradition: "The Objectivist theory was this: We had had 'Imagism' (*Amygism,* as Pound had called it), which ran quickly out. That, though it had been useful in ridding the field of verbiage, had no formal necessity implicit in it" (*Autobiography,* 264). Williams continues: "This was what we wished to imply by Objectivism, an antidote, in a sense, to the bare image haphazardly presented in loose verse" (265). Though H.D.'s work of the twenties is often classified as one of the "dilutions" of Imagism—and Williams, at least, would probably think as much—such dilutions as she engages in are conscious revisions of imagist possibilities just as powerful as the work of the more theoretically rigorous objectivists. The juxtaposition of H.D. ("Rhoda Peter") and Louis Zukofsky is a mark of contiguity in time and intent: they occupy almost the same space, and, though in many ways quite different, share a context uniting their work.

"Pontikonisi (Mouse Island)" is a story of disorientations, about a woman named Madelon who, on the deck of a ship in the Greek islands, speaks to a man named Paul Hampton. But, as she learns later, it is not really Hampton to whom she speaks; Madelon associates the appearance of his phantom with the appearance of Jesus to his apostles on the road to Emmaus:

> She would drop her head back into the shadow, her palms must turn black. As she stretched out palms, crucified to sunlight, her thought-under-her-thought

> informed her of Emmaus. Even when they brought sticks and dry olive leaves
> to build a fire, by just this boat, they didn't at first recognize him. If he could
> strip Hampton of Hampton, why shouldn't he galvanize the phantom into
> reality? She found afterwards, in the storm when she had talked to Hampton,
> that Hampton had been below deck. It couldn't be possible for Hampton to
> project himself or perhaps he had done. (7)

Though this event is the center of the story and the source of Madelon's
confusion, it appears only in passing; the rest of the story is made up of
Madelon's unorganized, hallucinated thought, passing back and forth between present and past, between "thought-under-her-thought" and
"thought over her thought" (8). The distortions through which Madelon
reveals her story, such as it is, make it practically impossible to determine
the status of any given occurrence; not only is the Hampton to whom Madelon speaks a phantom, but the very world within which she finds herself
partakes of the same visionary, hallucinatory aura: "No one had taught her
to think like that but she thought under her thought: it's moss-agate, it's a
sort of Poe-Baudelaire dope-dream frozen" (1). These dislocations are in
place from the beginning; the story opens with a statement defining not only
Madelon's state of mind, but also the means through which it comes to be
revealed: "I don't know what it's about but I have found a formula, she said"
(1). Madelon's "formula" is H.D.'s typical method of superimposing one
time upon another, melding the occurrences near Mouse Island with the
story of Jesus on the road to Emmaus. It is also a means of formulaic
response, a repetition of talismanic words (like "formula" itself) in an effort
to bring the discontinuities and disorientations of experience into some kind
of regularity. "Rhoda Peter" couches her description of this "formula" in
terminology drawn from psychoanalysis and H.D.'s *Notes on Thought and
Vision*:

> She recognized this as being what Fizz in the then new psycho-analytical jargon
> would have termed a suppression. She had said, Oh cut out old p.a., (as they
> called it) to Fizz. But P.A., become capitalized, it was comforting to know
> nowadays there were specialists in the thought-under-the-thought. Some day
> when she had time, she would find out why she had put the weights on the
> thought to keep it down that way. She had her formula, she was platinum
> sheet-metal over jelly-fish. The inside could get out that way, only when the top
> was broken. It was the transcendentalist inside that had met Hampton in the
> storm on deck, when Paul Hampton was downstairs in the smoking room. (8)

Madelon's formula is equivalent to the shell H.D. describes in her *Little
Review* response, a sign of individualized identity built up from the depths
of her own psyche. "Formula" is both a suppression of vision *and* a frame

within which to comprehend that vision. While H.D.—or Madelon—fears "being caught in any one set formula or set of circumstances," she simultaneously constructs an individualized formula as her "own particular line of defence" protecting herself from the pressures of a more generally defined "reason" (*Little Review*, 39–40).

H.D.'s most important exploration of the intersection between formula and vision in the late twenties and early thirties occurs in her writing on film—a genre which is perhaps the source for her new interest in the avant-garde and which certainly allows her to refocus and reconceive her work in poetry. In response to the *Little Review* question "What should you most like to do, to know, to be?" H.D. describes her involvement:

> Just at the moment I am involved with pictures. We have almost finished a slight lyrical four reel little drama, done in and about the villages here, some of the village people and English friends. The work has been enchanting, never anything such fun and I myself have learned to use the small projector and spend literally hours alone here in my apartment, making the mountains and village streets and my own acquaintances reel past me in light and light and light. At the moment I want to go on in this medium working with and around pure types, pure artists, pure people, experimenting with faces and shadows and corners. All the light within light fascinates me, "satisfies" me, I feel like a cat playing with webs and webs of silver. I should like for the moment to be what I am, to know a lot more about camera work and to have a little more sheer brawn for the lugging of things up hills. Yes, I should like more than anything to have some sort of workable little car that I could work myself and go off and on, on my own, more or less to Italy and wander in and about Italian and Swiss hills making light do what I want. I should like to work the Debrie camera which I can't. I can do a little work on the small cameras and some of it will be incorporated in the big film that we are busy on. (38–39)

The rhetoric of H.D.'s film writing reproduces her other work of the period and clarifies her response to avant-garde experimentation. Besides an anonymous pamphlet for the film *Borderline*, which starred H.D. and Paul Robeson, she wrote eleven articles for the journal *Close-Up*—edited by Kenneth Macpherson, the director of *Borderline*—between July 1927 and December 1929, ranging from discussions of the relationship between film and Hellenism to reviews of individual films. The most important of these in terms of H.D.'s other work is the first, "The Cinema and the Classics, I: Beauty," in which she discusses the art of film in terms reminiscent of her earlier essay on William Butler Yeats's *Responsibilities*, but with important changes in emphasis. Where the earlier essay makes it the responsibility of art to resist the "Juggernaut of planes and angles" of Futurism, and declares that such an artistic elite—rather than "the great mass of inert life, the so-called middle-classes"—is the enemy of art, the *Close-Up* essay defends the work of the avant-garde against the "lump" of philistinism; where H.D. herself had previously inveighed against the "Juggernaut," here the disparaging word comes from an unthinking mass: "The cinema or the movies is to the vast horde of the fair-to middling intellectuals, a Juggernaut crushing out mind and perception in one vast orgy of the senses" (23). For H.D., film is not limited by such a definition; rather, in the hands of the avant-garde, it is transformed into art, into a mode of vision which is both responsible and classic:

> I speak here, when I would appear ironical, of the fair-to-middling intellectual, not of the fortunately vast-increasing, valiant, little army of the advance guard or the franc-tireur of the arts, in whose hands mercifully since the days of the stone-writers, the arts really rested. The little leaven. But the leaven, turning in the lump, sometimes takes it into its microscopic mind to wonder what the lump is about and why can't the lump, for its own good, for its own happiness, for its own (to use the word goodness in its Hellenic sense) *beauty*, be leavened just a little quicker? The leaven, regarding the lump, is sometimes curious as to the lump's point of view, for all the lump itself so grandiloquently ignores it, the microscopic leaven. And so with me or editorially "us" at just this moment. Wedged securely in the lump (we won't class ourselves as sniffingly above it), we want to prod our little microbe way into its understanding. Thereby having the thrill of our lives, getting an immense kick out of trying to see what it is up to, what I am up against, what we all, franc-tireurs, have to deal with. (23–24)

The machine-worship of the earlier avant-garde has become the norm, the passion of the "lump"; the new avant-garde beauty of film stands against the "Juggernaut" of "mechanical efficiency" (a phrase which exactly repeats H.D.'s earlier essay):

> The lump heaving under its own lumpishness is perforce content, is perforce ignorant, is perforce so sated with mechanical efficiency, with whir and thud of various hypnotic appliances, that it doesn't know what it is missing. The lump doesn't know that it has been deprived of beauty, of the flower of some production or of the fine flower of some producer's wit and inspiration. The lump is hypnotized by the thud-thud of constant repetition until it begins to believe, like the African tribesman, that the thump-thump of its medicine man's formula is the only formula, that his medicine man is the only medicine man, that his god, his totem is (save for some neighbouring flat-faced almost similar effigies) the only totem. America accepts totems, not because the crowd wants totems, but because totems have so long been imposed on him, on it, on the race consciousness that it or him or the race consciousness is becoming hypnotized, is in danger of some race fixation; he or it or the race consciousness is so doped by mechanical efficiency and saccharine dramatic mediocrity that

he or it doesn't in the least know, in fact would be incapable (if he did know) of saying what he does want. (24–25)

In the value it places on beauty and the struggle for that beauty's preservation, this essay is interchangeable with H.D.'s review of Yeats. What changes is the definition of the tradition through which such preservation occurs; here, a newly conceived avant-garde stands in the place of the earlier "torch-bearers" resisting the destructiveness of mechanized art.

H.D.'s new interest in film reinvokes her earlier rejection of the mechanical. And yet, when this anti-mechanical terminology is set in the context of film, a curious irony develops, for the medium H.D. praises requires mechanism for its very existence. The movement of both projector—which she herself was able to operate—and camera are purely mechanical. H.D.'s new emphasis, however, allows her to sustain a distinction between mechanism and vision—between the machine and the play of light and dark on a screen which that machine makes possible. The fourth essay in the series, "The Cinema and the Classics III: The Mask and the Movietone"—published in November 1927 in response to the screening of a new sound film—confronts this dilemma with H.D.'s standard terminology. The possibilities generated by the advent of sound are, H.D. argues, functions of mechanism rather than of vision:

> Voice follows face, face follows voice, face and voice with all their subtle blending are accurately and mechanically welded. They are *welded*—that is the catch. The catch is that the excellent actress with all her beauty and her finished acting had a voice as beautifully finished as her screen image but it was (wasn't it?) *welded* to that image. Her voice and herself moving with so finished artistry were welded not (and this seemed some odd catastrophe) *wedded*. The projection of voice and the projection of image were each in itself perfect and ran together perfectly as one train on two rails but the rails somehow though functioning in perfect mechanical unison, remained separate,—separate entities, fulfilling different mechanical requirements. It seemed to me, astonished as I was at both (beauty of face and mellow finish of song) that each in some diabolic fashion was bringing out, was understressing mechanical and artificial traits in the other. Each alone would have left us to our dreams. The two together proved too much. (20–21)

H.D. puts her point simply later in the essay: "Mechanical efficiency, technique carried to its logical conclusion do not make divinity" (28); silent film is an instrument of vision rather than mechanical reproduction precisely because it avoids setting the mechanical in the place of the divine.

Despite this typical reaction to the mechanical extensions of film, H.D.'s response is much more equivocal than she openly suggests. She comes closest to admitting her equivocation when she concedes the efficacy of Movietone sound in certain contexts: "We must have refinement and perfection and more intricate machinery. Now I know that this is quite right. I do know. I know and utterly appreciate for instance the immense possibilities of the Movietone in certain circumstances. If it were used properly there would be no more misunderstandings for instance (or there shouldn't be) of nations" (24). Beyond her admission of the usefulness of Movietone sound for political ends—"elaborate and intimate propaganda" as she calls it (26)—the double nature of H.D.'s response to film sound shows most clearly in her parenthetical association of this advance to the art of her most significant classical precursor, Euripides:

> We feel fearful that our world may be taken from us, that half-world of lights and music and blurred perception into which, as I said earlier the being floats as a moth into summer darkness. Like a moth really we are paralysed before too much reality, too much glamour, too many cross currents of potentialities. There is too much really for the soul to cope with and all these out-reaching odd soul-feelers that you and I and Tom Jones and the shop girl and the barber and the knife boy have sometimes felt threatened with odd maladies. We want healing in blur of half tones and hypnotic vibrant darkness. Too mechanical perfection would only serve I fear, to threaten that world of half light. We hesitate to relinquish our old ideals and treasures, fearing we may lose our touch with mystery by accepting the new (this sort of Euripidean sophistication) in place of the old goat-herd and his ribald painted chorus. (31)

Though she dismisses the mechanical advance of movie sound as an impediment to vision, she simultaneously relates that advance with the very writer she most clearly admires.

Within three years of these first essays on film, H.D. would discuss the art of film as the very mode through which creativity and mechanism can be melded, calling it in her *Borderline* pamphlet the "new mechanical-creative film art" (33) and comparing it to Leonardo da Vinci's synthesis of scientific and artistic impulses. Such a notion of a combinatory art is of a piece with the governing metaphor of *Borderline* itself, which explores borderlines in both psychic and racial terms. The character H.D. plays "is and is not outcast, she is borderline," and the two black characters, played by Paul Robeson and his wife, "dwell on the cosmic racial borderline" (30). The film medium itself inhabits a kind of borderline state insofar as it is on the boundary between mechanically reproduced, repeated static images and the illusion of motion, the border between "mechanical efficiency" and vision. But, for the first time, the technology necessary to film requires that H.D. adapt battle rhetoric; this new-found art can never quite set itself against the machine, either as "mechanical efficiency" or as instrument of war. During and following the First World War she had rejected such terminology precisely for this reason; by 1930, she is able to praise Kenneth Macpherson in the *Borderline* pamphlet for his willingness to do battle, to become "a young gunner alone with his machine gun":

> Mr. Macpherson does not say, "there is no use doing this, I sweat blood for what use, if I ever do get across no one will understand me," he just goes on, his cadaverous frame getting more thin, his grey-steel eyes getting more glint and fire, his hands steady and his mind stable though his knees are shaking. It is funny to watch him work if you happen to have a mind for just that sort of humour. Like watching a young gunner alone with his machine gun. It is as if one knew all the time the sniper would at last get him. But it is a privilege, in no small way, to stand beside just such rare type of advanced young creative intellectual, waiting for the sniper to get oneself too. Pro patria indeed, if that pro patria is a no-man's land, an everyman's land of plausible perfection. Mr. Macpherson, like Mr. da Vinci is Hellenic in his cold detachment, his cool appraisal, his very inhuman insistence on perfection. (34)

The key to the correlation between mechanism and art allowed by film can be found both in the Rhoda Peter story and the *Little Review* questionnaire: the making of film—the actual physical work involved—is a strict application of something very much like Madelon's formula; and, just as her understanding of formula embraces both suppression and the ability to comprehend vision, the mechanical action of movie-making can be either mere empty mechanism *or* the motions of an art:

> The film relates to set measure and beat; it moves rhythmically or unrhythmically to certain measures, one-two-three or one-two-three-four or one-one, two-two, etc. etc. We used to set our metronomes when we pounded away at Czerney, to those various necessities. In the same way, it appears, some of the most spontaneous effects of the innovators of the Russian school of montage, were gained by being actually cut, re-cut, measured and re-measured with infinite pain and patience until just the desired time element was hit upon. It is needless to point out that metronome-cutting in the hands of a mere mechanic, becomes tedious and meaningless in the extreme. While in the hands of a creative artist, *any* desired emotional effect can be achieved. (38)

Like Madelon in "Pontikonisi (Mouse Island)," "the men and women in *Borderline* move, speak, turn, act in set formula to a set rhythm" (32), and it is precisely this formulaic action which marks them as inhabitants of the borderline.

One source for this new borderline is Eisenstein's innovation of montage:

It is easy to see that this form of montage required subtle alliance of patience, ingenuity, mechanical knowledge *plus* the creative impulse. That combination of psychological opposites is rare. The most perfect and now almost historical example of creative originality plus technical ingenuity is that in *Ten Days,* the soldier, the gun, the lightning-like effect of repeated firing. The lift, fire, pause, lift, fire, etcetera, were repeated in metronomic precision. The almost instantaneous effect was Eisenstein's meticulous innovation—the cutting and fitting of minute strips of soldier, gun, gun-fire, soldier, gun. (41)

While simple mechanical repetition deadens the spirit, artistic repetition is an eternal act of the spirit;[6] the repetition "in metronomic precision" of "soldier, gun, gun-fire, soldier, gun" creates new perception, transcends its own sheer weight of mechanism in order to become a talismanic formula unlocking what Eugene Jolas called in *transition* 3 "that sublimation of the spirit which grows imminently out of the modern consciousness" (179). Montage provides H.D. with the perfect metaphor for such a formula, combining radical repetition with radical discontinuity; proceeding by means of minute, frame-by-frame repetitions, montage links "cuts" jumping quickly from one vision to another.

In this context, the repetitions which Louis Martz finds so deadening in *Red Roses for Bronze*—and which define so much of H.D.'s work of this period—take on a new dimension. Martz's critique, to put it perhaps too bluntly, assumes that H.D.'s "pitiful" reliance on repetition and formula comes about through a diminishment of poetic control, as though she had lost touch with her work. There is some truth to this; as H.D.'s fiction of the period shows—"Pontikonisi (Mouse Island)" is a perfect example—the mechanical round of formula and repetition is in part sheer defense against the disorientations to which H.D.'s self-reflexive characters are subject. And yet, the pattern is so pervasive and so carefully pursued that Martz's characterization of it seems inadequate. H.D.'s continual repetitions in this period of her work are akin to what D. H. Lawrence, in his introduction to *Women in Love,* calls "continual, slightly modified repetition." In her work, as in his, "every natural crisis in emotion or passion or understanding comes from this pulsing, frictional to-and-fro which works up to culmination" (*Women in Love,* vii).

One story, "Narthex," published in 1928, suggests that H.D. herself was well aware of certain limitations of her formula. At the beginning of the story, Raymonde—the H.D. figure—attempts to conceal herself from her companion Gareth (Bryher) with a series of mechanical verbal repetitions:

"Saint Mark's Cathedral is a sort of Christmas-tree sort of church" . . . Raymonde went on mechanically putting the thing into mechanical destructive thought, into mechanical destructive language so that Gareth, sitting stiff and upright in the little tin chair of Florian's, should get no remotest inkling of what the thing meant (in all its connotations) now, to Raymonde. "Saint Mark's Square *is* Saint Mark's Square, the thing *is* Saint Mark's Square" was safe anyhow and it *was* rather surprising to see it here, after years, after wars; the same pigeons, rather plumper, the same people, rather funnier; the same come and go and the same three orchestras playing against each other in the separate niches behind the separate groups of carefully arranged chairs . . . and little tables. (226)

By the end of the story—filled with this kind of elaborate interior monologue slipping easily between past and present—Raymonde realizes that her protective formula must coexist with an acceptance of relationship, that "Reality" must coexist with "Dream": "'Dream is the reaching out feelers like a snail's horns. Reality is the shell or the thing of crystal boxes. We must have the two together'" (283). She moves to reunite herself with the reality she finds in Gareth:

If *go preach the gospel* was indicated so was *love one another.* When Greek meets Greek in Saint Mark's Cathedral, Saint Mark's Cathedral is another name for Delphi. *You have conquered O pale Gallilean,* but there was another Gallilean waiting for them in the moonlight. Moonlight made all of the Square a toy set there by some ardent child, corridor and space before corridor and little set of steps and columns set up carefully under arches. Saint Mark's Cathedral was a child's paste-board set of buildings, its toy village done to this columned pattern, forgotten in a garden. It was true that you could slit the thing to tatters, it had none of that quality Gareth liked . . . reality. Standing in the outer doorway of Saint Mark's Cathedral, Raymonde said to Daniel, "we must go back to Gareth." (283–84)

Returning to Gareth and reality, Raymonde "reach[es] out feelers" to her friend. But such a return—according to Raymonde's formula of "Dream is the reaching out [of] feelers"—is also a return to dream, re-implicating Raymonde in the conflation of reality and dream with which she began. The story's ending implicitly repeats the mode of repetition and defensive formula of its beginning in a new, more fully comprehended way. The project is not so much to find a way out of formula, to break the pattern of repetition, as it is to make it over into an instrument of vision. The mechanical in art takes on the function of what H.D. calls the palimpsest, a new text overwriting or rewriting an earlier text through obsessive repetitions. In a sense, this is literally H.D.'s favorite mode; in her critical memoir "H.D. by Delia Alton," written in 1949, she points out that all her fiction tells a single story again and again, that her texts are all, in effect, palimpsests of one another.[7] By extension, even the repetitions of a picture frame by frame in film or the verbal repetitions of Raymonde Ransome in "Narthex" are minute palimpsests, means through which the motions of the mechanical "formula" of a projector or an individualized "shell" gain artistic significance.

Appropriately, the central story of H.D.'s first published fiction of any significance, 1926's *Palimpsest,* is about this transmutation of destructive mechanism into the sublimations of art. The heroines of the three stories— Hipparchia in "Hipparchia: War Rome," Raymonde Ransome in "Murex: War and Postwar London," and Helen Fairwood in "Secret Name: Excavator's Egypt"—are versions of each other; as Deborah Kelly Kloepfer has pointed out in an excellent essay on *Palimpsest,* the three stories—the three women—take part in a single "hallucinated, layered cinema" through which H.D.'s own past, the antiquity of classical Rome, and the present of the novel's writing all exist together as an extraordinarily complex palimpsest (Kloepfer, 555).

The second of *Palimpsest's* three stories, "Murex: War and Postwar London," set "*circa* A.D. 1916–1926," explores the palimpsest in its microcosmic, verbal dimension; it is a story about the emergence of art from the obsessive mechanism of verbal repetition. As Melody M. Zajdel points out in her article "Portrait of an Artist as a Woman: H.D.'s Raymonde Ransom [*sic*]," the central motif of this story is the transformation of marching feet into poetic feet, a verbal play signifying both a metamorphosis in Raymonde Ransome's consciousness and a transmutation of destruction into creation. Within this context, the story is H.D.'s single most cogent investigation of the uses of repetition in her art.

The first story of *Palimpsest* sets the stage for the second by suggesting the ways in which repetition may have significance:

> When Verrus left her, Hipparchia kept repeating over and over and over like some trite charm "he is like young Philip." She was back, it appeared with the family problem, treading round and round and round. Like the donkey in the old grain-presser who walks round and round and round. So wandering round and round, would she finally evolve from the rough grain, the rough primitive matter that was her problem, meal fine-sifted, fit for nourishment or better still, for cakes for altar sacrament? Maybe. She was now numbing her fine sensibilities by wandering, mule-like, round and round. Treading the rough primitive stuff that was the very essence of her nature, into some fine sublimated matter, meal, ground fine that would finally (she must hold in her degradation to this hope) prove spiritual nourishment. (62)

This endless round of repetition may "prove spiritual nourishment" if it evolves properly. For Hipparchia, such evolution takes the form of creative work; the story ends as she returns to her translations of Greek poems into Latin. A young girl, Julia, seeks Hipparchia out because of these translations: "'I know them all by heart.' By heart? Again Hipparchia by some superhuman effort recalled herself, sat upright. 'What do you know by heart?' 'Poetry. Your poetry. All your poetry. All those rare translations. *Wind of the sea O swift—where Corinth, charm incarnate, are your shrines*—I know them all, all. They helped me to love Athens. All Greece, islands that no Romans ever yet saw'" (94).

If Hipparchia's art is translation, Raymonde Ransome's—under her pen-name Ray Bart—is poetry itself; she experiences the endless round of repetition both as physical threat and as a direct source of her creativity. In the very first paragraph of the story, she seeks to embrace the physical and psychic numbness of London:

> Raymonde didn't know what to think. But why think? London did this to her, blurred her acute perceptions so that inevitably at the end of her half-year visit (she always seemed to be in a state of expectation, of laisser-aller in London that made her feel, for all her definite little address, that she was a bird of passage) she would let go perception, let go arrow-vibrant thought. London did this to her. It blurred over too alert perception, it, so to speak, snuffed out vibration of too keen thinking. (95)

Raymonde takes this "last cocoon-blur of not-thinking" to be "her fixed and static formula for London" (96), where she comes to forget the First World War. But the city carries ineradicable, endlessly echoing signs of disaster, and she cannot escape the sounds of feet marching to death on the continent:

> Raymonde Ransome had wanted to drift and dream through this obliterating afternoon. Nothing to do but listen, nothing in London to do but wait. Listen to what? Wait for what? Her every heart and pulse-beat prompted her though she said she had forgotten. She wasn't listening. She wasn't waiting. She had utterly forgotten. There was a sound of feet. There were feet, feet, feet, feet passing up Sloane Street on the way to Victoria. London had forgotten. She was one with London. She had forgotten. She came to London to forget—feet, feet, feet, feet. There were feet passing up Sloane Street. She had thought she would be so happy. For these last few days so happy. She would have to remember, to think when she got to Cret-d'y-Vau. The clear Alpine air inevitably focussed, brought her mind to almost clairvoyant intensity of vision. She must think, work in Cret-d'y-Vau. But not there, not here. London blurred her over, permeated her and she (with London) had forgotten—feet—feet—feet—feet—feet—Feet were passing on the way to Victoria Station. Feet were passing on the way to Victoria. Carry on. Carry on. Carry on. She had forgotten. Feet, feet, feet, feet. (98–99)

This refrain moves like a juggernaut through the story, picking up more and more deadening associations as it goes.[8]

Ultimately, as Melody Zajdel points out, the "feet, feet, feet, feet" of destruction must be transmuted into poetry through the sheer force of all this association and repetition—and this is what the story is *about,* in both plot and structure. The plot itself is quite simple: a young woman, Ermentrude Solomon, visits Raymonde ostensibly to receive letters of introduction for her holiday in Florence. This initial connection, however, masks a more important affinity between the two. Ermentrude's young man, Martin, has been stolen from her by a third woman, Mavis—a situation exactly repeating a wartime encounter between Mavis and Freddie. This series of duplications and palimpsests structures the entire story. Raymonde Ransome is both Raymonde Ransome and the writer Ray Bart; the triangle of Raymonde, Freddie, and Mavis is repeated in Ermentrude, Martin, and Mavis; the war, Freddie's death, and a stillborn child are all versions of one another; even the nearly deadening verbal repetitions carry the weight of this elaborate structure.

Finally, as structuring principle of the story and as a given fact of Raymonde's consciousness, the very persistence of repetition comes to be an irrefutable sign of the possibility of poetic creation turning verbal and personal repetition to more positive ends. The transformation begins as the repeated "feet" takes on a doubled sense of destruction and vision: "Candles, desk drawers. Illumination, inspiration, feet, feet, feet, feet, feet. Freddie. Who had changed him? Feet, feet, feet, feet, feet" (119). Freddie, Raymonde's poet-husband who gives his attention to poetic feet, is changed by the marching feet of men fighting the war. Raymonde's change moves in the opposite direction—from obsession with the war to the more positive feet of the poem she spends the last half of the story writing.

As an ultimate embodiment of repetition, poetry bursts through the defensive repetitions of Raymonde's resistance. Raymonde Ransome becomes Ray Bart; poet repeats woman, with a creative change:

> That pain and that sound and that rhythm of pain and that rhythm of departure were indissolubly wedded. Or was it her heart beating? Feet, feet, feet, feet. No, Freddie, no Freddie not metres. Not poems. Not that kind of feet. Not trochaic, iambic or whatever, not verse, free or otherwise. I am listening to something. To feet, feet, feet, but not that kind, not your kind Freddie. No not iambic feet, not beat and throb of metre, no Freddie. I don't want to write it.
>
> *Now she may say that I adore her face——*

No Freddie, I don't want to think in metres. I'm tired of being a sort of lightning-rod for all the metres. Let someone with Joan of Arc hair, let Martin be a lightning rod—

> *O grave, O true——*

Who is grave and true? I don't want to write it.

> *I shall see mirrored back——*

O that eternal mirror, that eternal Ermy standing hypnotized, transfixed by this idea, this idea of betrayal. (145–46)

The poem, as Raymonde writes it, transforms dead repetitions into acts of discovery:

> *I shall see mirrored back, my own, just you,*
> *all grave and decorous and very rare,*
> *as one set with dull gold——*
> . . . .
> *set with dull gold and amber*
> *and with fair——*

fair, yes fair, they were dark but they were fair—Tyrian blue hyacinths—ah she had it—she now had it—she had always known it—now she had it, actually Freddie, a line I have always looked for—

> *as one set with dull gold and amber and with fair*
> *Tyrian blue hyacinths against hyacinth hair.* (147)

Raymonde experiences this act of creation as something coming in to her from the outside, as a forceful intrusion into her consciousness; it is as much a given revelation as the flickering images of film projected on a wall. Creative repetition cuts through her own deadening repetitions; echoing the vocabulary of the *Borderline* pamphlet, the beating of feet is the sound of an artist's metronome:

> Yet even as Raymonde argued in her determined logic and in her set determination to see both sides and to see clearly, the rhyme from outside broke across her set determination to be fair to Mavis, like an icy lance of cold rain across some low-lying feverish marsh-land. *Now she may say that I adore her face.* Something, some other metre, was about to tick, tick like some insistent metronome in the air above her; to tick-tick, penetrating even that very protective silver surface that was the helmet of Ray Bart resting where Raymonde would have worn small fragrant non-committal and eternal field flowers. (148)

A second recurring motif of the story gives an added dimension to the repetitions. As Raymonde works her way through the poem, she says to herself again and again "James Joyce was right"; through this single repeating element, H.D. situates her own work in relation to Joyce's in two ways. On the one hand, her fondness for minute verbal reiterations duplicates his—though she is more blunt in her usage, she is able to claim a formal kinship to his practice in *Ulysses,* where verbal elements (like "Throwaway" or "agenbite of inwit") filter in and out of the text giving it much of its structure. The second use of Joyce is more complex. As "Murex: War and Postwar London" progresses, the refrain "James Joyce was right" changes— Christ at one point takes the place of Joyce (158), as does Einstein (165). Joyce, then, even as he provides a structural model for the story, is himself a figure of the palimpsest—as he disappears, other figures are written over him, just as characters in *Ulysses* over-write figures from the *Odyssey,* and just as characters in *Palimpsest* over-write one another in historical and textual time. All of this provides H.D.—Raymonde Ransome—with a way of reading the eternal through the temporal, and of seeing the depth and significance of repetition:

> *Now she may say that I adore her face.* Raymonde must write that down carefully before she went on to anything else. Paper and pencil. Parchment and stylus. Delphic Helios who was competent to deal with a broken pencil, whose laws held inviolate over the merest dust heap. Laws like reading tea leaves. James Joyce was right. Inflexible laws were to be read in the meanest actions, the set of a ribbon (nowadays one didn't wear ribbons). Raymonde yawned. Scratched the first poem carefully on her fresh pad, regarded it, re-scratched. It was cold. No supper. There small sacrifices. (151)

Joyce is important to the story and to H.D.'s work in general—as film is important—because he at once destroys and re-invokes formula, breaks destructive patterns while rebuilding them as creative paradigms:

> Art was magic—but it had lost—had lost—its savour. Joyce was right. It had lost. Art was magic but it had lost. Must get back into art the magic it had had in Egypt, Greece even. Odd line in Egypt spelt exact and scientific formula. The amber eyes were set in the cat face that was drawn with its smile and whiskers like some geometric formula. For science and art and life in Egypt were represented by a formula. Ermy was a formula. Mavis was a blur. Mavis was the blur of some Celtic cloud, the incense of some banished Circe that rose in spirals toward an enchantress' cedar roof so that Greeks (thinking men) were blurred over and forgot their Greek formula. Greek formula must not be forgotten. Mavis blurred over, made one forget formula. It was easier to forget than to remember. To remember. Poetry was to remember. To remember Ermy and her odd eyes. Mnemosyne. The mother of—mother—feet, feet, feet, feet,

feet. It—will—be—James Joyce was right. Formula to be enduring must be destroyed. Mavis was right. Feet, feet, feet, feet—the absolute lack of the salt in the formula had sent them to die—where some buried Caesar bled. It had lost its savour when it sent them. "Tell the Lacedaemonians that we lie here obeying their orders." Greeks upon Greeks died that men might know that the formula must be re-formulated. Poetry. (155)

Like H.D. herself, Raymonde Ransom shuttles back and forth between acceptance and rejection of formula; in the end, poetry enacts formula even as it resists its more destructive capacities.

The story ends with a final embrace of this problematic creative impulse; Raymonde decides to go to Cret-d'y-Vau—the home of her working self rather than her drifting self—for the winter. Interestingly, her decision is accompanied by a momentary repudiation of Joyce and a reference to the avant-garde:

Sleep fumes to dull the perception, to dull over the lightning of vivid thought that was her Athenian inheritance, that was her so-treasured inheritance from those problematic States. Perceptions like lightning and lightning flash of bird-wings flashing up, up, up to the sun of inspiration. Banalities were the real facts. Fortunes in tea-leaves. James Joyce (she had found that the advance-guard of the intellectuals was usually on the right track) was in her inmost searching mind, repudiated. Fortunes in tea-leaves. The world in a grain of mustard seed. Imprisoned in a nut-shell and king of infinite space. Bad dreams, bad dreams. Save that I have bad dreams. London was a bad dream. London was a state of paradisial drifting that would become a bad dream if she so further drifted. (171–72)

The blur and drift of London tells Raymonde that the formula she has found in Joyce—and that her transmutation of repetition into poetry—is a bad dream. And it is, except that London is a much worse dream, from which she is saved by poetry. Her love of "paradisial drifting" repudiates Joyce and the avant-garde, and yet she must explore the psychic realms they open up if she is to be saved from drifting too far.

This realization informs H.D.'s new interest in experimental writing in the late twenties. If the 1925 *Collected Poems* suggests that her career is over, that any future work will only repeat past achievements, H.D.'s flirtation with the avant-garde turns this danger into a new ground of creativity. It is as part of this new ground that *Red Roses for Bronze* finds its place in H.D.'s oeuvre.

7

Red Roses for Bronze:
Toward the Mysteries

> *I only threw a shadow*
> *On his page,*
> *Yet I was his,*
> *He spoke my name;*
>
> *He hesitated,*
> *raised his quill,*
> *Which paused,*
> *Waited a moment,*
>
> *And then fell*
> *Upon the unblotted line;*
> *I was born,*
> *Claribel.*
>
> H.D., *By Avon River*

Though H.D. is largely remembered as the author of a few tiny gems—
"Oread" is the exemplary anthology piece—a substantial number of her
early poems are in fact works of some length, including several sequences
which stretch out over several pages, deliberately dodging the "few but
perfect" stance Ezra Pound had once defined for her.[1] For instance, the
third poem in *Sea Garden*, "The Shrine," contains four numbered sections
connected not by a clear narrative but by an associative pattern implying
rather than insisting upon the poem's argument. For her translations, too,
H.D. usually chooses choral sequences from Greek plays rather than
discrete lyrics;[2] in the *Collected Poems*, each item contained in the section
titled "Translations 1915–1920"—with the exception of a passage from the
beginning of *The Odyssey*—is such a sequence of dramatic choruses. Still,
despite H.D.'s clear willingness to explore larger gatherings of work, the

majority of her early poems are independent lyrics rather than longer groupings; when sequential, they tend with few exceptions to contain no more
than four or five numbered sections. And her collections—while clearly
conceived as coherent books—move obscurely and illogically; as *Heliodora*
would have it, each is a "maze of daedal paths" rather than a strict, logically
realized or rigorously defined sequence.

To suggest, however, that the H.D. who writes in a predominantly lyric
mode in her early career is simply the "Perfect Imagist," talented but
restrained by her own limited means, would be inaccurate at best. All the
poems—from the shortest to the longest—exist in context rather than in
isolation, both as part of the particular volumes in which they appear and
in the larger pattern of H.D.'s ongoing poetic explorations. Even the quin-
tessentially imagist "Oread" fits into such a context and is an important
component of a broadly conceived sequence.

1931's *Red Roses for Bronze* both extends and breaks from this pattern.
While the volume as a whole is clearly conceived as a cohesive sequence,
the *idea* of the poetic sequence changes from a vague way of building a
unified book to a more specific concern with individual poems; *Red Roses
for Bronze*, that is, is not simply assembled from discrete individual poems
but, for the most part, from gatherings of lyrics into larger groupings—it is
a book of sequences. One result of this is an intensification of the sequential
obscurity of the earlier volumes. The patternings and unifying concerns of
H.D.'s first three collections are sometimes difficult to discern as they
spread out over the course of a complete book; in *Red Roses for Bronze*,
this difficulty often occurs on the level of the individual poem. At the same
time, the means through which a volume is knotted together—thematic
echoes, verbal repetitions, and so on—are also reconceived in the terms of
the single sequentially structured poem. Thus, *Red Roses for Bronze* often
seems to be both H.D.'s most discontinuous and her most repetitive collection. In this regard, it is of a piece with H.D.'s new interest in the formal and
theoretical aspects of film and her new acceptance of avant-garde practice.

This is not to say either that the volume directly reflects these new
interests or that it is wholly successful in its maneuverings. Neither film nor
the avant-garde is an explicit part of *Red Roses for Bronze;* the book approaches
these interests only obliquely, filtering them through more or less explicit
versions of H.D.'s Hellenism. Though the poems of *Red Roses for Bronze* are
clearly different both technically and thematically from the work that came
before, even as astute a critic as Louis Martz, in his introduction to *Collected
Poems 1912–1944*, can claim—with some justification—that the book "shows
no development: the Greek mask is still holding, even more tightly" (xxiii).

But as early as the opening poem's first lines, the book breaks power-
fully from the bonds of H.D.'s "Greek mask":

If I might take a weight of bronze
and sate
my wretched fingers
in ecstatic work,
if I might fashion
eyes and mouth and chin,
if I might take dark bronze
and hammer in
the line beneath your underlip
(the slightly mocking,
slightly cynical smile
you choose to wear)
If I might ease my fingers and my brain
with stroke,
stroke,
stroke,
stroke,
stroke at—something (stone, marble, intent,
    stable, materialized)
peace,
even magic sleep
might come again.

(211)

In an article about the relationship between H.D. and Paul Robeson—her co-star in *Borderline*—Susan Stanford Friedman reads "Red Roses for Bronze" as a poem through which H.D. "explore[s] her attraction for Robeson" by inverting the traditional Pygmalion myth ("Modernism of the 'Scattered Remnant,'" 114). Friedman writes:

> What is interesting about the poem is the way H.D. rewrites the conventional script of such a forbidden love so as to avoid the cycle of the white woman's expiation of racial guilt, possession of blackness, and ultimate masochistic fantasy. H.D. avoids this cycle by her reversal of the Pygmalion tradition. Pygmalion, the sculptor whose desire for the woman he carves brings her to life, possesses and controls what he creates. H.D.'s sculptor, in contrast, carves the Lover in order to "sate my wretched fingers in ecstatic work." To fashion his face in bronze will bring her peace, will free her from the passion that cannot be fulfilled in life. (114)

What Friedman reads as a statement—as a desire realized through effective and successful transference of passion from the beloved to the art object— "Red Roses for Bronze" presents only as a conditional, perpetually unfulfilled desire: sleep or peace "*might* come." And this difference is central to any reading of the poem; whether it is specifically a poem about H.D.'s

sublimated love for Paul Robeson or not, it is also, and more directly, about
the relationship between the artist and her desire and about the transference of that desire from the human figure to the art object.[3] "Red Roses for
Bronze" updates the concern with passion and art which was so strong in
Notes on Thought and Vision and *Hymen*.

As in *Palimpsest*, though with significant differences, the verbal repetitions here are signs of the desired transformative powers of sculpture, and
thus of the poem. The very materiality of the art object establishes it as a
potential fulfillment of the artist's desires; and yet, the insistent use of
conditional verbs as well as the fixing of the brief catalogue of the stable,
material qualities of the sculpture into parentheses—not to mention H.D.'s
earlier critique of the imagist sculptural metaphor—effectively distances
such a fulfillment. While poetry enacts metamorphosis in *Palimpsest*, here
the sculpture is never more than a sign of *desire* for transformation. As "Red
Roses for Bronze" continues, making stronger and stronger claims for the
sufficiency and transformative power of art, this conditional function of desire remains; the poem ends as it begins, passionately affirming something
beyond its reach.

Still, the poem does pass through moments where it seems as though
all of its claims are fully justified; its second section, a single sentence,
makes claims not only for the sculpture, but for the sculptor herself:

> All very well
> while all the others smirked,
> to turn and smile:
> you thought that I might see your joke,
> would do
> (fault of a better)
> for the moment anyhow;
> you knew
> that I would prove too strange, too proud,
> for just the ordinary sort of come and go,
> the little half-said thing,
> the half-caught smile,
> the subtle little sort of differentiating
> between the thing that's said
> and that's said not;
> the "have I seen you somewhere else?
> forgot? impossible,"
> the half-caught back half-smile,
> the interrupted nod,
> "a clod
> may hold the rarest flower,

so I?"
the question that's an answer
and the thing
that means that what's said
isn't answering;
this,
this,
or this,
or this thing
or this other;
the casual sort of homage that you care
to flick toward this
or this odd passing whim;
the one above the second on the marble stair,
the smaller (or the taller) of those two,
chattering,
chattering
by the fountain-rim.

(211–12)

One critic, Vincent Quinn, gives an absurdly reductive assessment of *Red Roses for Bronze* through a reading of this portion of the title poem; he writes that "By using many short lines, divided into single words or phrases with frequent repetition, [H.D.] suggests a self-centered woman talking to herself" (91). On the contrary, this long passage *assumes* its authority through a flagrant borrowing of voices and vocabulary from T. S. Eliot;[4] the speaker is anything but a narcissistic woman disconnected from male reality. She is not one of the women who "come and go / speaking of Michelangelo" in Eliot's "Love Song of J. Alfred Prufrock," not one of the women "chattering / by the fountain rim" of Eliot's drawing room.[5] The very rhythms of the passage echo the cadences of *his* ladies, who perpetually speak without quite understanding the significance of the world around them. Suggestively— and as a corrective to Eliot's fixing of women in such inconsequential roles— much of this Eliot-like verse critiques the presumptions of the male figure; the "ordinary sort of come and go" trivializes the representative social scene within which the male may ask his banal questions—questions which presume female acquiescence—and make his sexual conquests.

Through the Prufrockian scene, H.D. also echoes another Eliot poem—one much closer in time to "Red Roses for Bronze"—for quite different ends. As the male figure appraises his female acquaintances, he "turn[s] and smile[s]," flicking his "casual sort of homage" toward a woman who is particular and yet anonymous: "the one above the second on the marble stair." The slightly involuted precision with which this line specifies the

woman on the stair is a transmutation of Eliot's 1930 poem "Ash Wednesday," with its "first turning of the second stair" and "second turning of the
second stair."[6] Furthermore, the Prufrockian women of H.D.'s poem chat-
ter "by the fountain-rim," echoing a later passage of "Ash Wednesday":

> But the fountain sprang up and the bird sang down
> Redeem the time, redeem the dream
> The token of the word unheard, unspoken.
>
> (Eliot, 64)

H.D.'s assumption of Eliot's words replaces the "Lady" of "Ash Wednesday" with the figure of the female artist. While Eliot's Lady "is withdrawn
/ In a white gown, to contemplation, in a white gown," H.D.'s speaker takes
on all the powers of artistic creation as her own proper possession. As the
final section of "Red Roses for Bronze" puts it, she "sets [the] bronze head"
of her object "in its place," reversing the process of sexual objectification
assumed by the male of the poem (215). H.D. reverses not only the Pygmalion myth—to return to Susan Friedman's reading of the poem—but the
masculinist spirituality of her most highly regarded contemporary.

Still, though "Red Roses for Bronze" stakes such a strong claim for
poetic authority, it does so only through a pervasively conditional voice.
The poem's final section specifies the working of art as an incarnation of
jealousy and hatred, directed both against the chattering women and against
the male figure who inspires the endeavour:

> such is my jealousy
> (that I discreetly veil
> with just my smile)
> that I would clear so fiery a space
> that no mere woman's love could long endure;
> and I would set your bronze head in its place,
> about the base,
> my roses would endure,
> while others,
> those, for instance,
> she might proffer,
> standing by the stair,
> or any tentative offers of white flowers
> or others lesser purple at the leaf,
> must fall and sift and pale
> in (O so short a space)
> to ashes and a little heap of dust.
>
> (215)

While the holy "Ash" of "Ash Wednesday" becomes nothing more than a small mound of ashen debris,[7] the passionate creation of art burns away the banalities of the drawing-room, producing a space in which the red roses of artistic desire might endure.

The sexual overtones of the first section's repeated "stroke" reaches an ultimate form in the highly eroticized statue, which may endure through time as a sign of the repeated strokes of the passionate artist. And yet, such consummation exists side by side with its own destruction: as the white flowers of the "mere woman" turn to "ashes and a little heap of dust" at the poem's end, the powerful artistic impulses themselves remain only conditional, desires which *"would* clear so fiery a space" for creation rather than the act of creation itself.

Red Roses for Bronze begins where *Heliodora* leaves off, tying desire for powerful song to doubts about the value of that song. The second poem, "In the Rain," like "Red Roses for Bronze," claims its own sufficiency only to call that claim into doubt. The poem recounts a confrontation between two former lovers with little left to say to one another. The ending of love brings welcome freedom to the woman who speaks the poem, and this freedom gives her poetic voice, allowing her to turn to the "one God" of song and to base her work in the earth rather than the heaven and hell of the more god-like man:

> Don't come there,
> don't come,
> you have all the world,
> go anywhere,
> everywhere,
> you have cloak and wings and a rod,
> all the paths are yours,
> all, all the altars
> save one,
> this one
> of my intimate God;
> don't come near,
> go here,
> there,
> where you will,
> you are Hermes,
> Lord-of-the-dead,
> you are a man,
> feigning the godhead,
> or a god pretending a man's weakness,
> a man's wiles;

> frowning
> or swift to smile,
> you are a god above
> and a god below,
> Hermes,
> treading the track of the dead;
> you said,
> "you were late yesterday";
> had a staunch heart bled
> at a casual word
> from a casual man?
> a god said,
> "you were late";
> you go to the under-world
> or the gate of heaven,
> while I tread
> an earth,
> devoid of your touch,
> (unutterable bliss)
> thank God,
> devoid of your kiss.
>
> (220–21)

The thankfulness with which this section of the poem ends provides a clue to its claim of poetic authority. The poet need not traverse the extremities of sky or underworld to find a legitimate place for her work. Such a constructive limitation, rather than constricting her, secures her bond with an "intimate God." Accepting a limited scope, "In the Rain" echoes 1917's "Eurydice," where the poet transforms Hell into a means of powerful expression:

> At least I have the flowers of myself,
> and my thoughts, no god
> can take that;
> I have the fervour of myself for a presence
> and my own spirit for light.
>
> (55)

But where Eurydice transforms her situation into a position of power through sheer will, the woman of "In the Rain" must content herself with a lesser demonstration. For one thing, the man against whom the poem is addressed is not the supremely arrogant Orpheus of "Eurydice," but someone named for H.D.'s own patron, the god Hermes; just as importantly, the altar to which the speaker turns is empty (220), inhabited neither by the

God nor by Eurydice's "flowers of myself." If the poem claims freedom from what Rachel Blau DuPlessis has called "Romantic Thralldom," it ends with an open admission that this claim has not been fulfilled, perfectly outlining a thralldom both to Love itself and to the figure of Hermes, who retains as his own the very power the poet seems to claim:

> a wreck,
> a circumscribed thing
> is a man's heart,
> touched by the wing
> of immortal ecstasy,
> we are maimed and weak,
> and yet—
>
> I was dead
> and you woke me,
> now you are gone,
> I am dead.

(222)

In both "Red Roses for Bronze" and "In the Rain"—as in much of *Heliodora*—the sufficiency of poetry is a function of power relations; where the title poem claims such power as its proper domain, the second reveals its own dependency on the strength of another. And the title of the poem which follows makes the poet's dependency almost painfully explicit, begging permission of the other for her very existence: "If You Will Let Me Sing" (222).

This terrible awareness of power as a determining factor of song—much more than the weight of deadening repetition Louis Martz finds in *Red Roses for Bronze*—is the force threatening to derail H.D.'s work of this period. *Heliodora* ends with a translation containing a threat of silence, followed by a silence of sorts in the seven years preceding *Red Roses for Bronze*; similarly here, a work of translation carries the burden of poetic threat. Following "If You Will Let Me Sing," a sequence of "Choros Translations from *The Bacchae*"—tracing the descent from the passionate ecstasy of the Bacchantes, through the dismemberment of Pentheus, to the final despair of his mother Agave as she realizes the significance of her act—fully mythologizes the threatened collapse of song into silence. The difference in tone between the beginning and the end of the sequence is stark. It begins as a song to an "intimate God":

> O cease
> from murmuring,

        for swift,
        I cry with every note
        of concentrated speech
        my song to Dionysos.

                                                    (223)

Passionate song, however, depends on power and violence, and the sequence
ends with Agave's repudiation of passion and an implicit denial of song:

            Take me,
            my guardians,
            where I shall look upon
            no,
            no,
            no Cithaeron;
            my sisters and me,
            one in our misery
            shall re-invoke no old
            passions and mysteries;
            the thyrsus shall pass on
            to other Dionysians;
            O let me never see
            haunted, mad Cithaeron
            nor Cithaeron
            see me.

                                            (230–31)

The "concentrated speech" of song becomes a concentrated repetition of
negation: "no, / no, / no Cithaeron." The sequence as a whole moves
through such repetitions, vainly attempting to achieve the kind of transformative magic discovered in "Murex: War and Postwar London." The terrible irony of Agave's cry informs the specific nature of these repetitions:

            O which of the gifts of the gods
            is the best gift?
            this,
            this,
            this,
            this;
            escape
            from the power of the hunting pack,
            and to know that wisdom is best
            and beauty
            sheer holiness.

                                                    (227)

If such repetition is—as Louis Martz would have it—"pitiful," it is not because H.D. has lost control of her poetry, because she is simply writing badly, but because Agave is in a pitiful state, claiming freedom from the "hunting pack" and yet leading such a pack herself, finding her ending in negation and silence.

The point that these poems make, though similar to the closing of *Heliodora,* is finally distinct; though they are themselves repetitious, they are not mere repetitions of that earlier volume. Where *Heliodora* ends by finding poetry and power at an impasse—built out of conflicting systems which cannot and yet must co-exist within a single work—*Red Roses for Bronze* sets out to make distinctions, to realize how the relations between the two can be negotiated. The threat of silence ending the "Choros Translations" is followed by the suggestion of just such a negotiation in "Chance Meeting," a poem which is a companion to "In the Rain" though with a quite different scenario. Here, the meeting is between two different modes of poetry as well as two different poets—the speaker searches out rarified vision while the other remains in the everyday realm of the "translatable":

> dip stylus in the beauty of the translatable
> > things you know;
> the things I have
> are nameless,
> old and true;
> they may not be named;
> few may live and know
>
> (232)

What takes place here is not *just* an engagement between song and power, but between two quite different systems of poetry. Where "In the Rain" leaves its speaker victimized by another's power—and *Heliodora* leaves its poet dominated and torn by song—"Chance Meeting" allows choice; the speaker exercises this choice, refusing to wield her ultimate power over the other:

> I thought my thought
> might spoil your thought,
> being fierce and rare,
> holding bright points
> as stars in the mid-air,
> slaying and hating
> that which it loves most,
> even as the sun
> the host of stars of night;
> even as the sun
> must slay the stars

by day,
I thought my thought
would slay.

(233)

Of course, the decision *not* to destroy the other's work by compelling an
acceptance of one's own alien, "untranslatable" truths is in itself a claim to
supreme poetic authority, but this new authority refuses the lure of destructiveness. Into *Red Roses for Bronze*'s exploration of power, "Chance Meeting" introduces a new argument—the poem transcends its function as an
invocation of power and becomes something else: an exemplum of the palimpsest, a mode which sustains awareness of something beyond itself. The
poem is neither an implement of power nor simply a pattern of words, but
is ultimately evidence of an untranslatable vision of the layers of the invisible palimpsest—a constatation. The final long stanza of "Chance Meeting"
suggests that this new sense of poetry is foreign to the male poet, something
which, in his hands, would lapse into an instrument of power over women.
In the speaker's hands, however, such a visionary poetry is an echo of the
divine rather than an occasion of domination:

> you did not sense the wings beyond the gate,
> you could not see,
> you could not touch and feel,
> actually the sea-sand
> and the sea-shell.
> If you had caught my hand,
> we would have dipped
> our fingers
> in an icy river,
> sipped
> a nectar
> that had spoiled your life,
> slain sister,
> daughter,
> mother,
> friend and wife,
> demanded headier loves
> than your heart knew.

(236)

Much of what remains of *Red Roses for Bronze* explores this aspect of
"Chance Meeting," attempting to retrieve song out of imposed silence, to
find a poetic mode which is powerful without being destructive. A poem
like "Wine Bowl" literalizes the project, allowing a sculpted wine bowl to

stand, not only as an emblem of the world, but as the world itself. The artist's vision creates a world; the bowl—the poem—engages power, but a fully creative rather than destructive power:

> men who travel afar
> will look up,
> sensing grape
> and hill-slope
> in the cup.
>
> (243)

"Wine Bowl," a small, very strange poem—unexpectedly and almost imperceptibly melding bowl and world in the same vision—marks *Red Roses for Bronze*'s first clear turn from a poetics of destructive power to one of creation, employing, for the first time, the vocabulary of rebirth, of Persephone's return from marriage and Hell:

> I will rise
> from my troth
> with the dead,
> I will sweeten my cup
> and my bread with a gift;
> I will chisel a bowl for the wine,
> for the white wine
> and red.
>
> (241)

"Wine Bowl" is central to *Red Roses for Bronze*'s attempt to allow song to emerge out of destruction and death, but the most complete transition takes place in a pair of extended sequences at the heart of the volume, "Myrtle Bough" and "Choros Sequence from *Morpheus*." These two sequences also constitute the most complete entrance of avant-garde and filmic techniques into the book and are without question the most problematic poems of the volume. Each takes a different element of montage as a structural given, and expands that element into a working poetics: "Myrtle Bough" utilizes the more discontinuous aspects of montage, while in "Choros Sequence from Morpheus" the repetition of minute verbal elements reaches its culmination. Through these quite different techniques, the two poems end on much the same note, with an apotheosis of the divine figure of Love.

"Myrtle Bough" begins with an epigraph, *"I'll wreathe my sword in a myrtle-bough,"* before undertaking a long series of strange transformations.[8] H.D. draws her epigraph from Callistratus's fragmentary "Song of Harmodius"; the classical song itself gives a brief version of the story of the tyrannicides, Harmodius and Aristogiton:

> I'll carry my sword in a myrtle-branch, like Harmodius and Aristogeiton when they slew the despot and made Athens free.—Dearest Harmodius, I know thou art not dead, because they tell me thou art in the Islands of the Blest, where Achilles lives still, and brave Diomed.—I'll carry my sword in a myrtle-branch, like Harmodius and Aristogeiton when at the Feast of Athena they killed the despot Hipparchus.—Your fame shall live in the earth for ever, dearest Harmodius and Aristogeiton, how you slew the despot and made Athens free. (J. M. Edmonds, *Lyra Graeca*, vol. 3, 567)[9]

Harmodius and Aristogiton free Athens from "the despot" just as *Red Roses for Bronze* attempts to free itself from the tyranny of song's power. But, though this particular historical reference sets a context and broadens the significance of "Myrtle Bough," it does not explain the poem, which more notably is about the "strange dissonance" (245) of its own transformations. Line by line, section by section, the poem unfolds irrationally, shifting from character to character, drawing the two tyrannicides together with Perseus, Narcissus, Hesperus, Hermes, and the poet herself into a single composite figure; each character is an image of the others, and they are all caught up in a system through which the poem's discontinuities resolve into a series of resemblances mirroring the act of the poet:

> Yourself in myself,
> mirror for a star,
> star for a mirror,
> water and wild, wild fervour,
> some night-bird
> crying to the impervious moon,
> Cynthia
> come soon,
> Cynthia
> come soon,
> come soon.

(247–48)

The poem's epigraph sheaths a sword in myrtle, blending the instrument of power with the work of the poem. Ultimately, the poet's voice stretches the boundaries of its authority, grafting the epigraph's myrtle with something quite different from a sword, bringing the vision of the sacred into actual visual incarnation:

sing
and your hell is heaven,
and your heaven less hell,
sing;
let my own retarded rapture tell
you of the pulse,
the throb,
the quivering
that bade great Helios
drop the golden string
and spurn the lyre for ever;
let song break
your icy cover,
O wild myrtle-frond
wild myrtle grafted
with a Syrian bud,
bud of dark purple
in an ivory cup
of fragrant petal;
O Tyrian shoot,
I would impregnate you
with sacredness
so that you never, never could be free
but loom
and waver
and waft terribly
white wings and wings of gold
across bright skies
be Eros to all eyes.

(252)

This ending mixes a powerful sexual authority with an acceptance of its own diminishment; the poet may "impregnate . . . / with sacredness," but only through the "retarded rapture" of her art. The poem's moments of focus, flowing one into another, reach an apotheosis in the projection of Eros across the screen of the skies. Still, though it stretches away from tyrannical song, taking as its starting point the historical death of such a tyranny, "Myrtle Bough" cannot fully avoid the poetics of power and demand; while the sword wreathed in myrtle becomes a "Syrian bud," and vision becomes actual sight, the transformation recreates the poet's servitude. Once invoked, the powers of song manifest a sacredness so powerful that "you never, never could be free." Vision prevails as terror.

"Choros Sequence from *Morpheus*," like "Myrtle Bough," begins in retreat from such terror, as a desire for drugged sleep which will demolish awareness of song:

Give me your poppies,
poppies, one by one,
red poppies,
white ones,
red ones set by white;
I'm through with protestation;
my delight
knows nothing of the mind
or argument;
let me be done
with brain's intricacies.

(253)

Like the London of "Murex: War and Postwar London," the sleep of Morpheus's poppies is anodyne, obliterating distinctions and levelling everything into a smooth but empty peace. "Choros Sequence from *Morpheus*" is the very poem Louis Martz chooses for his example of H.D.'s "pitiful" repetitions, and it is indeed riddled with deadening repetitions and futile graspings for significance through repeated insistence. But, as in "Murex" and "Choros Translations from *The Bacchae*," the endless repetitions are "pitiful" only because the poem explores a state which is itself "pitiful"; such a verbal treadmill—which from beginning to end resists pleasurable reading—is fully appropriate to the subject of the poem. More importantly, as in "Murex," these repetitions give way to something quite different. In "Myrtle Bough," disjunctive and discontinuous figures ultimately become indistinguishable from one another; here, sheer repetition blurs boundaries and leads to a similar vision. Minute verbal particles, echoing obsessively, transcend themselves as the minutiae of daily life begin to intimate the sacred. Out of dead language comes a kind of rebirth:

So having died,
raise me again,
again;
give me more poppies,
out of sleep, new flowers
rise fresh,
as rimming
river-wild Eurotas.

(262)

The "monotonous little song" (265) of repetition leads to the acceptance of a spiritualized quotidian existence echoing the "James Joyce" motif of "Murex":

> my room
> merges with precinct
> and the palace hall
> seems to lend lustre
> and ennoble
> all,
> all my trivial, simple little things.

(262–63)

The threads of this poetic fabric—birth, song, repetition, and love—come together in a single passage echoing the "Thetis" poems of *Hymen* and *Heliodora*:

> let me be the lover-mother,
> lay again
> your head here, here;
> there is no pain,
> no disenchantment, no, nor evil spell
> can ever touch you;
> see I tell
> and tell and tell the same thing over again
> over and over
> in monotonous tone,
> I love you,
> love you,
> love you,
> dear-my-own.

(266)

The "pitiful" repetitions of the long sequence ultimately replay the repetitions of a child's lullaby. While the poem at this point certainly retains elements of power relations—Achilles grows to the "lustihood / of warrior grandeur" and the mother weaves a powerful spell over her child as she sings to him (265–66)—it is a nurturing, unifying power:

> Achilles stayed a moment and is gone,
> man,
> man,
> and child,
> the warrior,
> all are one;
> I charmed the three
> to unity in my arms,
> I would re-make,

> re-break them
> and re-charm.

(266)

"Choros Sequence from *Morpheus*" abandons its quest for anodyne and forgetfulness as the poem's repetitions dissolve into the measures of song; as the bounds of dead repetition break, the sequence takes a distinct step into the future of H.D.'s poetry: "though I was tired of measures like deft oars / now I return" (268). Leaving behind "the shroud / of past" poetic "endeavour," the poem ends with a true apotheosis of Love and Song:

> love
> is a garment
> riven in the light
> that rises from Parnassus,
> showing
> the night is over;
> see
> He strikes,
> as sunlight through a purple cloud,
> and takes Love to him,
> lover
> and the shroud
> of past endeavour.

(269–70)

With this ritualized farewell, *Red Roses for Bronze* changes directions; where both "Myrtle Bough" and "Choros Sequence from *Morpheus*" are written in long, flowing free verse stanzas, the next poem, "Halcyon," is written in quatrains. While the free verse line does not disappear, the remainder of the volume—anticipating "Good Frend" (in *By Avon River*), *Trilogy*, "Vale Ave," and *Helen in Egypt*—tends toward stanzaic form. Perhaps as a result, the poems tend to be surer in their tracking of a poetic project. Poetic diminishment—the "retarded rapture" of "Choros Sequence from *Morpheus*"—remains a concern, but it is precisely through such a diminishment that the volume finally finds a place, a stronghold, for its workings.

"Halcyon" begins the process by welcoming a small creature—a gull—into its "vague, blurred" vision (270), finding that it clarifies that vision:

> O why, why, why
> am I fretful, insecure,
> why am I vague, unsure

until you are blown,
unexpected, small, quaint, unnoticeable,
a grey gull,
into a room.

(270–71)

The appearance of the gull allows H.D. to return to the imagery of *Sea Garden*, which she holds out as an offering of love for the gull:

what's left?
incomparable beyond belief,
white stones,
immaculate sand,

the slow move-forward of the tide
on a shallow reef,
salt and dried weed,
the wind's low hiss;

it's here in my skull
(leave your hand there)
for you—for ever—
mysterious little gull.

(277)

To replace power, "Halcyon" proposes simple reciprocal exchange as the basis for poetry's creation.

A shift also occurs at this point in the image structure of *Red Roses for Bronze*. Where the volume's title poem must make claims for a terrifyingly powerful art—one which turns the "tentative offers of white flowers" of the sculptor/poet's rivals into "ashes and a little heap of dust" (215)—"Songs from Cyprus" joins the red rose with the white rose in a vision of a purified, "unsevered" sexuality:

red rose, O wine,
fragrant, O subtly flavoured,
cyclamen stain,
how, how has your fire differed

from rose so white?
swift, swift, O Eros-favoured,
part, meet, part—then
rose, be rose-white, unsevered.

(278)

Though the final poem of this song sequence does return momentarily to a vision of simultaneous creation and threat, the dominant movement is toward a vision of the intact rose, acceptable in its diminishment; this movement ultimately finds a conclusion in a poem titled "White Rose," where, though it is "a stricken weary thing, / shaming the spring," the white rose embodies a simple wisdom:

> . . . white rose
> your wisdom is a simple thing,
> and must we grieve who found you very fair?

(285)

Like the flowers of *Sea Garden,* the rose appears as a curtailed life which nevertheless survives, but *this* flower is an originary, virginal thing, existing prior to hymeneal rupture and taking priority over both wild passion and a destructive incarnation of power. "Let Zeus Record" gives the conditions for this new melding of opposites. The second poem of the sequence puts it in terms of light and dark:

> Men cannot mar you,
> women cannot break
> your innate strength,
> your stark autocracy;
>
> still I will make no plea
> for this slight verse;
> it outlines simply
> Love's authority:
>
> but pardon this,
> that in these luminous days,
> I re-invoke the dark
> to frame your praise;
>
> as one to make a bright room
> seem more bright,
> stares out deliberate
> into Cerberus-night.

(282)

The very "slightness" of the verse makes it a mode fit to explore both light and dark; the two are aspects of the same "luminous" vision.

A later part of the sequence—originally a dedicatory verse for Bryher set at the beginning of *Palimpsest*—makes it clear that when the poet "stares

out deliberate / into Cerberus-night" she sees the weak but saving light of
a particular star:

> Stars wheel in purple, yours is not so rare
> as Hesperus, nor yet so great a star
> as bright Aldebaran or Sirius,
> nor yet the stained and brilliant one of War;
>
> stars turn in purple, glorious to the sight;
> yours is not gracious as the Pleiads' are
> nor as Orion's sapphires, luminous;
>
> yet disenchanted, cold, imperious face,
> when all the others, blighted, reel and fall,
> your star, steel-set, keeps lone and frigid tryst
> to freighted ships, baffled in wind and blast.
>
> (283–84)

The Mallarmean imagery of this poem, with its lone white star set as a nearly
invisible sign for ships lost in the blankness of the sea, designates the star—
an image related to all the other white objects of these poems—as a figure
for the poet's project, a figure anticipating the blank pages of *Tribute to the
Angels'* "unwritten volume of the new" (*CP*, 570). The equivalence between
the white flower and the act of writing provides a conclusion and title to
"Let Zeus Record":

> yet when Love fell
> struck down with plague and war,
> you lay white myrrh-buds
> on the darkened lintel;
>
> you fastened blossom
> to the smitten sill;
> let Zeus record this,
> daring Death to mar.
>
> (284)

Zeus records the offering of white flowers, making his mark, like the poet,
on the whiteness of a page; the offering itself is a kind of inverse of this, a
white mark on "the darkened lintel"—the poet melds the two, able through
her writing to both inscribe the white flower/page and leave it intact. "Let
Zeus Record," while it asks for a divine imprint of "white myrrh-buds / on
the darkened lintel," creates such a record on its own terms.

Curiously—since *Red Roses for Bronze* is contemporary with H.D.'s fresh interest in the avant-garde and her use, in *Borderline,* of militaristic metaphors—writing is no longer an act which can only be understood through metaphors of power, but is a natural act of inscription, something which finds itself in previously overlooked aspects of the world. "Let Zeus Record" discovers a writing in white flowers on a lintel, conjures a divine writing to acknowledge this discovery, and records both in its own act of inscription. "Birds in Snow" turns to a natural world, echoing Hermione's walk through the snow at the end of *HERmione* and finding a simultaneously natural and visionary imprint in the tiny footprints of birds:

> See,
> how they trace
> across the very-marble
> of this place,
> bright sevens and printed fours,
> elevens and careful eights,
> abracadabra
> of a mystic's lore
> or symbol
> outlined on a wizard's gate;
> . . . .
> hieratic, slim and fair,
> the tracery written here,
> proclaims what's left unsaid
> in Egypt of her dead.
>
> (292)

Writing becomes a search for these signs wherever they can be found—and they are found primarily in "what's left unsaid" in other, more powerful systems. *Red Roses for Bronze,* in its concluding passages, makes a nearly complete transition from the large art of powerful figures of its beginning to the art of finding and reading signs, the "carven hieroglyphs" of a natural and visionary world. It moves, in other words, from an art of domination and passion to an art of loving response.

The most important poem of H.D.'s new poetics—and, I think, the best sequence of the volume—takes this fascination with signs and turns it into a title defining the volume's ending much as "Red Roses for Bronze" defined its beginning: "Sigil." In the wake of such enigmatic poems as "Myrtle Bough" and "Choros Sequence from *Morpheus,*" the first section of "Sigil" is surprising in its simple eloquence as well as in its reliance on the natural world for images:

I come
as those parasites

out of frost almost,
Indian-pipe, hypatica
or the spotted snake-cup,

adder-root, blood-root,
or the white, white plaque
of the wild dog-wood tree;

each alone,
each separately, I come
separate parasite,

white spear-head
with implacable fragile shoot
from black loam.

                                                                    (295)

But "Sigil" is not just a simple poem reading its own signifying activity in the emergence of "white spear-head . . . from black loam"; like "Red Roses for Bronze," it traces the development of a relationship from difficult beginning to empowering end. The parasite invisibly infesting the tree draws sustenance from its host; the speaker of the poem depends on the other for whatever "fragile shoots" of writing may come from the connection. Though this is not quite a relationship based in power—it is more symbiosis than dominance—it *is* one of reliance. In this dependance, the sigil reveals an apotheosis of desire, a "secret / wild, / wild / wild fulfillment" as natural as a fish in water:

For:
I am not man,
I am not woman;
I crave

you
as the sea-fish
the wave.

                                                                    (296)

This apotheosis, however, is not quite as pure or direct as it may appear. If anything about the poem is "over-done"—a charge the speaker levels at her lover—it is the hyperbole and repetition of the "wild, / wild, / wild fulfill-

ment" leading to the image of the fish-in-water, a passage sounding like
D. H. Lawrence at the furthest reaches of his visionary rhetoric. And,
indeed, like Ursula in *Women in Love,* the speaker of "Sigil" slips away from
the definitions of love provided for "her" by the other to whom "her" words
are addressed.[10] The parasite, in one sense, relies on the tree for its existence, but it also is something different, something which, as parasite, is
beyond control; in other words, *it* controls what it draws from the tree and,
thus, in its diminished state, controls the tree. In the love affair traced by
the poem, the speaker is "something you can't grasp" (297), escaping envel-
opment and imposed definition—she is the sea-fish who slips away from the
wave.

    R. P. Blackmur, reviewing *Red Roses for Bronze* in *Poetry* in 1932,
dismissed the volume as a distinctly minor art: "For the lesser satisfactions
alone H.D. remains adequate" (Blackmur, 100). But "Sigil" itself answers
Blackmur's negative with a positive; as the poem's speaker turns from her
lover, she turns precisely to the "lesser satisfactions" of a minor art:

> that will be me
> to bid you recover
>
> every voice,
> every sound,
> every syllable
>
> from grass-blade,
> tree-toad,
> from every wisp and feather
>
> of fern
> and moss
> and grass,
>
> from every wind-flower,
> tethered
> by a thread,
>
> from every thread-stem
> and every thread-root
> and acorns half-broken
>
> above ground
> and under the ground.

                                                                 (297–98)

This new art is powerful through inclusion of the unnoticed—of "every voice, / every sound, / every syllable"—where the old works through exclusion; like Whitman, H.D. reaches to contain a totality, but shifts the emphasis from his myriad *Leaves of Grass* to a single "grass-blade." The sigil inhabits "what's left unsaid" by a more powerful art ignoring the "lesser satisfactions" of "thread-stem" or "thread-root." Such a turn to the small and the forgotten liberates *Red Roses for Bronze* from the monumental art of the title poem and sets in its place a fully sufficient poetics of the miniature.

The poem ends as the "measure" of its attention shifts from the unnoticed detail to the ineffable and undefinable:

> Confine
> your measure to the boundary of the sky,
> take all that, I
>
> am quite content
> with fire-fly,
> with butter-fly;
>
> take everything,
> I compensate my soul
> with a new role;
>
> you're free
> but you're only a song,
> I'm free but I've gone;
>
> I'm not here,
> being everywhere
> you are.

(298–99)

Where the "untranslatable" vision of "Chance Meeting" was withheld lest it destroy, this new poetic dimension empowers; at the same time, the poem's shift from H.D.'s earlier incarnational art into the ineffable has all the resonance of a mystic death. The poet, "not here," slips into a place without definition.

Appropriately, "Sigil" is followed by an "Epitaph":

> So I may say,
> "I died of living,
> having lived one hour";
>
> so they may say,
> "she died soliciting
> illicit fervour";

so you may say,
"Greek flower; Greek ecstasy
reclaims for ever

one who died
following
intricate songs' lost measure."

(299–300)

The measure extending to "the boundary of the sky" converts into the elusive "lost measure" of H.D.'s work. "Epitaph" fulfills the claim of "In the Rain," turning away from the extremities of sky and underworld in favor of a simple "earth." In one sense, the turn "Sigil" makes toward the powerful miniature reflects the suggestion of H.D.'s critics—Blackmur among them—that her work is one of excessive restraint and limited means; H.D. ends *Red Roses for Bronze* with an ironic acceptance of that position. And yet, the very intricacy of such small measure makes it something lost to the definitions of a dominant art. The act—the art—of being lost in intricate song extricates H.D. from the very limitation she seems to embrace. She lives through the workings of her art, and if the poems sometimes seem to slip from one's grasp, that is because the procedure of living through poems is very complex indeed, requiring a continual willingness to die and be reborn. And, as *Red Roses for Bronze* reaches its end, the poet passes through her own epitaph into a poem titled "The Mysteries: *Renaissance Choros.*" After this collection, H.D.—except for a few more-or-less obscure publications—was to remain publicly silent until *The Walls Do Not Fall* in 1944. The ending of "The Mysteries" makes that public silence sound very much like a chosen voice, a small death through which the mysterious workings of another kind of life, another kind of work, could still be heard. The chosen "death" of a poet is nothing if not fruitful:

"The mysteries remain,
I keep the same
cycle of seed-time
and of sun and rain;
Demeter in the grass
I multiply,
renew and bless
Iacchus in the vine;
I hold the law,
I keep the mysteries true,
the first of these
to name the living, dead;
I am the red wine and bread.
    I keep the law,

I hold the mysteries true,
I am the vine,
the branches, you
and you."

(305)

8

Eleusis Revisited:
From Silence to Constatation

Yet we must not step right over into the transcendental, we must crouch near the grass and near to the earth that made us.

H.D., ms. of *The Gift*

H.D.'s choice to end *Red Roses for Bronze* with a transition from the public address of "Epitaph" to the more private voice of "The Mysteries: *Renaissance Choros*" inaugurates her lengthy public silence during the transitional decade of the thirties. Where the poetic silence in the seven years between *Heliodora* and *Red Roses for Bronze*—years which are, in fact, filled with the publication of fictional and non-fictional prose—carried the disturbing suggestion of "a blood-stained throat / gone songless" with which the 1924 volume ends, the silence of the thirties is more a pause than a cessation; the time of a number of poems and short novels as well as H.D.'s work with Freud, it is a period of regrouping, a chosen silence out of which new strengths may emerge. And, indeed, the conclusion of *Red Roses for Bronze* suggests as much; "The Mysteries: *Renaissance Choros*" projects the generative and passionate poetics of H.D.'s earlier Eleusinian concerns into the still space of the years following 1931, years which, for H.D., are not only silent poetically, but are further tainted by premonitions of a new world calamity echoing the terrors of the First World War.[1]

The first lines of "The Mysteries: *Renaissance Choros*" clearly anticipate both the coming of the Second World War and H.D.'s own poetic disappearance:

> Dark
> days are past
> and darker days draw near;

darkness on this side,
darkness over there
threatens the spirit
like massed hosts
a sheer handful
of thrice-doomed spearsmen.

(300)

The pending duplication of the destructive First World War implies, for
H.D., a parallel lapse into silence; the looming "darker days" promise not
just the "thrice-doomed spearsmen" of battle, but a personal battle with the
war's threat to H.D.'s own spirit. By the forties, in *The Walls Do Not Fall*,
she would be able to testify to the capacity of both city and poet to survive
the darkness of war; significantly, in 1931, "The Mysteries: *Renaissance
Choros*" already finds such faith as an established poetic condition. The
ending of *Red Roses for Bronze*—the gesture with which the poet H.D.
retreats into public silence—implicitly promises renewal by way of that very
silence; such a silence—even lasting years—is a complex enactment of poetic impulse, a working of "intricate songs' lost measure."

Still, such a disappearing act *is*, in one sense, grounds for the surprise
of critics like Randall Jarrell at H.D.'s re-emergence more than ten years
later; even H.D.'s sympathetic readers have seen the thirties as a troubled
time for her, a time marked by a devastating writer's block. And certainly
she did write and publish less in this decade than in preceding or following
years, and was drawn to her analysis with Freud in part by the difficulty she
found in writing.[2] On the other hand, H.D.'s withdrawal is inseparable from
both the work which precedes it and the work which punctuates it. In the
terms of "The Mysteries: *Renaissance Choros*," a poet's silence is a chosen
darkness leading to new vision:

"Not to destroy,
nay, but to sanctify
each flame
that springs
upon the brow of Love;
not to destroy
but to re-invoke
and name
afresh each flower,
serpent
and bee
and bird."

(303)

The promised re-invocation which, for H.D., is poetry itself, emerges from the mysteries of darkness and silence; public speech—the act of the poet putting work into print—cannot be separated from a private vision bolstered by silence. They are forever intertwined in the measure of a poetic life.

Though to say this of H.D.'s comparative silence in the thirties romanticizes what must have been a very difficult time for her, it is still of a piece with her poetics, deeply informed as they are by a mythic pattern of escape and return—the mysteries of Persephone and Demeter. Raymonde Ransome's decision to return to Gareth at the end of "Narthex," for instance, is motivated at least in part by such an understanding of the mysteries. The vision through which H.D.'s narrator reaches her decision is not just an escape, in the words of *Notes on Thought and Vision,* to the ineffable realm of "over-mind," but is also an irreducible desire to remain in *this* world as well as out of it.

An unpublished 1933 short story, "Aegina," is about just such a transition between worlds. The unnamed speaker—clearly H.D.—is a member of a tour group on a small island when she experiences a vision dislodging her from the "real" world of the group:

> There was no division to me, as in Greece, there never had been, between God and the gods. *Kyrie eleison, Christe eleison, Kyrie eleison,* it was all God.
>
> I was in the heart of this—I was—I found I had a tiny pine-cone in my hand. I found I had stooped for a fragment of the pumice-stone that is washed up here. I remembered how the popular dean had been bargaining on this ledge, as the launch landed for a sponge. I had not bought a sponge. Peasants, with baskets were waiting for the return of the tourists above. It was so still. The island was curved like a sea-shell. I would walk to the next curve. Each curve made a special invitation, one could slide off. I did not want to slide off. Then I knew I had gone.
>
> I had expected some revelation at Delphi but it hadn't happened.
>
> It happened at Aegina.
>
> I just wasn't there now. (3)

"Aegina" takes quite seriously the possibility that vision or revelation can *actually* remove a person from the world; H.D.'s return to the tour group at the story's end—like Raymonde's return to Gareth in "Narthex"—is the result of conscious decision rather than any sense of the impossibility of escape into the metaphysical mist:

> [The tales of Christ and Asklepios] are spiritual facts. There is Virgo, that daughter; Virgo is that Christian mother. For a split second, they were superimposed and in that perfection of harmony, I could get out. I was fully expressed. If I paused one second, I could get out.

> I would be gone.
> I could go.
> Where would I go?
> There might be awkwardness.
> The boat would wait, the passengers would be distressed.
> Anyhow, I must go back. (4)

She "must go back," not because it is physically or psychically impossible
to do otherwise, but because there is something *in* the world which calls to
her as strongly as what she finds *out* of the world; she moves between the
world of physical fact and the world of spiritual fact, and "going back" is a
deliberate attempt to find the point at which these two worlds meet without
one dominating the other. In her 1949 memoir, "H.D. by Delia Alton,"
H.D. explains the dilemma, referring both to "Aegina" and "The Moment":

> But the experience of the Moment . . . though it offers escape, seems to bring
> its instantaneous message. Once "out," where are you? Will you come back?
> Will you stay "out"? And once "out," in any case, there is awkward dilemma.
> The spirit caught back into the old mysteries of Egypt and Greece, might be
> perfected, but on the other hand, it might, after the initial ecstasy of freedom,
> wander in some vague Limbo. (206)

Faced with the prospect of eternal entrapment in "some vague Limbo,"
H.D. chooses the world. Such a return carries with it the responsibility of
translating the terms of vision into the terms of the world, of testifying to
the efficacy of revelation in a world which would otherwise deny it. In other
words, the public work of the poet is to bear witness to the fruits of vision,
to re-write silence, making it over into the legible measures of poetry.

Two stories written between 1931 and 1934 outline this transition from
private to public in terms which move from the deeply hermetic and puzzling to the almost flippantly accessible. These stories center around the
figure of H.D.'s only male pseudonym, John Helforth.[3] *Kora and Ka*, written by "H.D.," features Helforth as the character through whose consciousness the meager narrative is filtered; it was published in an edition of only
100 copies by Imprimerie Darantière in Dijon, France in 1934 along with
another, unrelated story titled "Mira-Mare." *Nights*—published in a similar
edition in 1935—is divided into two sections; the second of these is a series
of twelve diary-like prose sketches written by "Natalia Saunderson" on the
twelve nights preceding her suicide by drowning. Helforth does not figure
in this portion of the novella. The book does, however, carry his name on
the title page in the place of H.D.'s, and he is the author of its first section,
a "Prologue," also divided into twelve portions, giving a history of the story
itself and explaining how it came to be published. The two novellas trace a

very specific modulation from disappearance into the darkness of a death, through the mysteries, back into the world of public language.

Natalia Saunderson's narrative, a "purple sex story" written, as John Helforth says, with "the realism of white lightning" (26), explores Natalia's psychic reactions to the departure of her husband Neil with his male lover and to each night of her own brief love affair with a young man named David Leavenworth.[4] It is clear from the first of the "Nights" that one of Natalia's goals is precisely the kind of escape from the world recounted in "Aegina"; during intercourse with David, she blacks out, fainting into vision:

> How could anyone live, who didn't know this? But what did she, Natalia, know—only—surely it was not a failure! Why, she had almost got "out," she had never been so "out of the world" with Neil, but it was another world, this was the catch, she was "out" in. (44–45)

As the twelve nights pass, Natalia continues her erotic and spiritual search for escape, for the unimpeded "flow of white electricity" (52) which is one part orgasm and one part break from the set formula of habitual mental and social response.

Natalia comes closest to her goal one night after David Leavenworth has left her room when she brings herself to orgasm, transforming herself through masturbation into nearly perfect "radium":

> Her deity was impartial; as the radium gathered electric current under her left knee, she knew her high-powered deity was waiting. He would sting her knee and she would hold muscles tense, herself only a sexless wire that was one wire for the fulfillment. She was sexless, being one chord, drawn out, waiting the high-powered rush of the electric fervour. It crept up the left side, she held it, timed it, let it gather momentum, let it gather force; it escaped her above the hip-bone, spread, slightly weakened, up the backbone; at the nape, it broke, distilled radium into the head but did not burst out of the hair. She wanted the electric power to run on through her, then out, unimpeded by her mind. (51)

Still, even without the interference of David, she cannot quite reach the state she seeks, and is brought back by the impeding force of her own mind:

> She was happy to find her face, salt-wet with tears. Mind yet checked the flow of white electricity. But she was nearer than she had ever been to the source of this power. Evil? Sin was the damning of this force until it ate back into the fibre of existence, turned foul, in spite and suppression of maniacal repudiation. Yet how judge? She hated the spend-thrift of beauty, as much as the miser. Each must find his own high-road to deity. To-night, she was not far off. (52)

The ecstasy she almost reaches is both promise and danger. At the beginning of the following night, Natalia picks up the thread of her narrative and wonders whether her escape may be simply an avoidance of life, a movement not into vision, but into a terrible death:

> ... the Greek is radium. The Egyptian is the gold beetle, the Greek the white, escaped butterfly. . . . She saw no force for it but death, and as the aura of radiant life sped through her, she saw that she was not so much healed as shocked back, re-vivified, for fresh suffering. Would she die sometime in some such shock-aura of pure light? And if so, would she be flung into a medieval hell, filled with the most hideous of refuse, come to life, the horrors of the unconscious? Was her fervour, after all, an illicit escape, an inhuman intolerance of the casual, tiresome things of this life? (53)

Unlike the nameless narrator of "Aegina," Natalia feels the lure of escape so strongly that it leads her to suicide. Her manuscript ends just before her ultimate passage "out" into the darkness below the ice of lac de Brey.

If the risk of Natalia's approach to erotic vision through her own resources is death—or such a disappearance into the self that her public identity vanishes—then the risk of the same approach with David is absolute and destructive transformation; on the fifth night, with him, she feels the danger:

> She was in so many pieces. The hand held her; she was in many, many pieces. The fingers held her, did not move, went taut, as her hand went limp and she herself allowed all the rest of herself to drift out, to become amorphous, while he held her. Had he saved her from this last, most desperate drowning or was there some other form of regeneration to be learned? Chemical change seemed to take place, as his mouth held hers. She seemed to breathe a new substance into her lungs like those ridiculous hydrangea roots that turn blue in—she couldn't remember what people poured over the earth, so that white hydrangeas were blue. Something was poured into her, volatile, potent as ether, that was turning the very marrow of her bones into another substance. He was melting her bones. (72)

Though David may keep Natalia from disappearing into herself, he does not have the right kind of power to bring her "out" into a visionary world. She brings herself close to ecstasy; the transformation he represents, on the other hand, is rape—she can go "out," but only by way of a violence threatening to destroy the very vision she seeks:

> It seemed from the beginning of time, one had been told not to touch things—*touch things.* Hands. His hands were reaching. Hands were reaching, superim-

posed on his hands. They re-valuated her torse. Here, they seemed to say, is authentic fragment. Hands.

There was a black sort of sweat that broke out. David knew all about it, he was so stolid but he knew that. He turned and his shoulders were wind-screen, she lay under boulders. Over his left shoulder, wind howled and she dragged feet in, out of the cold. His feet found and pinned hers, rape out of stone-age. He was stone, out of stone-age. (74)

Natalia's "Nights" examines her need to choose between "drowning" into herself and the even more destructive subordination of herself to another's intended or unintended violence. Given the choice, she follows the option which most completely conforms to the dictates of a visionary or—as the narrator of "Aegina" puts it—"Delphic" sensibility; she goes out of the world in a "last, most desperate drowning" from which David could never save her, skating out onto the frozen lac de Brey to collapse through the ice and fall into its measureless waters.

John Helforth, in his introduction, interprets her suicide as an attempt to find the perfect visionary relationship, one impossible under the geometric laws governing this world:

> But evidently, for all her erotic experiments, she could not make an equation that answered, only that last one, *two parallel lines meet.*
>
> They were very straight lines, Renne [Natalia's sister-in-law] tells me. It was their chauffeur, Georges Crox, who explained, with the acumen of his kind, that Madame had scuffled a little with her skates; the powdered snow on the ice, showed every gesture of the take-off; the finish was, as if it were, cut by diamond, on glass. The two lines ran straight out, two parallel lines—they met in a dark gash of the luminous ice-surface. She had demonstrated perfectly. (4–5)

Such a perfectly impossible meeting, Helforth's reading implies, can take place only at the deadly labial "gash" in which the suicidal ice-maiden finds her ultimate auto-erotic ending. And the other gesture of Natalia's exit gives Helforth a conclusion for his introduction:

> Her skates on the lac de Brey, that winter afternoon, made a simple statement. It was a mathematically simple statement. So with these pages. She had put down something that happened as it happened. The catch is, that it doesn't read as if it ever happened, because such things don't happen to other people or if they happen, I am sure, they don't happen like that. But, then, neither would anyone else, I am sure, have chosen that particular lake on that particular plateau, on the road between Avignon and Laugy, on the way to Trois Couronnes, for an exit. And neither would anyone else, I am sure, have spoiled such an utterly concentrated and beautifully abstract gesture, by leaving (God help us all) somebody's borrowed watch, at the last, on an old muff. (29)

Natalia leaves time—in the guise of the watch, something foreign to her, not her own—behind her as she dives into the eternity of a lake whose depth has never been measured.

Though Helforth's reading of the suicide accounts for much of its significance—it *is* an auto-erotic escape from time and from the violence Natalia finds in her compulsive heterosexual "erotic experiments"—the final sentences of the "Nights" manuscript make it clear that it means much more to Natalia than this:

> [David] would drag her down; she would perceive fronds of fern, but that was the pattern on Neil's pyjamas; she would perceive pattern of unfamiliar sub-tropic bush and trees, but her mind zigzagged off, went triangular course like a dragon-fly on the surface of stagnant water. She was hovering over a stagnant pond, while the sea was waiting, while it had only to draw her—out—— (106)

On one level, Natalia Saunderson's "Nights" is a fairly simple story—like Kate Chopin's *The Awakening*—of a woman's choice of suicide over an even more deadly life. And yet, even a cursory look at the "white lightning" of the oblique interior narrative complicates such a straight-forward reading. Neither the suicide itself nor any clear awareness of its impending occurrence filters through Natalia's elaborate mythopoeic account; as her text would have it, the choice to skate dangerously far out onto lac de Brey—something to which she never directly refers—is nothing more or less than an ultimate way of going "out" to the place for which she has been searching all along. We are only able to read her manuscript's ending as a suicide note of sorts because that is how John Helforth tells us to regard it.

As with H.D. herself, Natalia's very name complicates matters further. Both Helforth and Natalia begin their texts with the question of names, but Helforth's account simply tells us that they are masks for real people:

> I can not do better than use the names in this manuscript, as Natalia Saunderson used them. Her name is not Natalia nor Saunderson, neither is her sister-in-law called Renne, nor her husband, Neil. The last two are living, Natalia is dead. (3)

However, in Natalia's opening, the choice of a name, like her passage "out," takes on mythic resonance:

> Natalia, they had called her; but it was Nat or Neith now. Neit or Neith is what he called her; he said, "Neith" and she felt rhymes go with the word; sheathe, unsheathe—claws certainly. He says "you have no need to be so cruel. You bully me." He says "it was cruel." (33)

Natalia—"Neit or Neith" as she is called—is not only a woman struggling in the human world, but a goddess who controls or creates her own mythic and eternal domain. Neith, according to E. A. Wallis Budge, "was one of the oldest of all the Egyptian goddesses" (Budge, 450), whose devotees "declared that she was the mother of the gods, and the creator of all the heavens and the earth, and of everything which is in them" (Budge, 93), and associated her with Isis.[5] Budge goes on to point out that "at an earlier period she was certainly a personification of a form of the great, inert, primeval watery mass out of which sprang the Sun-god Ra" (Budge, 451). In this context, Natalia's last "Night"—her final paragraph before skating "out"—makes new sense. The differences between the details of the suicide as Helforth gives them and Natalia's own account are striking; as Helforth suggests, "She had put down something that happened and as it happened. The catch is, that it doesn't read as if it ever happened" (29). This is because it never quite happens in the real world of Helforth and the reader but rather in the mythic world of Neith. Natalia's text ignores the frozen lake over which her skates carve their parallel lines and substitutes a "surface of stagnant water" so that her death may more clearly incarnate the mythic creation of the sacred out of "the great, inert, primeval watery mass" which is Neith in her oldest form. Natalia's choice of death—like H.D.'s choice of silence following *Red Roses for Bronze*—is less a suicide than a powerful passage into the darkness of the mysteries.

Even the title Natalia Saunderson gives her text belongs to this mythic story; in the simplest sense, she calls her narrative "Nights" because it recounts the passage of twelve literal nights, but in a deeper sense—a sense suggested by the similar sounds of "Nights" and "Neith"—the title ties the text to the mysteries of Neith. Budge, quoting Herodotus, provides an important gloss:

> At Sais in the temple of Minerva [i.e. the temple of Neith], in a base Chappell, are standinge certayne greate brooches of stone, whereto is adioyninge a lowe place in manner of a Dungeon, couered over wyth a stone curiously wroughte, the vaute it selfe being on euery side carued with most exquisite arte, in biggnesse matchinge with that in Delos, which is called Trochoides. Herein euery one counterfayteth the shadowes of hys owne affections and phantasies in the nyghte season, which the Aegyptians call Mysteryes. (453)

Natalia's "Nights," then, carries her through the shadows of her own "affections and phantasies in the nyghte season," or—to put it another way—traces her passage through twelve stages of erotic initiation into the mysteries. Her narrative is exactly equivalent to the "first step in the Eleusinian mysteries" which, H.D. is careful to point out in *Notes on Thought and Vision*, "had to do with sex" (29).

Still, as Natalia explores this first stage of the mysteries, even as she searches out its most solitary and intense form, she finds that her "mind yet check[s] the flow of white electricity," that her intellect keeps her from her goal. Her death, apart from being an acceptance of darkness, is in an important sense an attempt to side-step the limits of the intellect. The irony of Natalia's choice—and a sign that her quest ultimately fails—is that H.D.'s reading of the mysteries *requires* the mediation of the intellect as a necessary second stage. Natalia refuses to undergo this second step and thus—though clearly she herself has a different understanding of her act—surrenders before she reaches her goal.

Kora and Ka takes this stage of the mysteries as its textual terrain, putting the story into John Helforth's hands. The "Ka" of the title is an internalized, ghostly double—an "overmind" in the terms of *Notes on Thought and Vision* (and, indeed, Helforth explicitly refers to his Ka with this word)—or an intellectualized *doppelgänger* for Helforth. The problematic nature of this second stage of the mysteries is immediately apparent in the opening of the story; the Ka, speaking with the voice of Helforth, begins with a direct reference to the difficulties of the intellect: "There are two things mitigate against me, one is my mind one is the lack of it" (7). The Ka goes on:

> Kora brought me here. She thinks that I am overworked. I am overworked. Kora is exquisite and helpful. I follow her as a child follows its mother. But she is more to me than any mother could be to any child. She is to me what a materialized substance is to a shadow. Without substance, shadow cannot exist. I cannot exist without Kora. But I am more to Kora than a shadow. I am that sort of shadow they used to call a Ka, in Egypt. A Ka lives after the body is dead. I shall live after Helforth is dead. (7)

Helforth—with his Ka—is, to put it simply, split into two parts, the man and his double each striving for dominance. The story of *Kora and Ka*—there is no real plot to speak of—follows the course of a gradual re-integration of the two in the terms of a transition from a visual to a visionary setting. And this transition precisely re-enacts the intellectual stage of H.D.'s mysteries. In "Helios and Athene," H.D. writes, "The mind grips the statue as the bird grips the rock-ledge. It would convince itself that this is its final resting place" (*CP*, 328). In *Kora and Ka*, it is Helforth himself who fills in for the statue; in the beginning he is seen by the Ka as a dead, nearly sculptural figure:

> I look across a space of grass that is the colour of the chiffon scarf that Kora wore last night at dinner. The grass is the colour of tea-roses. From the burnt

grass, there is a slight burnt fragrance like tobacco scattered across pot-pourri. The hand of Helforth lies affectedly across the grey knee of his lounge suit. The clothed knee is a dummy knee in a window. The shod feet are brown leather lumps. They rest in the grass like amputated dead feet. The hand of Helforth lives the more markedly for this. It is a long hand, affectedly flung there, living. I, this Ka, cannot see the face of Helforth. (7)

And yet, though deadened, Helforth—as seen in his hands—has a living core which re-emerges as he takes the internal narration over from the Ka; the story's second section begins with an echo of the Ka's first statement melded with an unacknowledged memory of Natalia Saunderson's suicide, here referring to the split in Helforth's mind:

> There are two things that mitigate against me. One is my mind, one is the lack of it. I, John Helforth, go on existing in that beam of sunlight. As I stand now, stretching, the bar of light that underlined that triangle, (sun-serpent) is exactly parallel to the threshold of the doorway. Parallels, parallels . . . are two things that travel along, equidistant, and never quite meet. Parallels? I am John Helforth, I say, yawning and I endeavor to banish, in that yawn's exaggeration, the monster I call, for lazy lack of definition, "Ka." Ka is far off now; Ka partook of symptom, was neurotic breakdown; Ka, it is true, led me, made me, having made me, preserved me—but yawning, I say, for what? If I, Helforth, get rapt back into this Ka thing, contemplating vine-green leaf, Helforth will be good for nothing. (21)

Helforth and his Ka are the two parallel lines which inhabit the same space and yet never meet; as the figure of the triangle seen by Helforth suggests, however, there is a third term making up the scene of *Kora and Ka*—the woman Kora, through whose mediation Helforth's intellectual split is bridged. Helforth himself points out the intimate ties between the three:

> Kora is everything. Without Kora, Ka would have got me. Sometimes I call Kora, Ka, or reverse the process and call Ka, Kora. I am on familiar terms with Kora, with Ka, likewise. We are, it is evident, some integral triple alliance, primordial Three-in-One. I am Kora, Kora is Helforth and Ka is shared between us. Though she repudiates affiliation with Ka, and refuses to discuss it, yet the fact remains. Ka is Kora, Kora is Ka. The waif must be shared between us. (21–22)

Helforth's re-integration with the Ka comes through Kora but—as in *Nights*—this reconciliation takes place more on a mythic plane than on the quotidian level of the "real" Helforth. One passage late in the story—a passage just as confused and opaque as the character of Helforth himself—presents a series of revelations concerning Kora and her husband and Helforth's dead brother Larry:

Surface anger can be got at, can be demolished with a like flare of anger. Kora's anger is not like Helforth's anger, but it allays and stills it. But Kora was not really angry. On the surface, Kora tells me she was angry. She sits beside me, she says, "must we ever be angry again, Helforth?" I say, "Kora it's like this. If I could have had bouts of resentment, anger, hatred, all through those ten years, these great volcanic break-downs wouldn't happen." Kora says "yes, Helforth. I too. If I could have hated Stamford, known what he was, if I could have loathed him, I might have loathed the children." (36)

Helforth translates Kora's situation into his own, allowing her realization to lead him back to his obsession with his brother:

Her profile is hard. Sometime, somewhere, there was a jab, a sort of slice was taken out of Kora. You feel a certain sort of tenderness was removed, as one might have one's appendix removed, on an operating table. The stability of Kora is not really stable. It is the stability of a frozen rabbit that hears the hounds not far off. She seems to be listening, to be waiting. "But Kora, they can't ever take the children." She does not accept me, she is looking far off. She says, "it's odd. I would never have minded, none of it would have mattered, if I had ever loved him." I say, "Kora you did love him." I say even, "you do love him." I feel with one last flagrant tendril that binds me to the past, that this is somehow what Larry would have said. I have forgiven Larry, now, for dying and even as I said, "I will let Larry go," Larry stood there near me. I feel, "this is what Larry would have said to Jeanette." I feel with one last fibre that binds me to that past, that I must now (having discarded Larry) be once more with him, just this once, this once, Larry. I say "you do really, Kora, love him."

My eyes are filmed over. I feel, in death, only the tenderness of dismissal. Kora has done this for me. Well, Kora reconciled me to death, I, appositely, will try to reconcile her to life. (37–38)

Just as Helforth is able to take Kora's situation as a kind of parallel to his own, he is also able to apply her admission that she did not love her husband—appropriately—to himself:

I had not kissed her, after that first kiss of my condonation as I smoothed red poppy-heads about her. I condoned not this present lapse but the fact that, till now, she had astonishingly hidden the fact that she had not loved me. (40)

At the denouement of the story, as these revelations and sudden understandings follow—inexorably if obscurely—one after another, Helforth's Ka returns, now transmuted from symptomatic sign of "neurotic breakdown" to instrument of vision. The Ka's ability to see the deadened Helforth at the story's opening becomes a new power to "see" Kora in mythological guise; through a subtle shift in her name, the entire situation changes from the world of breakdowns, husbands, and dead brothers to the eternal world of the mysteries and rebirth:

> Ka, it appeared however, still belongs to Helforth, his personal little dragon; it seemed, with the assistance of this personal little pest, that I could see around and, as it were, through walls and into tree-trunks. I could see through the wall behind Kora and I saw Kora sitting in a Florentine frame, her head encompassed with an aura of lilies. I saw Kora then just as the Kore-Persephone and I realised that I too have proper affinity with her. (42)

As exemplum of the intellectual stage of the mysteries, Helforth undertakes a transformation from a man lost in the stasis of too much thought into the eternal man signified by his name: Hell-forth, the one capable of harrowing hell, of emerging from the underworld along with Persephone through the medium of his "symptomatic" visions. His story ends in apotheosis; he concludes, shifting his verb tenses from deadened past to resurrected present: "We were Kora of the Underworld and Dionysus, not yet risen" becomes "Now we are Kore and the slain God . . . risen" (43).

In the world of the mysteries through which H.D. takes *Kora and Ka* and *Nights* the goal, as in *Notes on Thought and Vision*, is the creation of art; the end result of the entire process, in other words, is constatation—the initiate's declaration of the truth. Thus Helforth, having experienced not only his own intellectual transformations in *Kora and Ka*, but—through the agency of Natalia Saunderson's "Nights"—the "radium" of the initial sexually charged mysteries, acts appropriately as the channel by means of which constatation occurs; in his section of *Nights* he plays the role of publisher, making known to the public both Natalia's and his own obscure journeys. Read together, the stories merge into a single account of passage through the darkness of personal mysteries back out into the voicing of poetic vision. In this sense, publication is enactment of that impossible mathematic equation sought by Natalia, the point at which two parallel lines touch, bringing together escape and re-engagement, sex and intellect, the private and the public.

A Dead Priestess Speaks:
H.D.'s Answer to Lawrence

> *... that wistful ghost look of someone who has been right past the door of the tomb. ...*
>
> H.D. describing Freud,
> letter to Bryher, 14, 15 March 1933

H.D.'s poems of the thirties play out a fascinating if curious version of her interest in the meeting point between private vision and public constatation; though these poems—many directly concerned with the passage from the mysteries into speech—make up a good one hundred pages of *Collected Poems 1912–1944*, and though a number of them were published in the late thirties in journals such as *Life and Letters Today, The New Republic,* and *Poetry,* H.D. apparently made no effort to collect them into a volume until the winter of 1948–49, when, "in response to the sensitive advice of Norman Holmes Pearson," she sorted out nine poems from "the hay-stack of notes and loose leaves and old MSS" provided by Bryher into a collection which she titled, after one of the poems, *A Dead Priestess Speaks* (*CP,* xxiv). And, even though this collection now has a place in H.D.'s archives as a discrete volume clearly intended for publication—or at least for a kind of private publication—it did not see print as a whole until 1983.[1] Though it is in many ways a culmination of H.D.'s prewar work, it is not quite a "great lost book" of her poetry; while some of the poems—particularly a continuation of *Red Roses For Bronze*'s "Sigil"—are quite good, it is a problematic collection. H.D. herself wrote of these poems that they are "left over," "even more difficult to assess" than her earlier work ("H.D. by Delia Alton," 208). She herself suggests their place in her oeuvre, finding that, though they remained unpublished, they must be taken into account:

The nine poem-sequences or choruses of [*A Dead Priestess Speaks*] belong in technique and emotional content, exactly to this transitional period. So I leave them. They are hardly a bridge, they are threads in a tapestry. Somewhere, they fill in or fill out a shadow. Somewhere, they lead, each taken separately to the final pattern.

Somehow, their aspect and intention can not be wholly disregarded. ("H.D. by Delia Alton," 217)

The "shadow" which they fill out, the pattern they complete, is that realm of the mysteries so important to H.D. between the two world wars. The very title of her gathering designates it positively as a work of the mysteries, implying in its four words a realized transition from darkness to constatation. And the title poem, set at the opening of the collection, gives some indication of what is at issue:

> O never, never, never write that I
> missed life or loving;
>
> when the loom
> of the three spinning Sisters stops,
> and she,
> the middle spinner, pauses,
> while the last
> one with the shears,
> cuts off the living thread,
> then They may read
> the pattern
> though you may not,
>
> I, being dead.
>
> (371)

The figure of life as a text or "thread" to be read—or, more accurately, *not* to be fully read by any but the eternal fates—lends an oddly paradoxical quality to the speech of the dead Priestess. On the one hand, the poem concerns the relation of her public life as Herald to her quite different secret life "in the arms of an angry lover" (376); it is a poem which resolutely separates the misunderstandings of a public from the actualities of a life. The post-mortem speech of the Priestess first of all rectifies this distance—it is poem-as-constatation, setting the record straight following her descent into death. On the other hand, the pattern of her life remains unreadable despite her telling of it. Giving the name of Delia—Delia Alton, one presumes—to the Priestess, the poem implicates her as a figure for the poet herself and makes her death an emblem for the poet's years of silence; with that silence, the poem becomes, not public constatation, but an instance of the very silence and mis-apprehension it would claim to overcome, moving as obscurely as the mysteries it proclaims.

The act of writing itself is central to the poem, in an image which similarly reveals and conceals. In the second section, Delia's role as Priestess is related to her earlier role as a poet who once found herself unable to write a standard Homeric tribute to a dead soldier (371–72); she is a writer, but her act of inscription, scratching "the tablet-wax / with a small broom" (371), could just as easily be an erasure, sweeping the slate clean to make room for her own text:

> no one could write, after his *wine-dark sea*,
> an epitaph of glory and of spears;
>
> I watched the years go on
> like sun on grass,
> and shadow across sunlight,
>
> till they said,
> O—you remember? trumpets,
> the fire, the shout, the glory of the war?
>
> I answered circumspectly,
> claiming no
> virtue
> that helped the wounded
> and no fire
> that sung of battle ended,
>
> then they said,
> ah she is modest, she is purposeful,
> and nominated for the Herald's place,
> one
> Delia of Miletus.
>
> (372)

Delia's—H.D.'s—work as a poet or a priestess, even as it emerges from the silence of death or non-publication, is inextricably caught up in the web of such a paradox. The title poem, caught in this web, has as its implicit textual territory not only the post-Homeric world of Delia, but the specifically contemporary world of H.D. herself. While Delia sweeps away the heroic Homeric tradition to make room for her own work, H.D. performs an equivalent act with the writing of one of her own peers. "A Dead Priestess Speaks" is a direct response to D. H. Lawrence's *The Man Who Died*.

That *The Man Who Died* is an important work for H.D. is clear from the "Advent" section of *Tribute to Freud*, written in the spring of 1933 during her time with Freud, where she tells the story of Stephen Guest's claim that she is Lawrence's priestess of Isis:

> For one day in the year, H.D. and D. H. Lawrence were twins. But I had not actually realized this until after his death. He was born September 11, 1885: I was born September 10, 1886.
>
> Stephen Guest brought me a copy of *The Man Who Died*. He said, "Did you know that you are the priestess of Isis in this book?"
>
> Perhaps I would never have read the book if Stephen had not brought it to me. Actually, I might have had at first a slight feeling of annoyance. I had told friends of a book that I wanted to write, actually did write. I called it *Pilate's Wife*. It is the story of the wounded but living Christ, waking up in the rock-tomb. I was certain that my friends had told Lawrence that I was at work on this theme. My first sudden reaction was, "now he has taken my story."
>
> It was not my story. George Moore, among others, had already written it. There is the old myth or tradition that Christ did not die on the Cross. (141–42)

Implying that Lawrence's working of the same material she worked in *Pilate's Wife* is less an instance of theft than one of synchronous inhabitation of tradition, H.D. writes herself into Lawrence's book, implicating herself not only as the priestess but also as the dead titular figure:

> Yes, I was "Buried Alive."
>
> Is this why my thoughts return to Lawrence?
>
> I can only remember that last book he wrote. *The Man Who Died* was buried alive. (139)

In "A Dead Priestess Speaks," this melding of figures—this conjunction of H.D. and Lawrence into "twin" writers undertaking parallel projects within a single tradition—is central, though it takes place below the surface, fusing the Priestess of Isis with Christ in the character of Delia of Miletus, buried alive and still telling her story.

The poem reconstructs and revises Lawrence's story through the subtle manipulation of a number of details. Both take place in a typical H.D. setting, a temple overlooking a harbor. And, as *The Man Who Died* nears its end, the Priestess of Isis anoints Christ's wounds with oil:

> "Let me anoint you!" the woman said to him softly. "Let me anoint the scars! Show me, and let me anoint them!"
>
> He forgot his nakedness in this re-evoked old pain. He sat on the edge of the

couch, and she poured a little ointment into the palm of his hand. And as she chafed his hand, it all came back, the nails, the holes, the cruelty, the unjust cruelty against him who had offered only kindness. The agony of injustice and cruelty came over him again, as in his death-hour. But she chafed the palm, murmuring: "What was torn becomes a new flesh, what was a wound is full of fresh life; this scar is the eye of the violet." (204)

Similarly, Delia is known for her healing ointments:

> they spoke of honours,
> the line I drew with weaving,
> the fine thread,
> they told of liniments, I steeped in oil
> to heal the burns of those washed here ashore,
> when that old ship took light from a pine-torch,
> dropped by a drunken sailor.
>
> (377)

The Man Who Died is about Christ's late attempt to come into "touch with the flesh" (175) and sexuality with the priestess of Isis. In H.D.'s poem, the secret of the Priestess's life is a sexual tryst with a man who "waited too long" for her:

> how was it I,
> who walked so circumspectly, yet was caught
> in the arms of an angry lover,
> who said,
> late,
>
> late, I waited too long for you, Delia,
> I will devour you,
> love you into flame,
> O late
> my love,
> my bride,
> Delia of Miletus.
>
> (376–77)

Without calling attention to itself as a palimpsest or as a reworking of Lawrence's story, the poem inhabits the same space as that story while shifting its emphasis from Christ himself to the words of the Priestess.

Still, the apparent insignificance of H.D.'s appropriations from Lawrence—an answer perhaps to his seeming borrowings from her own *Pilate's Wife*—is belied by the significance of this change of focus from Christ to

Delia. To hint at the distance between the two characters, H.D. borrows one of the story's details only to alter it slightly. Lawrence's priestess wears a saffron robe; H.D. makes it clear that hers does not:

> I walked sedately at the head of things,
> who yet had wings they saw not;
> had they seen,
> they would have counted me as one of those
> old women who were young when I was young,
> who wore bright saffron vestments;
>
> I wore white,
> as fitting the high-priestess.

(372)

This difference masks another, more important, change; the shift from "man who died" to "dead priestess" involves an important new understanding of the meaning of both death and poetic speech. Both Lawrence's Christ and his Priestess of Isis are necessary for the discovery of the story's passions, but Christ unquestionably dominates; his Priestess is naive, perhaps even a bit laughable in her role:

> And he could not help smiling at her, in her naive priestess' absorption. This was her dream, and he was only a dream-object to her. She would never know or understand what he was. Especially she would never know the death that was gone before in him. But what did it matter? She was different. She was woman: her life and her death were different from his. Only she was good to him. (204)

The rebirth unveiled in *The Man Who Died* is the rebirth of the *man;* the woman—a woman H.D. was able to read as a stand-in for herself—is ultimately no more than a vehicle, a medium through which this rebirth may take place.

Clearly, for H.D. to write a poem like "A Dead Priestess Speaks," a poem which takes up the challenge of *The Man Who Died* and applies it to the Priestess herself, the very possibility of rebirth must shift from the male to the female. The man of Lawrence's story is, after all, *The* man, from the beginning a locus of significance in and of himself. The title of H.D.'s poem not only changes male to female, but rewrites "The" as "A," implicitly criticizing Lawrence's subtle belittlement of the Priestess and creating a new character who casts off the anonymity of her role through an act of speech. This new Priestess—a woman who tells her own story rather than being part of another's—not only understands "the death that was gone before in him," having undergone something very much like it herself, but also the deaths of others and the secrets they have revealed:

> ah, at night—
> I had my secret thought, my secret way,
> I had my secret song,
> who sang by day,
> the holy metres that the matrons sang,
> sung only by those dedicate to life
> of civic virtue
> and of civic good;
>
> I knew the poor,
> I knew the hideous death they die,
> when famine lays its bleak hand on the door;
> I knew the rich,
> sated with merriment,
> who yet are sad,
> and I was ever glad,
> and circumspect
> who never knew their life,
> nor poor nor rich,
> nor entered into strife,
> when the new archon spoke of a new war.
>
> (373)

The circumspection and subtlety of "A Dead Priestess Speaks" are missing from the three poems which follow, two dialogues—one between Electra and Orestes concerning the murder of Clytemnestra and one between Calypso and Odysseus, an angry denunciation of man as "a brute and a fool" (396) on the heels of Odysseus's subjugation of Calypso—and one dramatic monologue in which a man named Menexeus hires an assassin "in the long-shoreman's inn, before the Egilian breakwater" (396). The first two of these extend the implicit male-female dialogue of "A Dead Priestess Speaks" into the more recognizable mythic realm of H.D.'s Greece, while the third, "In Our Town," is practically unique in its barely submerged violence and odd setting. One passage of this third poem extends the exploration of the public and the private begun in "A Dead Priestess Speaks." The setting for the poem is public, and yet the business at hand is a secret violence; in the midst of this sordid scene comes a woman's song:

> We will wait;
> I hear my sister singing by the lion-gate;

> she thinks no one goes there;
> she hasn't much to fear,
> no one can understand anyhow,
> her metre's too intricate;
>
> she sings of blue-prows,
> she sings of black prows,
> she sings of a sword so white,
> so luminous, that its own light
> alone must slay;
> she sings of a sword, a sword, a sword,
> and I creep away;
>
> I mustn't listen to this.
>
> (399)

Menexeus's dismissal of his sister's song recalls—with a more sinister note—Christ's smile at the Priestess's naive "absorption" as she anoints his feet. And the sister's care lest her song be overheard by those who would not understand echoes the gulf in "A Dead Priestess Speaks" between the Priestess's actual life and the public misunderstanding of that life.

In "H.D. by Delia Alton," H.D. calls the sister's song "a startling prophecy" (213). One of the predecessors of this prophetic woman, *Heliodora*'s Cassandra, must endure the curse of the public's eternal disbelief; the situation here is the same, but while *Heliodora* ends in despair over the workings of song, the overlay of the Eleusinian mysteries onto *A Dead Priestess Speaks* makes that despair over into the dark ground from which further song may spring. Menexeus's sister may not be believed, but the realization of this disbelief leads not to the terrors of *Heliodora*, but to a further engagement with the prophetic mode of poetry. The two poems which follow "In Our Town"—"Delphi" and "Dodona"—trace the emergence of such song as a type of prophecy, an inscrutable yet empowering act of impassioned speech, as—to put it another way—constatation.

The first of these, "Delphi," focuses on the unpredictable nature of the god upon whom poetry-as-prophecy depends. While the poem's title makes it clear that such unpredictability is a given of the prophetic mode—the god of Delphi, as revealed in his prophetic utterances, is by nature inscrutable, speaking in riddles—the poem itself implicitly applies this sense to the work of the poet;[2] coming in the midst of H.D.'s silence, "Delphi" functions as a defense of silence and a statement of faith that the silence will not endure:

> his word
> is withdrawn,

hieratic,
authentic,
a king's,
yet all may receive it;
he turns at a whim,
who answers no threat,
no call of the flute,
no drum-beat of the drum;
you may bargain
and threaten,
the prophet
is distant and mute;
yet one day
he will speak
through a child or a thrush
or a stray in the market.

(402)

Furthermore, the presence of the god—the presence of poetry—depends neither on the labor of study nor on a conscious struggle with tradition—both of which are strengths of H.D. throughout her career—but is an unexpected present, a gift beyond demand and beyond rational control:[3]

I entreated the grove and the spring,
the bay-tree in flower,
I was wise on my way,
they said I was wise,
I was steeped in their lore,
I entreated his love,
I prayed each hour;
I was sterile
and barren
and songless.

I came back:
he opened my door.

(404)

This gift is a terrifying presence in "Delphi," an "ecstasy [which] will betray" (405) and which can bring death in the place of song. "Dodona" shifts the scene slightly, retaining the inscrutability of the god but turning the accompanying terror to the service of constatation through the figure of the High Priestess, a version of the volume's titular figure who here negotiates a successful act of prophetic exchange with the god. This Priestess,

who—like the Dead Priestess herself—has "lain / with strange lovers" (408),
stands at the end of the poem as an emblem of inspired prophecy:

> I stand by your portal,
> a white pillar,
> luminous.
>
> (411)

Acknowledging her status, the voice of Zeus speaks "THROUGH THE
ORACLE," dismissing all trace of the unease Christ felt over the "absorption" of the Priestess of Isis in *The Man Who Died,* and endorsing that
absorption as empowering fervor:

> luminous,
> unfearful;
>
> high-priestess,
> your fervor,
> shall banish
> all evil.
>
> (410)

Lawrence's Priestess is a woman—a little ridiculous, perhaps—who is
finally little more than a means to a particular end; after their tryst, after
he has impregnated her, Christ leaves to find his own destiny:

> "I have sowed the seed of my life and my resurrection, and put my touch
> forever upon the choice woman of this day, and I carry her perfume in my flesh
> like essence of roses. She is dear to me in the middle of my being. But the gold
> and flowing serpent is coiling up again, to sleep at the root of my tree.
> "So let the boat carry me. To-morrow is another day." (211)

Lawrence's Christ sets off into the future, into a "To-morrow" where he
may find another lover, a new "choice woman" through whom he may once
again discover the "middle of [his] being." The Priestess of H.D.'s poems,
on the other hand, works to achieve spiritual or poetic presence, a "to-day"
rather than a "to-morrow," where the god need not be sought because he
is always already present.

Following "Dodona," a sequence appears which continues *Red Roses
for Bronze's* "Sigil"; the first poem of this sequence is a direct rejoinder to
Lawrence's "To-morrow":

There is no sign-post to say
the future is there,
the past lies the other way,
there is no lock, no key;

there is no bell on the door,
there is no door-mat before
the wide-open door:

there is no "he and me,"
there is no "you and she,"
there is no "it must be";

there is one mystery, "take, eat,"
I have found the clue,
there is no old nor new:

wine, bread, grape and sweet
honey; Galilee, Delphi, to-day.

(411)

The imperative leading Christ into the future at the conclusion of *The Man Who Died* is replaced by the "sign-post" or sigil merging Greek and Christian traditions within a single contemporary mystery of presence; in the terms H.D. used as early as 1921 and which still seem appropriate in the late thirties, to write the odd, seemingly anachronistic poems of *A Dead Priestess Speaks*—in which ancient traditions meld with a running critique of D. H. Lawrence—is to "Paint It To-day," to create a poetics of constatation, by definition a simultaneously modern and eternal "Sigil."

Appropriately enough, the twelve sections of "Sigil" included in *A Dead Priestess Speaks* both continue and amend the sequence as begun in *Red Roses for Bronze*. As it appears in the earlier volume, "Sigil" is content with the limitations of a miniaturist art, accepting them as a paradoxically empowering mode of being; the poet, holding herself to the tiny, the unseen or forgotten, maintains a vision inaccessible to the more expansive poet who measures "the boundary of the sky." But, because "Sigil" does not end in 1931, it finally reaches a quite different conclusion. By means of a direct revision of another D. H. Lawrence text—this time, his 1916 novel, *Women in Love*—"Sigil" both extends the critique begun in "A Dead Priestess Speaks" and makes new claims for the validity and strength of the female poet's constatation.[4]

In *Tribute to Freud*'s "Advent," H.D. notes her inability to come to terms with the Lawrence of *Women in Love:* "I have carefully avoided coming to terms with Lawrence, the Lawrence of *Women in Love* and *Lady Chatterley*" (134). But the ending of "Sigil" in *A Dead Priestess Speaks*, directly confronting a text of this particular Lawrence, is exactly such a "coming to terms" with him and his work.

After the poem reiterates H.D.'s acceptance of the miniature—and neatly encapsulates her use of Lawrence's Priestess of Isis as a replacement of the more dominant figure of Christ—as a way of "perceiving the other-side of everything" (413), it turns to a new, expansive reach of poetic power. The final five sections of "Sigil"—which, as Louis Martz notes, originally formed a sequence on their own (620)—undertake this change, beginning with a transformation of the poet herself into a figure stretching out to encompass "the boundary of the sky":

> So if you love me,
> love me everywhere,
> blind to all argument
> or phantasy,
> claim the one signet;
>
> truly in the sky,
> God marked me to be his,
> scrawled, "I, I, I
> alone can comprehend
>
> this subtlety."
>
> (414–15)

The poet capable of this kind of claim is also capable of asking for a forceful love which, in its strength of declaration, is akin to the powerful visions of Rupert Birkin in *Women in Love*:

> shall we rise,
>
> wing-tip to purple wing,
> create new earth,
> new skies?
>
> (415)

The final portions of "Sigil" echo *Women in Love* not only in such Birkinesque hyperbole,[5] but also in a number of details—images of snow, the moon, "the northern gloom" (416)—even, at one point, a recapitulation of the climactic moment of the novel in a plea for oblivion at the hands of the powerful and deadly lover:

take me,
let your hand

gather my throat,
flower from that land
we both have loved,
have lost;

O wand of ebony, keep away the night,
O ivory wand,
bring back the ultimate light
on Delphic headland;

take me,
O ultimate breath,
O master-lyrist,
beat my wild heart to death.

(417)

But this Lawrentian hyperbole—recalling the near strangulation of Gudrun Brangwen by Gerald Crich in *Women in Love*—shifts in the poem's final section to an exact reversal; the ecstatic finality of near death becomes something very different:

"I love you,"
spoken in rhapsodic metre,
leaves me cold:

I have a horror
of finality,
I would rather
hazard a guess,
wonder whether
either of us
could for a moment
endure the other,
after the first fine flavour
of irony
had worn off.

(418)

This conclusion not only—like Lawrence's Birkin—dismisses the sterility and stasis of conventional love, but also takes up the role of the novel's Gudrun, erasing her final, bitter irony at the end of her destructive love-affair. H.D.'s lines depend for much of their impact on an exact verbal echo of a passage late in *Women in Love*. Lawrence writes:

> But even as [Gudrun] lay in fictitious transport, bathed in the strange, false sunshine of hope in life, something seemed to snap in her, and a terrible cynicism began to gain upon her, blowing in like a wind. Everything turned to irony with her: the last flavour of everything was ironical. When she felt her pang of undeniable reality, this was when she knew the hard irony of hopes and ideas. (408)

In H.D.'s hands, Gudrun's final irony becomes a mere beginning, a "first fine flavour" rather than a "last flavour of everything"; it is nothing more than a sign of indecision at the beginning of a doomed relationship, a perceived limitation in the place of a crushing final bitterness. H.D.'s revision of Lawrence's words transforms the attack on Gudrun into her own "let your hand / gather my throat," and transfers the scene from inexorable and terrible climax to an early stage of the failed affair. Where *Women in Love* ends with the irony of Gudrun's despair—and with Birkin's knowledge of the impossibility of his visions of love—"Sigil" is a necessary trivialization of such grandiose notions. It allows, in a sense, the figure of Gudrun to have the last laugh, to escape the domination of Gerald. Or—to put it another way—it allows H.D. to move beyond, to revise the destructive sexual poetics of Lawrence and create a place for her own constatation through a reading of the underside—the "other-side" as "Sigil" would have it—of that other modernist "master-lyrist."

What the Dead Priestess—the "silent" H.D.—says in the nine poetic sequences of *A Dead Priestess Speaks* depends on the significance of the sigil as it appears to the poem's initiate. The only direct manifestation of the sigil—or sign—in the poem is in the guise of a "signet" of poetic power written across the sky, a writing which leads to the Birkinesque vision of a potent love creating "new earth, / new skies":

> God marked me to be his,
> scrawled, "I, I, I
> alone can comprehend
>
> this subtlety."

(415)

The sigil—while H.D. does finally forsake it, claiming "But it won't be that way, / I'm sane, / normal again" (415)—sets the stage for the large poetic claims implicit in the closing of both "Sigil" and the volume as a whole. As the volume works its way to an ending, H.D. undertakes a final radical revision of Lawrence's *The Man Who Died* into a vision of a Christianity which, like Lawrence's, does not deny the body but which, unlike his, depends on the efficacy of the Priestess's speech rather than on the sheer male potency of Christ for its power; *A Dead Priestess Speaks,* in other words, fulfills the quest of *Pilate's Wife* for a religion which does not leave out women.

The penultimate poem, "Priest," centers around a meeting between a woman and a man—now a priest—who had known each other fifteen years earlier.[6] The man has apparently turned to the priesthood following the death of his wife, and the poem's debate focuses on this decision, strongly criticizing the falseness of his new life in the church:

> no,
> you prefer a woman under the earth,
> you heap roses above a grave;
> a woman under the earth
> is safe,
> a woman dead
> is beloved;
> it's all neat,
> but God is not neat.
>
> (423)

The woman who speaks is an incarnation of the Priestess who, having regained her powers of speech in the volume's title poem and explored the significance of such power throughout the rest of the volume, can now claim a full physical life in comparison to the cold dead wife:

> yet Death and I were equal;
> I have walked with like fever, with like fervor,
> but
> I,
> I did not die.
>
> (428)

The Priestess, through the sheer power of her speech, lives; the failure of the Priest—like the failure of the underworld figure of Menexeus in "In Our Town"—lies in his refusal to recognize this living power when he sees it:

> But you will not say you lie,
> and I,

> I will not die,
> and you will not praise me that I live,
> nor give signification,
> nor recognition,
> nor any sort of sign,
> nor hail me
> who wear
> a breast-plate,
> difficult to bear,
> radium,
> with radium on my thighs,
> and greaves
> of white luminous power,
> white as a knife
> that eats through me.
>
>   (422)

Implicit in this criticism is a notion carried over from the volume's initial revision of *The Man Who Died*, that any division which sets Christ apart from the physical—and from the physical, sexual incarnation of love—is inherently false; the priest's choice of a dead woman over a living Priestess is, in fact, such a fraudulent division. "Priest" is, H.D. notes in "H.D. by Delia Alton," "a lyric rendering of the [1935] story *Jubilee*" (215), and a passage from this story makes the criticism very clear; she condemns the man because of "the specific treason of him in his aspect to the church, in insisting on the separation of Christ from Love" (7).[7]

Christ in *The Man Who Died* discovers the flesh through intercourse with the Priestess of Isis. In *A Dead Priestess Speaks*, He is taught that this discovery must not lead to an abandonment of the female. And, just as the volume begins with a new incarnation of the Priestess of Isis—a corrected version, as it were, returning to her the powers of speech Lawrence was never quite willing to give her—it ends (in a poem originally titled "Master" and later given the title "Magician" to distinguish it from a poem written to Freud) with a new incarnation of Christ, seen through the eyes and the visionary constatation of the Priestess herself. Lawrence presents the Priestess by way of the man who died; H.D. gives us Christ by way of the woman who died and came back to testify to the mysteries of death and poetic speech. The poem begins with a plea for the abandonment of the violent trappings of traditional Christianity:

> pull out the nails,
> fling them aside,
> any old boat,

left at high-tide,
(you yourself would admit)
has iron as pliable;

burn the thorn;
thorn burns;
how it crackles;
you yourself would be the first to seek
dried weed by some high-sand
to make the land
liveable;
you yourself;
would be the first to scrap
the old trophies
for new.

(432–33)

In the place of this old system—like Lawrence moving beyond the terror of Christ crucified—"Magician [Master]" conceives of a new religion of vision. This new religion is equally a poetics—the conjunction is inescapable for H.D., in Christianity as in the Delphic mysteries; *A Dead Priestess Speaks* ends with a beautiful passage in which the Priestess has a vision of what Christ sees, a passage in which the poetics of the miniature begun in *Red Roses for Bronze* comes to fruition through an unfolding of a tiny piece of glass into an emblem of eternity:

He liked jewels,
the fine feel of white pearls;
he would lift a pearl from a tray,
flatter an Ethiopian merchant
on his taste;
lift crystal from Syria,
to the light;

he would see worlds in a crystal
and while we waited for a camel
or a fine Roman's litter
to crowd past,
he would tell of the whorl of whorl of light
that was infinity to be seen in glass,

or a shell
or a bead
or a pearl.

(439)

By the end of 1944 and the end of *The Flowering of the Rod*, this unfolding "whorl of light" would come to stand as the culmination of H.D.'s *Trilogy*, Kaspar's vision in the "flaw or speck of light" in Mary's jewel:

> And the flower, thus contained
> in the infinitely tiny grain or seed,
>
> opened petal by petal, a circle,
> and each petal was separate
>
> yet still held, as it were,
> by some force of attraction
>
> to its dynamic centre;
> and the circle went on widening
>
> and would go on opening
> he knew, to infinity;
>
> but before he was lost,
> out-of-time completely,
>
> he saw the Islands of the Blest,
> he saw the Hesperides,
>
> he saw the circles and circles of islands
> about the lost centre-island, Atlantis;
>
> he saw what the sacrosanct legend
> said still existed,
>
> he saw the lands of the blest,
> the promised lands, lost;
>
> he, in that half-second, saw
> the whole scope and plan
>
> of our and his civilization on this,
> his and our earth, before Adam.

(601–2)

In both *The Flowering of the Rod* and "Magician [Master]," the final vision comes through the eyes of a man, either Christ or Kaspar, but is made possible only through the example and constatation of the Priestess—

and Mary belongs, clearly, in the chain of H.D.'s Priestess figures. It is only because of the process undertaken throughout H.D.'s career, the entire exploration of the meanings of poetic speech and of constatation emerging from the mysteries, that this ultimate vision is possible. And this is H.D.'s final, most complete revision of *The Man Who Died*. Lawrence's Christ makes use of the Priestess of Isis only to leave her behind; H.D.'s Christ— and her Kaspar—are able to see what they see through the medium of the Priestess, and it is *only* through her powers of speech that their visions come into being, only through H.D.'s act of making that speech legible through poetry that any record of their visions is extant.

The path taken by Lawrence's Christ leads from public engagement and constatation in the role of Messiah through death to the privacies of his sexual afterlife. H.D.'s Priestess moves in the opposite direction. She begins in death, in the knowledge that her private visions have no meaning in the public realm, that she is destined to be misunderstood; as she passes through death, however, she is able to forge a public stance, able to become the visible Priestess of Zeus in "Dodona" and to criticize the Christian priest for *his* withdrawal from engagement. The Christ of the final poem is not the figure who disappears from sight in Lawrence's story, but the public man, the one who "spoke to the rabble" in the Sermon on the Mount (437). It is the Dead Priestess's passage through mystery which makes this new Christ accessible and which makes Him possible following the retreat in *The Man Who Died*. And it is precisely her powerful transition from private vision to public constatation, from silence to poetry—even though *A Dead Priestess Speaks* in fact remained unpublished during H.D.'s lifetime—which generated H.D.'s new capacity in the forties and after for her most powerful and successful poetry, for the brilliant and beautiful prophecies of *Trilogy* and *Helen in Egypt*.

Afterword

And suddenly, I saw it fair,
How Love is God, how Love is strong,
When One is Three and Three are One,
The Dream, the Dreamer and the Song.
                              H.D., *By Avon River*

This book began with an ellipsis of sorts, taking up the story of H.D.'s poetry only after *Sea Garden*, that nearly definitive imagist collection of poems presided over by the patron of Imagism, Hermes of the Ways. In one sense, the omission of *Sea Garden* is regrettable; the book does, after all, establish H.D.'s vocabulary—sets the terms which she then spends the rest of her career exploring and expanding. And yet, it seems also to be necessary. That earliest part of H.D.'s story is well known; her anthologized poems are almost all drawn from that first book, and Ezra Pound's creation of "H.D. Imagiste" in a tea room at the London Museum is, as she herself suggests, the stuff of modernist mythology:

> I was 21 when Ezra left and it was some years later that he scratched "H.D. Imagiste," in London, in the Museum tea room, at the bottom of a typed sheet, now slashed with his creative pencil, "Cut this out, shorten this line."
> H.D.—Hermes—Hermeticism and all the rest of it. (*End to Torment*, 40)

In the particular story which I have chosen to tell—or, more accurately, the aspect of H.D. I have emphasized—I have found it necessary simply to *assume* this beginning, to take it as part of the common heritage of modernism. What has interested me is perhaps a bit more arcane, or at least not quite so well known: the story of H.D.'s unique journey beyond her beginnings, of what she wove from the threads of Imagism she took as her own and made into a pattern, a fabric unlike any other in the modernist canon.

But, if this book begins with an ellipsis, it ends with one which is even more emphatic; winding up with the poems of *A Dead Priestess Speaks*, poems pointing emphatically to the future, it holds the work for which H.D. has been most celebrated at a distance. The body of work made up by *Trilogy, By Avon River, Helen in Egypt,* "Vale Ave," and *Hermetic Definition*—to many the definitive H.D.—is beyond the scope of this book. That late work comprises, as it were, the final stitches of H.D.'s pattern, and puts the finishing touches on whole poetic tapestry she had begun many years earlier.

This is not to suggest that H.D.'s writing of the twenties and thirties— the work to which I have directed my attention—is merely a preliminary to the undeniably major writing of her late years. H.D.'s work is—through-out her career—an interesting and unique variation on modernist concerns; and certain poems of the twenties and thirties—"Hippolytus Temporizes," "Heliodora," "Red Roses for Bronze," the two parts of "Sigil," among oth-ers—stand out as wonderful examples of H.D.'s particular genius. Even the weaker poems of the period, whatever their failings, are never less than fascinating embodiments of that genius, irreducible, necessary "threads in a tapestry," parts of a whole fabric ("H.D. by Delia Alton," 217). If her work is—as such a metaphor would have it—a tapestry of sorts, then it is one which is stitched over time, one which thus emerges only through the passage of an entire life. In such an undertaking of discovery and process, the late additions are inconceivable without the earlier. To put it in another way—to encapsulate H.D.'s entire career with one of her favorite words—it is a palimpsest, a collection of writings set one on top of another. The late work does not so much obscure the earlier or consign it to oblivion as it rewrites or revises—it takes its discoveries, its framework and makes them over into a new pattern based upon the old.

And yet her work in the years between the wars certainly is a prelimi-nary in an important sense. The writing from *Hymen* through *A Dead Priest-ess Speaks* does not, it is true, exist apart from the context of what precedes and follows it, but neither do *Trilogy* or *Helen in Egypt* reveal their secrets apart from the full pattern of H.D.'s career. From the beginning, H.D.'s poetry moves dynamically from volume to volume, building upon itself and drawing upon its own lessons as it moves. The problematic conclusions reached by the sexually charged poetics of *Hymen* require the shift to a poetics of masks in *Heliodora*, which in turn suggests H.D.'s transition from a poetics of grand gesture to one of the unexplored detail in *Red Roses for Bronze*. And the ending of *Red Roses for Bronze*, with its emphasis on the silent workings of the mysteries, makes way for the thorough exploration of silence and constatation of *A Dead Priestess Speaks*. Similarly, the nine poems of that unpublished volume make possible the prophecies of *Trilogy*.

Indeed, H.D.'s acknowledged masterpieces are unthinkable without her lesser-known, sometimes tentative explorations of the twenties and thirties. *Helen in Egypt*, of course, reaches back to H.D.'s ecstatic reading of Euripides' *Helen* and, even earlier, to her reading of Yeats's *Responsibilities*. The sequences of "Vale Ave," *By Avon River*, and *Hermetic Definition* would not be what they are—either formally or thematically—without H.D.'s earlier historical and poetic palimpsests and her career-long practice of building poetic structures transcending the individual poem, of making each volume into a single, coherent sequence.

And, perhaps most importantly, *Trilogy* depends both conceptually and poetically on everything which precedes it—Kaspar's unfolding vision at the end of "The Flowering of the Rod" is of a piece with the poetic lessons and revelations of H.D.'s earlier writing, as is the sustaining faith that "The Walls Do Not Fall." And the vision of the Lady in "Tribute to the Angels" is in an important sense a revelation of the perfect sigil, the perfect sign of all that H.D. has learned through her workings of poetic fabric. The book which she carries, "written / or unwritten" (*CP*, 571), is, in this regard, the book of a career, bringing together in a single image all that has been written—the entire range of work from "Hermes of the Ways" through "Sigil"—with all that remains to be written. It is not—as *Trilogy* is not, as *Helen in Egypt* is not—so much a culmination or apotheosis of H.D.'s prophetic spirit as it is an acknowledgment of the unity of her career, of the literary and historical palimpsest she has made her own, stretching as it does into both past and future. Thus, the ellipses with which I begin and end this study are already written—or, to return to the metaphor of the tapestry, stitched—into H.D.'s career. To look at any point of her career is to acknowledge, if only silently, these ellipses, to recognize that her career is, like the book of the Lady, a whole fabric with extensions beyond the specific reach of one's gaze. In that book, in that sigil of a career, the lost books of H.D.'s Greek precursors—Heliodora, Lais, and Nossis—are metaphorically recovered from obscurity and joined with H.D.'s own overlooked writings into a single, powerful oeuvre, a constatation of the highest order out of the mysteries of her poetics.

Notes

Introduction

1. See for instance Ford Madox Hueffer's assessment of H.D.'s anthology work in an article published in the *Outlook* on July 10, 1915 and reprinted in Hughes's *Imagism and the Imagists:* "Of the six poets printed in this anthology, only two—H.D. and Mr. F. S. Flint—have the really exquisite sense of words, the really exquisite tranquility, beauty of diction, and insight that justify a writer in assuming the rather proud title of Imagist—of issuing, that is to say, that challenge, that they will rouse emotions solely by rendering concrete objects, sounds, and aspects" (Hughes, 47).

2. For the "laconic" appellation, see Pound's famous letter of October 1912 to Harriet Monroe in *The Letters of Ezra Pound* (45).

3. A third book, Barbara Guest's *Herself Defined*, is a biography emphasizing H.D.'s life at the expense of her work, and a fourth, Janice Robinson's *H.D.: The Life and Work of an American Poet*, while valuable for extensive quotations of unpublished work, is questionable at best in its critical and biographical claims.

Chapter 1

1. "Helga Dart" is one of H.D.'s many pseudonyms, others of which include "John Helforth," "Delia Alton," "Rhoda Peter," "Helga Doorn," and "Edith Gray." On the typescript of *Paint It To-day*, the name has been typed and subsequently crossed out.

2. For an account of Vorticism and its relation to Cubism and Futurism, see Reed Way Dasenbrock's *The Literary Vorticism of Ezra Pound and Wyndham Lewis: Towards the Condition of Painting*, particularly the first chapter, "Vorticism among the Isms," 13–27.

3. As H.D. points out on her manuscript, the "Ion" portion of her study of Euripides was published in her 1937 translation, *Euripedes' Ion*. The choruses from *The Bacchae* were published in *Red Roses for Bronze*, and the portion of her Pausanius essay titled "People of Sparta" was published in the December 1924 issue of *The Bookman*. More recently, an early draft of one of the essays on Sappho was published as "The Wise Sappho" in *Notes on Thought and Vision*.

4. Although Yeats's book was published in 1914, the fact that the review is bound with writings dating from ca. 1919 to 1920 suggests that it may have been written several years after the book it purports to review.

5. Indeed, one of the vorticist painters, Charles Wadsworth, was fascinated with military airplane designs, even developing a vorticist camouflage for warships.

6. For an overview of critics' views of H.D. as an "escapist," see E. B. Greenwood's "H.D. and the Problem of Escapism." Robert Duncan also addresses the question in several chapters of his "H.D. Book" in response to criticism leveled by Randall Jarrell and Dudley Fitts, particularly in chapter 9 of part 2.

7. See the interview with Norman Holmes Pearson in the 1969 special H.D. issue of *Contemporary Literature*, where he says "Like Pound and Gertrude Stein she was . . . completely an American. She never thought of herself as anything but that, and she often told me that her nature imagery, for example, was never really Greek but came from her childhood reminiscences of Watch Hill and the coasts of Rhode Island and Maine, which she used to visit with her friends as a child" (437).

8. Of course, as Pound's interest shifts from "Imagisme" to Vorticism, his use of the sculptural metaphor changes accordingly, reaching what is perhaps its culmination in his description of Brancusi's work as "a revolt against one sort of solidity" (*Literary Essays*, 443). The vorticist sculptural figure is motile rather than static.

9. For the Yeats passage, see his introduction to *A Vision*, 8. See also Friedman's *Psyche Reborn*, where she suggests that H.D.'s disagreement with Freud stems from her "non-materialist, nonrationalist perspective" (87).

10. H.D.'s choice of Yeats's poem "about" Helen furthermore places this review in the center of a long history of her interest in the figure of Helen, an interest which is itself a palimpsest of sorts. Her most famous use of the figure, of course, occurs in her late epic, *Helen in Egypt*, but as early as 1918 she writes about Euripides' *Helen* in her "Notes on Euripides, Pausanius, and Greek Lyric Poets." In addition, H.D.'s mother was named Helen, and she writes in her 1944 portion of *Tribute to Freud*, "Writing on the Wall": "The Professor translated the pictures on the wall of a hotel bedroom in Corfu, the Greek Ionian island, that I saw projected there in the spring of 1920, as a desire for union with my mother. I was physically in Greece, in Hellas (Helen). I had come home to the glory that was Greece. Perhaps my trip to Greece, that spring, might have been interpreted as a flight from reality. Perhaps my experiences there might be translated as another flight—from a flight" (44). Thus the figure of Helen is central, if only implicitly, in my discussion of H.D.'s poetics here.

11. See Eliot's "Tradition and the Individual Talent" in *Selected Prose of T. S. Eliot*.

12. In fact, H.D., in *Tribute to Freud*, ascribes an autobiographical—and war-related—source to her other, seemingly historical novels: "I have tried to write the story or the novel of my war experience, my first, stillborn child and the second. . . . I have rewritten this story and others have 'ghosted' for it, as in the case of *Pilate's Wife* and *Hedylus*, both historical or classic reconstructions" (148).

Chapter 2

1. All of my citations to H.D.'s poetry are to *Collected Poems 1912–1944* unless otherwise noted.

2. Very little is in fact known concerning the actual procedure of the mysteries, though at least one scholar, George E. Mylonas, divides—as does H.D.—the initiation into three parts, "the preliminary initiation into the Lesser Mysteries, the initiation proper into the

Greater Mysteries, known as the *telete,* and the *epopteia,* or highest degree of initiation" (239). See Mylonas's *Eleusis and the Eleusinian Mysteries,* 237–85, for a good overview of these stages. On the other hand, Mylonas, unlike H.D. and Harrison, dismisses the idea that a "Sacred Marriage" was an element of the mysteries (270).

3. H.D. repeats this in different terms in an unpublished review of Edwin Marion Cox's 1924 translation of Sappho included in "Notes on Euripides, Pausanius, and Greek Lyric Poets," criticizing his work for being a Sappho in "a cap and gown" rather than "with a close-bound chaplet of wild cyclamen or fragrant orange-buds or even . . . the frail, silver leaf of the bright, scentless and immortal olive" ("Winter Roses," 4).

4. Jane Ellen Harrison notes that "it is abundantly clear that at Eleusis the Marriage and the Birth were the culminating ritual acts, acts by which *union with the divine,* the goal of all mystic ceremonial, was at first held to be actually effected, later symbolized" (563).

Chapter 3

1. Though *Hymen* is the second major collection, H.D. published three smaller volumes (two of translation and one of original verse) between 1916 and 1921: *Choruses from* Iphigeneia in Aulis (1916), *The Tribute and Circe, Two Poems by H.D.* (1917), and *Choruses from the* Iphigeneia in Aulis *and the* Hippolytus *of Euripides* (1919).

2. For a reading of the *Sea Garden* as such a line of intersection and merging, see my "The Identity of 'H.': Imagism and H.D.'s *Sea Garden,*" to be published in a forthcoming issue of *Sagetrieb.*

3. Eileen Gregory, in "Scarlet Experience: H.D.'s *Hymen,*" suggests rightly that "The wedding-rite, the rite of Hymen, is the governing metaphor of the whole volume: 'marriage' is the mythic domain of all these poems" (91).

4. The recent *Collected Poems 1912–1944* restores the dedication.

5. For an account of this period, see Barbara Guest's *Herself Defined,* 105–12.

6. In the unpublished novel *Asphodel,* the goddess also initially appears as a figure marked by an insurmountable distance; the young Hermione, talking to her brother, hears his "a goddess" as "a God-less" (pt. 1, 43–44). A similar distance occurs in *Sea Garden,* particularly in the poem "Cliff Temple."

7. Alicia Ostriker, in *Writing like a Woman,* suggests something similar. Finding a poem which seems at first to be "the most prettily ritualized celebration of feminine sexuality since Edmund Spenser's 'Epithalamion,'" she also discovers what she calls a negative "aftertaste": "that a polarized active-passive, plunderer-prey pattern in sexuality makes the 'object' of love faceless, voiceless, blank" (20–21).

8. Jane Ellen Harrison notes that Bromios—frequently referred to in Euripides (413)—is a name given to Dionysos in his guise as "son of Demeter the Corn-Mother before he becomes god of the grape and son by adoption of Olympian Zeus" (416).

9. See Vincent Quinn, who rather simplistically writes that "Demeter seems resentful that other goddesses have been preferred before her" (49).

10. As Susan Friedman points out, H.D. more often places her mother in the role of Demeter, with herself as Persephone (*Psyche Reborn,* 139, 141). For one instance of this, see *HERmione,* where "Eugenia" rescues Her from the destructive mathematics of her father: "Demeter ('such a dear nurse') had driven the raging storm back . . . had saved them from

the numbers" (90). Similarly, Eugenia is associated with Eleusis: "Eugenia was not Hellenistic, she was Eleusinian" (31).

11. For an account of H.D.'s separations from both men at the time of Perdita's birth, see Guest, 95, 101.

12. The second edition of the *Oxford Classical Dictionary* lists two Evadnes, the first of whom comes from Pindar's *Olympian Odes*, and is clearly H.D.'s figure; she is "a daughter of Poseidon, who became by Apollo mother of Iamus, ancestor of the prophetic clan of the Iamidae in Olympia." The second, from Euripides' *Suppliant Women*, is the one most often cited in dictionaries of mythology. (*OCD*, 425). She is, in Robert Graves's words, "Capaneus's wife [who], seeing that her husband had been heroized by Zeus's thunderbolt, would not be parted from him. Since custom demanded that a lightning-struck man should be buried apart from the rest, and his grave fenced off, she flung herself on the general pyre, and was consumed alive" (*The Greek Myths*, vol. 2, 18). The palimpsest of these two women suggests that H.D.'s poem may not be as affirmative a vision of the erotic as my reading suggests.

13. In the first edition of *Hymen*, this poem is titled "The Whole White World," a phrase which also appears in D. H. Lawrence's *Aaron's Rod*—a novel he began when living with the Aldingtons at 44 Mecklenburgh Square—in an interesting context. Aaron, remembering his wife Lottie, sees that she had always seen herself "as woman, and particularly as mother," in the role of "the first great source of life and being, and also of culture." Lawrence's sardonic remark follows: "Sure enough, Lottie had never formulated this belief inside herself. But it was formulated for her in the whole world. It is the substantial and professed belief of *the whole white world*" (169, emphasis mine). It is impossible to know who is echoing whom in this exchange, but the connection adds an unsuspected irony to H.D.'s poem.

14. Another bee appears in H.D.'s 1927 novel, *HERmione*, as a sign to Her that she can become a writer: "Music might have caught the trial of the grass as she ran on across the meadow and the deep note made by a fabulous bee that sprung into vision, blotting out the edge of the stables, almost blotting out the sun itself with its magnified magnificent underbelly and the roar of it sort of booming. The boom of the bee in her ears, his presence like an eclipse across the sun brought visual image of the sort of thing she sought for . . . it had not occurred to Her to try and put the thing in writing" (13).

15. See Vincent Quinn's more specifically realized but less accurate reading: "Each stanza begins with a declaration of loyalty to the goddess, but the remainder of the stanza is a parenthetical outpouring of desire for Phaedra" (50).

16. The substitution of a relationship between two women in the place of the parent/child paradigm here recalls and, I would argue, depends upon the dedication to Bryher at the volume's head. The unity which the Eleusinian mystic finds between Christ and his mother is, then, equally a sign of unity in other types of passionate relationship—particularly the "marriage" between H.D. and Bryher and the verbal overlay of Hippolyta and Phaedra.

17. Since "Helios and Athene" remained unpublished until 1981 (when it appeared with an important essay by Adalaide Morris in *Iowa Review* 12), this connection is evident only in a private—rather than a public—context.

18. This double sense of H.D.'s use of the figure of the Hesperides also occurs in the October 1921 issue of *Poetry*, where she collects three poems under the collective title

"Hesperides" (26–30). Of these, the first—"Fragment XXXVI"—was later to appear in *Heliodora*, while the other two—"Song" and "At Baia"—are from *Hymen*. "Song" presents an essentially positive vision, while the other two deal with loss and abandonment and are deeply equivocal.

Chapter 4

1. See Susan Friedman's "Palimpsest of Origins in H.D.'s Career" as well as my "The Identity of 'H.': Imagism and H.D.'s *Sea Garden*" for discussions of H.D.'s discovery of persona and identity within image.

2. See her "Palimpsest of Origins in H.D.'s Career" for the juxtaposition of "Hilda's Book" with *HERmione*. The complete text of "Hilda's Book" is included at the end of H.D.'s *End to Torment*, with a short bibliographic note by Michael King.

3. Shari Benstock, in *Women of the Left Bank: Paris, 1900–1940*, pursues a fascinating reading of *HERmione*, reaching a very different conclusion. She suggests that it is a post-Imagist excursion in which H.D. reverses "the principles that bound word to image from a post-Poundian, post-Imagist perspective" (337). I would argue that H.D.'s "Imagism" is always already "post-Poundian," that from its earliest incarnations it problematizes any simple understanding of what Imagism is about. See also L. S. Dembo's reading of the novel, where he reaches the conclusion that "The story of Hermione Gart is . . . that of the future Imagist poet whose 'imagism,' far from being limited to certain formal characteristics such as those listed by Flint and Pound, would be set in a psychological and philosophic context that would allow it to deal with a broader and deeper range of experience" (214).

4. D. H. Lawrence uses a version of the same story for his *The Man Who Died*. In chapter 9 I explore the significance of this connection through a parallel reading of Lawrence's story and H.D.'s *A Dead Priestess Speaks*.

5. See Rachel Blau DuPlessis's important "Romantic Thralldom in H.D." for a discussion of this alienation.

6. Thus reads one draft of *Pilate's Wife*. In a reading of the novel in *Psyche Reborn*, Susan Stanford Friedman cites a significantly different draft which reads "'I am Veronica,' said Veronica, realizing at last, that she was *a* person" (*Psyche Reborn*, 181, emphasis mine). Because of the textual difference, Friedman's reading of the novel is quite different from mine.

7. Rachel Blau DuPlessis, in her book *H.D.: The Career of That Struggle*, suggests that "'Greece' function[s] in an interlocking fashion: as a sign of female cultural authority, and as a set of associations sufficient to encode issues of sexuality" (24). While I would agree, it will become clear in the following discussion that H.D.'s understanding of "Greece"— as well as sexuality and "female cultural authority" is more problematic than this would suggest.

Chapter 5

1. Dale Davis, in her article "*Heliodora*'s Greece," explores the literal sense of *Heliodora*'s translations, studying the poems in relation to their sources. I am indebted to her work at several points.

2. Mirror imagery is pervasive in *HERmione*. See, for one example, H.D.'s description of the entrance of Fayne Rabb playing the role of Pygmalion in a production of the play: "Everything is great seen in its right perspective, but George will never see that. George had said 'Oh rot, what rot is this you're talking' when for a moment she had realized her head—the bit here, the bit there, the way it fitted bit to bit—was two convex mirrors placed back to back. The two convex mirrors placed back to back became one mirror . . . as Fayne Rabb entered" (138).

3. See Davis, 150.

4. Dale Davis points this out (152).

5. The two epigrams read as follows in Aldington's translation:

A GIRL
Now the white violet blooms and the rain-loving narcissus blossoms and the mountain-haunting lilies are flowering; even the sweet amorous rose of Persuasion, flower among flowers, Zenophile, now blooms.

Meadows! why do you laugh so gaily and so rashly under your tresses? She is lovelier than your sweet-breathing garlands.

THE GARLAND
I will bind the white violet and the gentle narcissus with myrtles, laughing lilies and the soft crocus; and I will bind with them the dark-blue hyacinth and the amorous rose so that the garland about the temples of myrrh-tressed Heliodora may strew flowers on her bright loose hair. (25)

For other translations of these epigrams, see Dale Davis's "*Heliodora's* Greece" (153–54).

6. See Barbara Guest's *Herself Defined*, 37–92.

7. See the *Oxford Classical Dictionary*, 835, for a short account of Piraeus.

8. This passage of Pausanius appears here in the translation by J. M. Edmonds, from his *Lyra Graeca*, first published in 1924, the same year as *Heliodora*.

Chapter 6

1. See, for instance, Harriet Monroe's almost elegiac review of the *Collected Poems* in *Poetry* of August, 1925, where, though she hopes "that [H.D.'s] work is not yet half done," she also refers to the volume as "her whole record" and suggests that the later poems "[enrich] her fame though scarcely advancing it." See also Vincent Quinn's assessment of the collection; he writes that the implication of the end of H.D.'s career does her a "disservice," but that it is also "justified" (30).

2. The essay is included in *Writing like a Woman*. For an example, see p. 8, where Ostriker simply omits *Red Roses for Bronze* from a list of H.D.'s collections.

3. See the advertisement for *Blues* in the final pages of *transition* 16–17, calling the journal "a magazine of a *more complete revolt* against the cliche and commonplace welcoming poetry and prose radical in form, subject or treatment" (n.p.).

4. In addition to these poems, a prose fragment by H.D. appears in this issue of *transition* in an advertisement for Kenneth Macpherson's novel *Poolreflection*. This fragment is not noted in the checklist of H.D.'s publications in *Contemporary Literature*, and deserves quotation in full, since it too explores an irrational psychic realm in which the physical and spiritual writhe, joining in an undefinable unity:

Has the ripe grape been frosted, or has the frozen ice lily been drenched as with Falernian? This is the problem that confronts us with our first breathless wonder at the clarid perception of this urbane poet. The lyric quality of Mr. Macpherson hides, as it were, under a robe of very tangled worldliness. The robe however does not obstruct the free play of white limbs beneath it. Heavy with riotous colour, and at the same time chaste as some Olympian victor. . . . Phrase after phrase of penetrating psychic power. . . . The scientific and the lyric meet in a super-ecstasy that reduces to a "magnesium ribbon flared out." Superhuman effort toward parental appreciation leads to "kick the young cub into the army." Affection and hypercritical detachment tied in indissoluble love knots. Gorgon knots that must be severed with the casting away of the fretting physical encumbrance. The physical and spiritual writhe, unrelated yet indisseverable. Laacoon [*sic*]. (n.p.)

5. In a 1930 article, Zukofsky—though he has some reservations about H.D.'s work—includes her in a list of poets who have never been constrained by the limits of Imagism: "Pound, Williams, Eliot, Marianne Moore, H.D. (when she does not suffer from an Anglicized dilution of metric and speech, defeating her double effort towards emotional expanse and condensation) did not stop with the monolinear image; they extended it to include 'a greater accessibility to experience' (Marianne Moore, 'N.Y.'). They are thus not a gang-plank for a younger generation to step onto. Or, if they are, their individual rungs matter, and Cummings is maybe on shore or sometimes certainly on board" (*Prepositions*, 130).

6. As Bruce F. Kawin has pointed out, repetition has, by its very nature, this doubleness: "It can lock us into the compulsive insatiability of neurosis, or free us into the spontaneity of the present tense" (5). Together with some of Gertrude Stein's explorations of the repetitive mode, H.D.'s work defines the possibilities of the practice for modernism.

7. See, for instance, her account of the genesis of *Bid Me to Live* (which she calls *Madrigal*): "I had been writing or trying to write this story, since 1921. I wrote in various styles, simply or elaborately, stream-of-consciousness or straight narrative. I re-wrote this story under various titles, in London and in Switzerland" ("H.D. by Delia Alton," 180).

8. See Zajdel, 129–31, for her account of this accumulation of associations.

Chapter 7

1. For Pound's complaint that H.D. "has . . . let loose dilutions and repetitions, so that she has spoiled the 'few but perfect' positions which she might have held on to," see his August, 1917 letter to Margaret Anderson in *The Letters of Ezra Pound 1907–1941*, p. 114.

2. The exceptions are to be found in the incorporation of translated lyric fragments in the poems of *Heliodora*, where they do not stand as units on their own but as integrated parts of H.D.'s own work.

3. Claire Buck, using the theories of Jacques Lacan, makes a similar point about Friedman and DuPlessis's reading of H.D.'s poem to Freud "The Master" and *Helen in Egypt*: "The fact that [H.D.'s] language of 'hieroglyphs' always remains a foreign script to be translated or interpreted, or else is given a conditional status . . . precludes any claim . . . for a simple unmediated relation to the body outside the Symbolic" (61). In "Red Roses

for Bronze," the artist's relation to her own body and to the body of her object are both inescapably mediated by the concrete, static figure she proposes to sculpt, and her approach to the entire project is deeply ambivalent.

4. In the unpublished "Compassionate Friendship," her 1955 "diary" in honor of her friend/ therapist Erich Heydt, H.D. runs through a list of "Erics" from her dead half-brother to Dr. Heydt. In this list, T. S. Eliot comes to be a substitute for Eric Doolittle; at the same time, this short mention of Eliot—as far as I know the only explicit reference to him anywhere in H.D.'s writing—makes it clear that H.D. was aware of his writing and did follow it with keen interest: "Eric III was possibly a distant fantasy of kinship with T. S. Eliot; I never knew him very well but through the years, have followed his career and read his books. From time to time, I have had remarkable visual dreams in which Eliot manifested. I always thought that this dream-Eliot was a 'screen,' but I did not identify him with Eric I" (90).

5. It is perfectly possible to read the entire poem in such a modern setting; however, it is also possible to read it in a typically classical setting. Beyond a reference to "the Olympieum" and the classical form of the sculpture itself, the poem does not specify its own timeframe, and is a palimpsest of several possible periods.

6. The figure of the woman on the stair also anticipates the vision of the Lady in *Tribute to the Angels*, who enters the poem "standing there, / actually, at the turn of the stair" (562).

7. H.D.'s "little heap of dust" also echoes one of the most famous lines of Eliot's "The Waste Land": "I will show you fear in a handful of dust" (38).

8. For a straightforward, section-by-section reading of the "plot" of "Myrtle Bough," see Thomas Burnett Swann's *The Classical World of H.D.*, 101–3. Though Swann does see the poem's shifts and sudden transitions, he reads it as a reversal "of H.D.'s usual viewpoint," a poem accepting sexuality and passion. Though the reading reflects Swann's own obsession with H.D.'s aloofness and asexuality more than it does the poem itself, it is still a handy paraphrase.

9. Interestingly enough, a fuller version of the story given by Thucydides changes the possible significance of the two in H.D.'s poem. In Thucydides' story, Aristogiton and Harmodius are lovers, who plot against the tyrant's *brother* because of his attempt to seduce Aristogiton. Ironically, though the song celebrates the two men as liberators of Athens, Thucydides makes the point that "After [the killing of the tyrant's brother] the tyranny became harsher for the Athenians" (Thucydides, 285). H.D.'s choice of the celebratory version of the story, however, occludes the very real oppression which followed.

10. I call the speaker "her" because, though she is "not man" and "not woman," she has a dower, and clearly takes the woman's role—both as dependent in the poem's early stages and in "her" emergence from this dependence later—in the "marriage" which the poem examines.

Chapter 8

1. Just two years after the publication of *Red Roses for Bronze*, H.D. began her work with Freud, some of which is recorded in the "Advent" section of her *Tribute to Freud*, written as a diary in March of 1933. This record of her analysis—which includes reports of dreams, and memories as well as details of her daily encounters with Freud—is dark with the Nazi presence in Vienna. See for instance H.D.'s mention of "fresh Nazi atrocities" (174)

or her account of swastikas chalked on the pavement leading to Freud's door in "Writing on the Wall" (58–59).

2. In *Psyche Reborn*, Susan Friedman notes that "H.D.'s letters to Bryher while she was in analysis openly discuss the writer's block in 1933 and 1934" (30). She also, however, suggests that this difficult period was, in retrospect, a period of growth: "the relative latency of the thirties [was] a sort of 'incubation' period out of which the new H.D. emerged" (9).

3. Another pseudonym of the time, D. A. Hill, the "author" of a story titled "Ear-Ring" which appears in the summer, 1936 issue of *Life and Letters To-day,* is, like "H.D." itself, not gender-specific. The story is set in a stylish restaurant in Athens and follows the reveries of a woman named Madelon Thorpe, who is apparently the same Madelon of "Pontikonisi (Mouse Island)."

4. In a letter to her friend Viola Jordan written in 1927 or 1928—cited by Susan Friedman in *Psyche Reborn* (6)—H.D. calls "Hipparchia," the first story of *Palimpsest,* a "purple sex story (though highly spiritualized) about a Greek girl in Rome." The description fits Natalia Saunderson's "Nights" perfectly.

5. Neith also puts in an appearance in the "Advent" section of *Tribute to Freud* in this guise: "The Professor says that Athene is the veiled Isis, or Neith the warrior-goddess" (187).

Chapter 9

1. Martz, in his introduction to *Collected Poems 1912–1944,* gives an account of this gathering of material, pointing out that H.D. did consider other orderings and other poems for her volume (see xxiv–xxvii). One tentative inclusion not noted by Martz is the "Prose Chorybantic," H.D.'s experimental prose work of the late twenties and early thirties.

2. In the poem, the identity between the god and poetry is implicit; in her commentary on the poem in "H.D. by Delia Alton," H.D. makes the connection explicit, writing that "He (song) can not be cajoled, bribed, threatened" (214).

3. A memoir written in the early forties though not published until 1982 (and even then in bowdlerized form), *The Gift*—in the midst of delightful stories about H.D.'s childhood and about the Moravian visions of her grandmother—makes it clear that H.D. took this connection between prophecy and the arts very seriously indeed, thinking of it as a "gift" of the spirit.

4. In "H.D. by Delia Alton," H.D. suggests that there may be some small connection between "Sigil" and "A Dead Priestess Speaks": "Perhaps *Sigil* 17 relates back to the death-love motive of the *Priestess*" (215). I am here suggesting a much more intimate, much more significant and deliberate connection, one which turns the volume as a whole into an integrated sequence rather than a mere collection of disparate poems.

5. The "new earth / new skies" of "Sigil" also echoes the title of Lawrence's poem "New Heaven and Earth," a poem which, appropriately enough, is about the passage from sexuality through the mysteries of death into a new, expansive life:

> Yet rising from the tomb, from the black oblivion
> stretching out my hand, my hand flung like a drowned
>   man's hand on a rock
> I touched her flank and knew I was carried by the

> current in death
> over to the new world, and was climbing out on the
> shore,
> risen, not to the old world, the old, changeless I, the
> old life,
> wakened not to the old knowledge
> but to a new earth, a new I, a new knowledge, a new
> world of time.

(Selected Poems, 80)

6. The man of this poem is the "Peter Van Eck" of *Tribute to Freud*, who was central to H.D.'s on-ship visionary experience of 1920. See "Advent," pp. 153 ff. for H.D.'s telling of the story. "Priest" is, then, also related to the earlier story "Pontikonisi (Mouse Island)," which revolves around this experience without ever quite recounting it.

7. H.D.'s curious reading of "Priest" in "H.D. by Delia Alton" suggests a very different scenario, placing blame on the speaker of the poem for the "psychological fault or flaw" of transferring "her human contact or emotion" to the powers of poetry, thus reducing herself "to quicksilver, radium," and dehumanizing herself (215–16). I think, however, that "Priest"—as well as "Jubilee"—makes it very clear that something quite different is at stake, that the destruction of "human contact or emotion" is a result of the man's religion rather than the woman's retreat into the efficacies and powers of song.

Bibliography

there are the old prints in my uncle's book,
but I need not consult them any more.

H.D., *"Vale Ave"*

Aldington, Richard. *Life for Life's Sake: A Book of Reminiscences.* New York: The Viking Press, 1941.

Arthur, Marylin B. "Psychomythology: The Case of H.D." *Bucknell Review* 28, 2 (1983), 65–79.

Benstock, Shari. *Women of the Left Bank: Paris, 1900–1940.* Austin: University of Texas Press, 1986.

Blackmur, R. P. "The Lesser Satisfactions." *Poetry* 41, 2 (1932), 94–100.

Bryer, Jackson R., and Pamela Roblyer. "H.D.: A Preliminary Checklist." *Contemporary Literature* 10, 4 (1969), 632–75.

Bryher, Winifred. "Spear-Shaft and Cyclamen-Flower: *Hymen,* by H.D." *Poetry* 19, 6 (1922), 333–37.

Buck, Claire. "Freud and H.D.—Bisexuality and a Feminine Discourse." *M/F: A Feminist Journal* 8 (1983), 53–66.

Budge, E. A. Wallis. *The Gods of the Egyptians: Or Studies in Egyptian Mythology.* 2 vols. 1904. New York: Dover Publications, Inc., 1969.

Burnett, Gary. "H.D. and Lawrence: Two Allusions." *H.D. Newsletter* 1, 1 (1987), 32–35.

———. "The Identity of 'H.': Imagism and H.D.'s *Sea Garden.*" Unpublished ms. Forthcoming in *Sagetrieb.*

———. "A Poetics out of War: H.D.'s Responses to the First World War." *Agenda* 25, 3–4 (1987), 54–63.

Bush, Douglas. *Mythology and the Romantic Tradition in English Poetry.* 1937. New York: Norton, 1963.

Chopin, Kate. *The Awakening.* Chicago and New York: H. S. Stone & Co., 1899.

Coleridge, Samuel Taylor. *Biographia Literaria,* in *Selected Poetry and Prose of Coleridge.* Ed. Donald A. Stauffer. New York: The Modern Library, 1951, 109–428.

Collecott, Diane. "Images at the Crossroads: The 'H.D. Scrapbook.'" *H.D.: Woman and Poet.* Ed. Michael King. Orono, Maine: National Poetry Foundation, 1986, 319–67.

———. "Remembering Oneself: The Reputation and Later Poetry of H.D." *Critical Quarterly* 27 (1985), 7–22.

Collins, H. P. *Modern Poetry*. New York: Houghton Mifflin Company, 1925.

Cork, Richard. *Vorticism and Abstract Art in the First Machine Age*. Berkeley: University of California Press, 1976.

Crosby, Harry. "Aeronautics." *transition* 15 (1929), 19–21.

Dasenbrock, Reed Way. *The Literary Vorticism of Ezra Pound and Wyndham Lewis: Towards the Condition of Painting*. Baltimore: Johns Hopkins University Press, 1985.

Davis, Dale. "*Heliodora*'s Greece." *H.D.: Woman and Poet*. Ed. Michael King. Orono, Maine: National Poetry Foundation, 1986, 143–56.

Dembo, L. S. "H.D. *Imagiste* and Her Octopus Intelligence." *H.D.: Woman and Poet*. Ed. Michael King. Orono, Maine: National Poetry Foundation, 1986, 209–25.

Des Imagistes: An Anthology. New York: Albert & Charles Boni, 1914.

Duncan, Robert. "From the Day Book—Excerpts from an Extended Study of H.D.'s Poetry." *Origin* 10, First Series (1963), 1–47.

——— . "The H.D. Book, Part One: Beginnings." Published in sections in *Coyote's Journal* 5/6 (1966), 8–31 (chapter 1); *Coyote's Journal* 8 (1967), 27–35 (chapter 2); *Tri-Quarterly*, 12 (1968), 67–98 (chapters 3–4); *Stony Brook* 1 (1968), 4–19 (chapter 5, "Occult Matters"); *Caterpillar* 1 (1967), 6–29 (chapter 6, "Rites of Participation," part 1); *Caterpillar* 2 (1968), 125–54 (chapter 6, part 2).

——— . "The H.D. Book, Part Two: Nights and Days." Published in sections in *Sumac* 1, 1 (1968), 101–46 (chapter 1); *Caterpillar* 6 (1969), 16–38 (chapter 2); *Io* 6 (1969), 117–40 (chapter 3); *Caterpillar* 7 (1969), 27–60 (chapter 4); *Sagetrieb* 4, 2/3 (1985), 39–85 (chapter 5); *The Southern Review* 21 (1985), 26–48 (chapter 6); *Credences* 2 (1975), 53-94 (chapters 7–8); *Chicago Review* 30, 3 (1979), 37–88 (chapter 9); *Ironwood* 22 (1983), 47–64 (chapter 10); *Montemora* 8 (1981), 79–113 (chapter 11).

——— . "H.D.'s Challenge." *Poesis* 6, 3/4 (1985), 21–34.

——— . "In the Sight of a Lyre, A Little Spear, A Chair: *Selected Poems* by H.D." *Poetry* 91, 4 (1958), 256–60.

DuPlessis, Rachel Blau. "Family, Sexes, Psyche: An Essay on H.D. and the Muse of the Woman Writer." *H.D.: Woman and Poet*. Ed. Michael King. Orono, Maine: National Poetry Foundation, 1986, 69–90.

——— . *H.D.: The Career of That Struggle*. Sussex: The Harvester Press, 1986.

——— . "Romantic Thralldom in H.D." *Contemporary Literature* 20, 2 (1979), 178–203.

Edmonds, J. M. *Lyra Graeca*. Cambridge: Harvard University Press, 1924.

Eliot, T. S. *The Complete Poems and Plays 1909–1950*. New York: Harcourt, Brace & World, Inc., 1962.

——— . *Selected Prose of T. S. Eliot*. Ed. Frank Kermode. New York: Harcourt Brace Jovanovich & Farrar, Straus and Giroux, 1975.

Engel, Bernard F. "H.D.: Poems That Matter and Dilutations." *Contemporary Literature* 10, 4 (1969), 507–22.

Firchow, Peter E. "Rico and Julia: The Hilda Doolittle–D. H. Lawrence Affair Reconsidered." *Journal of Modern Literature* 8 (1980), 51–76.

Fletcher, John Gould. *Goblins and Pagodas*. Boston: Houghton Mifflin Co., 1916.

——— . "H.D.'s Vision." *Poetry* 9, 5 (1917), 266–69.

Freibert, L. M. "Conflict and Creativity in the World of H.D." *Journal of Women's Studies in Literature* 1, 3 (1979), 258-71.

Friedberg, Anne. "Approaching *Borderline*." *H.D.: Woman and Poet*. Ed. Michael King. Orono, Maine: National Poetry Foundation, 1986, 369–90.

——— . "The POOL Films: What They Are, Where They Are, How to See Them." *H.D. Newsletter* 1, 1 (1987), 10–11.

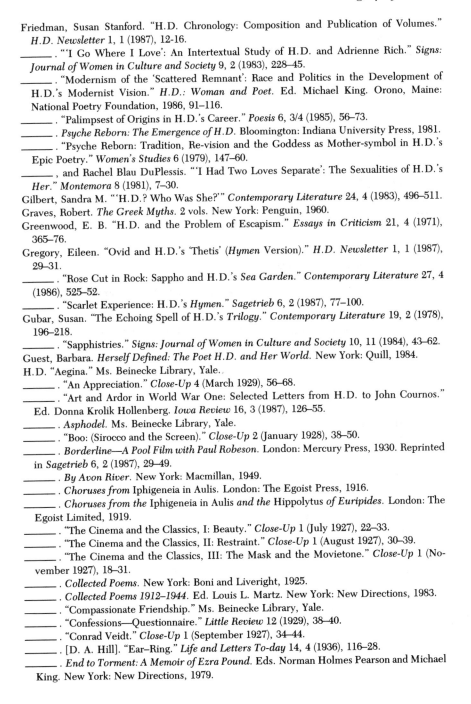

Friedman, Susan Stanford. "H.D. Chronology: Composition and Publication of Volumes." *H.D. Newsletter* 1, 1 (1987), 12-16.

_____. "'I Go Where I Love': An Intertextual Study of H.D. and Adrienne Rich." *Signs: Journal of Women in Culture and Society* 9, 2 (1983), 228–45.

_____. "Modernism of the 'Scattered Remnant': Race and Politics in the Development of H.D.'s Modernist Vision." *H.D.: Woman and Poet.* Ed. Michael King. Orono, Maine: National Poetry Foundation, 1986, 91–116.

_____. "Palimpsest of Origins in H.D.'s Career." *Poesis* 6, 3/4 (1985), 56–73.

_____. *Psyche Reborn: The Emergence of H.D.* Bloomington: Indiana University Press, 1981.

_____. "Psyche Reborn: Tradition, Re-vision and the Goddess as Mother-symbol in H.D.'s Epic Poetry." *Women's Studies* 6 (1979), 147–60.

_____, and Rachel Blau DuPlessis. "'I Had Two Loves Separate': The Sexualities of H.D.'s *Her*." *Montemora* 8 (1981), 7–30.

Gilbert, Sandra M. "'H.D.? Who Was She?'" *Contemporary Literature* 24, 4 (1983), 496–511.

Graves, Robert. *The Greek Myths.* 2 vols. New York: Penguin, 1960.

Greenwood, E. B. "H.D. and the Problem of Escapism." *Essays in Criticism* 21, 4 (1971), 365–76.

Gregory, Eileen. "Ovid and H.D.'s 'Thetis' (*Hymen* Version)." *H.D. Newsletter* 1, 1 (1987), 29–31.

_____. "Rose Cut in Rock: Sappho and H.D.'s *Sea Garden*." *Contemporary Literature* 27, 4 (1986), 525–52.

_____. "Scarlet Experience: H.D.'s *Hymen*." *Sagetrieb* 6, 2 (1987), 77–100.

Gubar, Susan. "The Echoing Spell of H.D.'s *Trilogy*." *Contemporary Literature* 19, 2 (1978), 196–218.

_____. "Sapphistries." *Signs: Journal of Women in Culture and Society* 10, 11 (1984), 43–62.

Guest, Barbara. *Herself Defined: The Poet H.D. and Her World.* New York: Quill, 1984.

H.D. "Aegina." Ms. Beinecke Library, Yale.

_____. "An Appreciation." *Close-Up* 4 (March 1929), 56–68.

_____. "Art and Ardor in World War One: Selected Letters from H.D. to John Cournos." Ed. Donna Krolik Hollenberg. *Iowa Review* 16, 3 (1987), 126–55.

_____. *Asphodel.* Ms. Beinecke Library, Yale.

_____. "Boo: (Sirocco and the Screen)." *Close-Up* 2 (January 1928), 38–50.

_____. *Borderline—A Pool Film with Paul Robeson.* London: Mercury Press, 1930. Reprinted in *Sagetrieb* 6, 2 (1987), 29–49.

_____. *By Avon River.* New York: Macmillan, 1949.

_____. *Choruses from* Iphigeneia in Aulis. London: The Egoist Press, 1916.

_____. *Choruses from the* Iphigeneia in Aulis *and the* Hippolytus *of Euripides.* London: The Egoist Limited, 1919.

_____. "The Cinema and the Classics, I: Beauty." *Close-Up* 1 (July 1927), 22–33.

_____. "The Cinema and the Classics, II: Restraint." *Close-Up* 1 (August 1927), 30–39.

_____. "The Cinema and the Classics, III: The Mask and the Movietone." *Close-Up* 1 (November 1927), 18–31.

_____. *Collected Poems.* New York: Boni and Liveright, 1925.

_____. *Collected Poems 1912–1944.* Ed. Louis L. Martz. New York: New Directions, 1983.

_____. "Compassionate Friendship." Ms. Beinecke Library, Yale.

_____. "Confessions—Questionnaire." *Little Review* 12 (1929), 38–40.

_____. "Conrad Veidt." *Close-Up* 1 (September 1927), 34–44.

_____. [D. A. Hill]. "Ear–Ring." *Life and Letters To-day* 14, 4 (1936), 116–28.

_____. *End to Torment: A Memoir of Ezra Pound.* Eds. Norman Holmes Pearson and Michael King. New York: New Directions, 1979.

———. *Euripides' Ion.* 1937. Redding Ridge, Connecticut: Black Swan Press, 1986.

———. "Expiation." *Close-Up* 2 (May 1928), 38–49.

———. "'The Farmer's Bride'." *The Egoist* 3 (1916), 135.

———. *The Gift.* New York: New Directions, 1982.

———. "'Goblins and Pagodas.'" *The Egoist* 3 (1916), 183–84.

———. "H.D. by Delia Alton" ["Notes on Recent Writing"]. *Iowa Review* 16, 3 (1986), 174–221.

———. *Hedylus.* 1928. Redding Ridge, Connecticut: Black Swan Press, 1980.

———. *Helen in Egypt.* 1961. New York: New Directions, 1974.

———. *Heliodora and Other Poems.* Boston: Houghton Mifflin, 1924.

———. *HERmione.* New York: New Directions, 1981.

———. "Hesperides." *Poetry* 19 (1921), 26–30.

———. *Hippolytus Temporizes.* 1927. Redding Ridge, Connecticut: Black Swan Press, 1985.

———. *Hymen.* New York: Henry Holt and Co., 1921.

———. "Joan of Arc." *Close-Up* 3 (July 1928), 15–23.

———. "Jubilee." Ms. Beinecke Library, Yale.

———. "King of Kings Again." *Close-Up* 2 (February 1928), 21-32.

———. *Kora and Ka* [originally published in 1934 with "Mira Mare"]. Berkeley: Bios, 1978.

———. "Marianne Moore." *The Egoist* 3 (1916), 118–19.

———. "The Moment." Ms. Beinecke Library, Yale.

———. "Narthex." *The Second American Caravan: A Yearbook of American Literature.* Eds. Alfred Kreymborg, et al. New York: The Macaulay Co., 1928, 225–84.

———. [John Helforth]. *Nights.* 1935. New York: New Directions, 1986.

———. "Notes on Euripides, Pausanius, and Greek Lyric Poets." Ms. Beinecke Library, Yale.

———. *Notes on Thought and Vision.* San Francisco: City Lights Books, 1982.

———. *Paint It To-day.* Ms. Beinecke Library, Yale. The first four chapters published in *Contemporary Literature* 27, 4 (1986), 444–74. Eds. Susan Stanford Friedman and Rachel Blau DuPlessis.

———. *Palimpsest.* 1926. Carbondale: Southern Illinois University Press, 1968.

———. *Pilate's Wife.* Ms. Beinecke Library, Yale.

———. [Rhoda Peter]. "Pontikonisi (Mouse Island)." *Pagany: A Native Quarterly* 3, 3 (1932), 1–9.

———. "Prose Chorus Four." *Caravel* 5 (1936) n.p.

———. "Prose Chorus Two" and "Prose Chorus Three." *Blues* I (1929), 107–8, 138–39.

———. "Responsibilities." *Agenda* 25, 3 / 4 (1987), 51–53.

———. "Russian Films." *Close-Up* 4 (March 1929), 18–29.

———. *Tribute to Freud.* 1974. New York: New Directions, 1984.

———. "Turksib." *Close-Up* 5 (December 1929), 488–92.

———. Untitled advertisement/review of Kenneth Macpherson's novel *Poolreflection. transition* 4 (1927), n.p.

———. "Vale Ave." *New Directions* 44 (1982), 18–68.

Harrison, Jane Ellen. *Prolegomena to the Study of Greek Religion.* 1922. New York: Meridian Books, 1955.

Hughes, Glenn. *Imagism and the Imagists: A Study in Modern Poetry.* 1931. New York: The Humanities Press, 1960.

Hulme, T. E. *Further Speculations.* Ed. Sam Hynes. Lincoln, Nebraska: University of Nebraska Press, 1962.

———. *Speculations: Essays on Humanism and the Philosophy of Art.* Ed. Herbert Read. London: Routledge and Kegan Paul, 1924.

Jackson, Brendan. "'The Fulsomeness of Her Prolixity': Reflections on 'H.D., "Imagiste."'" *The South Atlantic Quarterly* 83 (1984), 91–102.

Jaffe, Nora Crow. "'She Herself Is the Writing': Language and Sexual Identity in H.D." *Literature and Medicine* 4 (1985), 86–111.

Jarrell, Randall. *Kipling, Auden and Co.: Essays and Reviews, 1935–1964*. New York: Farrar, Straus, & Giroux, 1980.

Jolas, Eugene. "Preface" to the "Vertical Age" issue. *transition* 21 (1932), 6.

———. "Proclamation" to the "Revolution of the Word" issue. *transition* 17 (1929), 13.

———. "Suggestions for a New Magic." *transition* 3 (1927), 178-79.

Joyce, James. *Ulysses: The Corrected Text*. Ed. Hans Walter Gabler. New York: Vintage Books, 1986.

Kawin, Bruce F. *Telling It Again and Again: Repetition in Literature and Film*. Ithaca: Cornell University Press, 1972.

Keats, John. *Selected Poems and Letters*. Ed. Douglas Bush. Boston: Houghton Mifflin, 1959.

Kerenyi, C. *The Gods of the Greeks*. London: Thames and Hudson, 1951.

Kloepfer, Deborah Kelly. "Fishing the Murex Up: Sense and Resonance in H.D.'s *Palimpsest*." *Contemporary Literature* 27, 4 (1986), 553–73.

———. "Mother as Muse and Desire: The Sexual Politics of H.D.'s *Trilogy*." *H.D.: Woman and Poet*. Ed. Michael King. Orono, Maine: National Poetry Foundation, 1986, 191–206.

Lawrence, D. H. *Aaron's Rod*. London: Martin Secker, 1922.

———. *The Letters of D. H. Lawrence*. Vol. 2, June 1913–October 1916. Ed. George J. Zytaruk and James T. Boulton. Cambridge: Cambridge University Press, 1981.

———. *The Letters of D. H. Lawrence*. Vol. 3, October 1916–June 1921. Ed. James T. Boulton and Andrew Robertson. Cambridge: Cambridge University Press, 1984.

———. *St. Mawr and The Man Who Died*. New York: Vintage Books, 1953.

———. *Selected Literary Criticism*. Ed. Anthony Beal. London: William Heinemann Ltd., 1955.

———. *Selected Poems*. Ed. Kenneth Rexroth. New York: Penguin Books, 1980.

———. *Women in Love*. 1933. New York: Penguin Books, 1976.

Levertov, Denise. "H.D.: An Appreciation." *Poetry* 110, 3 (1962), 182–86.

Loy, Mina. *The Last Lunar Baedeker*. Ed. Roger L. Conover. Highlands, North Carolina: The Jargon Society, 1982.

Mallarmé, Stephan. *Mallarmé: The Poems*. Trans. Keith Bosley. New York: Penguin Books, 1977.

Mandel, Charlotte. "Garbo/Helen: The Self-Projection of Beauty by H.D." *Women's Studies* 7 (1980), 127–35.

———. "The Redirected Image: Cinematic Dynamics in the Style of H.D. (Hilda Doolittle)." *Literature/Film Quarterly* 11, 1 (1983), 36–45.

Mathis, Mary S. and Michael King. "An Annotated Bibliography of Works about H.D.: 1969–1985." *H.D.: Woman and Poet*. Orono, Maine: National Poetry Foundation, 1986, 393–511.

Monro, Harold. *Some Contemporary Poets (1920)*. London: Leonard Parsons, 1920.

Monroe, Harriet. "H.D." *Poetry* 25, 5 (1925), 268–75.

———. *Poets and Their Art*. New York: Macmillan, 1926.

Morris, Adalaide. "The Concept of Projection: H.D.'s Visionary Powers." *Contemporary Literature* (25, 4), 411–36.

———. "Reading H.D.'s 'Helios and Athene.'" *The Iowa Review* 12, 2/3 (1981), 155–63.

Mylonas, George E. *Eleusis and The Eleusinian Mysteries*. Princeton: Princeton University Press, 1961.

Olson, Charles. "Projective Verse." *Poetics of the New American Poetry*. Ed. Donald Allen and Warren Tallman. New York: Grove Press, 1973, 147–58.

Ostriker, Alicia. "What Do Women (Poets) Want?: Marianne Moore and H.D. as Poetic Ancestresses." *Poesis* 6, 3/4 (1985), 1–9.
_____ . *Writing like a Woman*. Ann Arbor: University of Michigan Press, 1983.
Oxford Classical Dictionary. 2nd ed. Ed. N. G. L. Hammond and H. H. Scullard. Oxford: Oxford University Press, 1970.
Pearson, Norman Holmes. "Norman Holmes Pearson on H.D.: An Interview." *Contemporary Literature* 10, 4 (1969), 435–46.
Pondrom, Cyrena. "H.D. and the Origins of Imagism." *Sagetrieb* 4, 1 (1985), 73–97.
Pound, Ezra. *The Cantos of Ezra Pound*. New York: New Directions, 1972.
_____ . *Gaudier-Brzeska: A Memoir*. New York: New Directions, 1970.
_____ . *The Letters of Ezra Pound 1907–1941*. London: Faber & Faber, 1951.
_____ . *Literary Essays of Ezra Pound*. 1935. New York: New Directions, 1968.
_____ . *Personae: The Collected Poems of Ezra Pound*. New York: New Directions, 1926.
_____ , and Dorothy Shakespear. *Ezra Pound and Dorothy Shakespear: Their Letters 1909–1914*. Eds. Omar Pound and A. Walton Litz. New York: New Directions, 1984.
Prins, Johanna H. "H.D.'s Sappho." Unpublished essay, 1985.
Quinn, Vincent. *Hilda Doolittle (H.D.)*. New Haven: College & University Press, 1967.
Rexroth, Kenneth. *World Outside the Window: Selected Essays*. Ed. Bradford Morrow. New York: New Directions, 1987.
Robinson, Janice S. *H.D.: The Life and Work of an American Poet*. Boston: Houghton Mifflin, 1982.
Sarton, May. "Letters from H.D." *H.D.: Woman and Poet*. Ed. Michael King. Orono, Maine: National Poetry Foundation, 1986, 49–57.
Seiffert, Marjorie Allen. "Glacial Bloom: *Heliodora and Other Poems*, by 'H.D.'" *Poetry* 25 (1924), 160–64.
Smith, Paul. "H.D.'s Identity." *Women's Studies* 10 (1984), 321–37.
_____ . *Pound Revised*. London: Croom Helm, 1983.
Stein, Gertrude. *Geography and Plays*. 1922. New York: Something Else Press, 1968.
_____ . "Portraits and Repetition." *Look at Me Now and Here I Am: Writings and Lectures 1909–45*. Ed. Patricia Meyerowitz. Baltimore: Penguin Books, 1971.
Swann, Thomas Burnett. *The Classical World of H.D.* Lincoln, Nebraska: University of Nebraska Press, 1963.
Thucydides. *History of the Peloponnesian War*. Vol III: Books 5 and 6. Trans. Charles Forster Smith. Cambridge: Harvard University Press, 1952.
Whitman, Walt. *Complete Poetry and Collected Prose*. Ed. Justin Kaplan. New York: The Library of America, 1982.
Williams, William Carlos. *The Autobiography of William Carlos Williams*. 1951. New York: New Directions, 1967.
_____ . "Kora in Hell." *Imaginations*. Ed. Webster Scott. New York: New Directions, 1970.
Yeats, William Butler. *The Collected Poems of W. B. Yeats*. New York: Macmillan, 1956.
_____ . *Mythologies*. 1959. New York: Collier Books, 1969.
_____ . *A Vision*. New York: Macmillan, 1956.
Zajdel, Melody M. "Portrait of an Artist as a Woman: H.D.'s Raymonde Ransom [*sic*]." *Women's Studies* 13 (1986), 127–34.
Zukofsky, Louis. *Prepositions: Collected Critical Essays*. 1967. Berkeley: University of California Press, 1981.

Index